D1487178

ONE

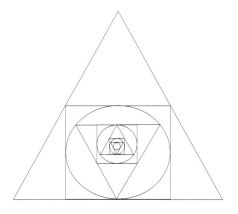

Copyright © 2021
All rights reserved. This book or any portion thereof may not
be reproduced or used in any manner whatsoever without the
express written permission of the publisher except for the use
of brief quotations in a book review.

Book cover design by Rupa Limbu
Book interior design by Tom Howey

Printed in the United States of America
First Printing, 2021

ISBN: 978-1-7366035-0-5

ONE

An Intellectual Odyssey to Rediscover the
Most Powerful Being in the Universe: YOU

JEROME MICHAEL McLAUGHLIN

Dedicated to my brother, who taught me:

*Sometimes life hands you a bag of shit.
You pick it up, throw it over your
shoulder, and soldier on.*

The following is a pedestrian's guide to the imprecise, a wide-ranging, bumpy ride along the third rail of uncertainty for the rewired mind.

It is to be sifted through like a junk drawer of oddities, a collection of loose screws and misshapen thing-a-ma-jigs organized into a random pattern for reflection and perhaps potential action.

It may contain passages, perspectives, and opinions that tweak a nerve or twist a tendon. Through our own lived experience, we develop certain convictions that stretch tight over time, predispositions we may find difficult to now loosen and adjust.

I ask only one thing:

Come to the table with a clean plate, an open mind, and some room to roam.

CONTENTS

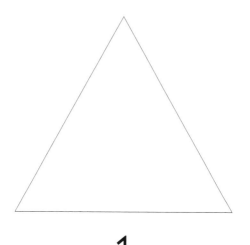

1

IN THE BEGINNING

A stranger appears upon the hill.

"Who the hell are you?!!"
—ANONYMOUS

Once, there was no You.

In fact, there wasn't even the possibility of You. A "You" as we know it today did not exist, could not exist.

How is that possible? The earth was teeming with Us. Each one of Us a unique and embodied being with a set of traits that make up what we refer to today as "an individual." And yet, despite this apparent abundance, You were not yet one of them. Why?

The context for understanding was not available. It wasn't time.

> In the past, the color blue did not exist. At least not in the way we know it today. Ancient languages did not have a word for it—not Greek, not Chinese, not Hebrew. And without a word for the color, people could not describe it.
>
> In fact, they might not have been able to see it at all.
>
> A researcher traveled to Namibia in Africa to investigate this phenomenon. An experiment was conducted with the Himba tribe whose members speak a language with no word for blue, or more precisely, no distinction between blue and green. When shown a diagram with eleven green squares and one blue, the Himba could not pick out which one was different from the others.[1]

For much of our past, the concept of You as an individual, remained in a state of immature adolescence. The language, the knowledge, the cultural conditions, and the configuration of the human mind had not advanced to the point that it could fully comprehend the individual—an independent, autonomous, and sovereign being, one free to make choices. We could not intellectualize the individual as an entity with a unique and separate identity, a distinct set of personal beliefs, and a flourishing sense of self-understanding.

Today, it is hard to imagine the possibility of being so dislocated within conscious experience, to be trapped inside yourself without the ability to assert your own agency in the world. Yet, the thought of You as an independent, autonomous, and sovereign being is strictly a modern notion unsuitable for consideration when discussing us in the past, for it was not always possible to grasp such an abstraction. Upon the long stretches of the timeline of modern humans, the capacity for a full understanding of the concept of You was absent, or at a very minimum, impossible to be articulated.

So, where did the concept of You originate?

Did You just one day magically appear? Or did the concept of You evolve over time?

And if so, what are You *evolving* into?

As an individual, are You predetermined, or more, open for interpretation?

And most importantly, what is the ultimate destiny of this thing called You?

◆

One, and only one.

Today, within the vast herd of humanity there are many variants, but only one You. You exist distinctly and uniquely as a separate and knowable thing. And all others share one thing in common: they are not You.

Every group, be it the family, the tribe, the clan, the commune, the collective, the city-state, the nation, or the entirety of civilization, are all social configurations made up of the single atom of humanity, the building block of all humankind: You, the individual.

Yet this You, the you that you know now, is not as you once were. You have been carved out of time—recombined from an elaborate and shifting genetic puzzle, forged through a long process of repeated experimentation, and shaped through the lineage of lived experience by your ancient ancestors.

Across thousands of generations, a wealth of human knowledge, what we might refer to as "our inherited wisdom", has been painstakingly mined, processed, and refined. It is the most advanced product of the pinnacle of evolution: the human mind, now housed within the crown of the most intelligent, widespread, and irrepressible species ever known.

And with each new edition of this vast book of knowing, an improved version of the concept of the individual has slowly emerged. With every new season, a more distinct and empowered being has gradually surfaced until it assumed its current recognizable form: You.

◆

Usher us across.

Yet despite this vast wealth of knowledge and the advancements that have come along with it, we now find ourselves in a rather precarious position. We stand together yet alone at an unfamiliar and unnerving evolutionary junction.

How do we know so much yet still understand so little?

How have we learned so much yet believe it still not enough?

Why do we find ourselves still unable to answer life's most basic questions?

How did we lose the thread that wove wisdom out of mere knowing?

What is it we are supposed to come to know?

What are we destined to become?

> *"Judge a man by his questions, not by his answers."*
> — VOLTAIRE

The arrival of human consciousness initiated a confounding conundrum, a persistent and nagging problem that we demand be solved. We have endeavored to understand Us as a species then establish a harmonious working order, a livable arrangement in which we can all not only survive but thrive. To dissolve our angst and locate a sense of inner peace, we have sought a resolution to the enigma that is Us, the most complex structure in the universe

And so, we have experimented with an array of ideas, ideologies, inventions, and institutions that might somehow reveal the final answer to Us. We have put our collective minds to work to formulate a solution out of the knowledge we have gained.

To date, none have proven effective…or even satisfactory.

We have found no prescription, no salve, no formula, no system, no theory, no principle, no discovery, no belief, nor any physical or metaphysical force that is able to thoroughly and completely solve us, protect us, comfort us, save us, or even spare us from the travails and troubles of daily life.

As a species, we have come so far but seem unable to cross the last river to enter the place we have long envisioned—a place without pain, without hate, without strife, without injustice, without fear, and without the unraveling sense of futility.

We have become entangled in our own complexity. We seem trapped in a perpetual cycle of toil, epiphany, euphoria, and disappointment repeating the same pattern over and over only to invariably return to the beginning. It has wearied our walk and clouded our mind. At the risk of both under and overstating our predicament, a sense of purposelessness has invaded the human spirit.

Intelligent yet uncertain, fearful yet hopeful, exhausted yet resolute, together yet alone, we seek a path, a map, a bridge, or a potential guide who might usher us finally across.

◆ ◆ ◆

First, clear the mind.

To better understand the origin of Us and the beginning of You, we must venture back as far the limited set of available facts might allow. As always, when traveling back in time in an attempt to intellectually relocate within the period of human history that remains regretfully unknowable, we must erase the bias of what is known of Us today, in the present. We must attempt to reset the patterns of our mind to enter the infinite realm of uncertainty, for the mind that existed back then is different from what it is today.

def: **PRESENTISM** – interpreting past phenomena in terms of current beliefs and knowledge[2]

Upon our journey backward, we will envision much but actually come to know little, for nearly the entirety of the human story remains buried, fragmented, or disappeared. Much of our human story has been lost altogether. We have yet to even discover a discernible edge to the scattered puzzle that might provide a clearer image of Us as we once were in the deep past.

The true source of our beginning remains woefully incomplete, but we must begin somewhere. So let us begin here.

◆

A shared blood.

When we climbed down from the trees, we found the flatness of the ground plentiful but unsettling. Going solo into this vast new openness meant certain death, quick and often horribly violent. It was imperative to construct a means to protect ourselves from the perilous "out there" including our potentially murderous neighbors. So, we gathered together in small groups bonded together by relations of the primary order—a shared blood.

We also learned that we needed to safeguard ourselves not just from the external, but our own inherent nature—competitive and prone to violence. Since our beginning, we have been on a perpetual quest for power. Within each of us stirs the latent desire to be recognized for the potent uniqueness we all possess. Certain norms for living had to be established early. Modes of behavior needed to be set in place to manage the threats of the external world and the animal still living within. A few basic "don'ts" were sufficient to begin.

Working methods were established to forge each member into a working asset who could assist in the daily operation of the tribe and, if lucky, perpetuate the longevity of this new collective. Orientations, rituals, and ceremonies were instituted to ensure that each member performed as expected and each new generation perpetuated the learned patterns of the past. An acceptable order of operation within the tribe began to take shape.

Within the tribe, the individual was considered subordinate to and indistinguishable from the whole. Every individual played a vital role in the tribes' singular focus: survival. Aberrant behavior was unacceptable and immediately tempered with swift corrective measures. There was neither time nor tolerance for the greedy. The individual did what was expected, as directed, without hesitation, to ensure the bloodline of the tribe did not come to an end and vanish into the soil.

◆

The roots of the family tree.

Imagine five people moving together along a river. As they walk, they leave their footprints in the soft mud. These prints appear to have been made by one adult male, one female, two young adults, and a small child.

A team of archaeologists from the British Museum would discover these fossilized footsteps along the coast of England nearly 800,000 years later. They are believed to be the oldest known evidence of humans outside of Africa.

Even though these prints are referred to as "human," they weren't made by us. Homo sapiens, or anatomically modern humans, appeared on earth about 200,000 years ago, and in this part of the world, only around 40,000 years ago.

A species called Homo antecessor, a hominid that lived in Europe more than a million years ago and believed to be the ancestor to both Neanderthals and Homo sapiens, is the leading candidate for the footprint makers.[3]

According to one archaeologist: "The glimpse of the past that we are seeing is a family group moving together across the landscape."

What was the early familial or social structure of our ancestors? How did it operate? Would we find their configurations familiar, or would they seem more closely related to those still living in the trees today?

To gain a clearer picture of our original social grouping, we might examine a few of our closest genetic relations who demonstrate a rather wide range of possibilities.

Orangutan males, for example, live alone and mate with any female who wanders into their claimed territory. Gibbons, on the other hand, break into monogamous male and female units, and along with their offspring, establish and monopolize a particular region of the jungle. Chimps evolved with smaller bodies making them more vulnerable to predators, so they band together in large and rather promiscuous groups to compensate for their physical size. Apes live in cohesive social groups that usually include one dominate alpha male who mates with many females. Humans are much closer anatomically to the great apes and thus our tendency is to equate our early family origins along the same line as the ape.[4]

From our present situation, it might be a bit difficult to imagine our earliest social structure mirroring that of the great ape. But in the end, all we can do is sift through the dirt for clues and make educated (but often erroneous) guesses about what life was like in these unrecorded days. Or, as we have done recently, we can apply the magic of science to construct mathematical models using mitochondrial matching or genetic sequencing to offer views that fit more comfortably with nostalgic visions we might hold of our early forefathers and foremothers.

Yet all we can really say is: the truth is uncertain. We can weave a tale that best suits our story, yet the details remain but a figment of the imagination, long gone and eternally indecipherable.

Despite this sparse historical record and the dearth of viewable physical evidence, it could be argued that the individual in those early days was not viewed as a distinct and autonomous being. Instead, each member was tightly embedded within the group, interwoven into the social fabric of the whole. The individual remained bound in subordination disallowed from emerging or developing in any particularly unique way. "You" as a single entity was predetermined by the needs of the many.

One distinguished member might stand out as more capable of protecting the group altogether, or perhaps assert themselves as more adept at leading the tribe toward the next meal or more suitable shelter. But for the remaining individuals, the extraction and distinction of the singular self from the fabric of the communal whole was perhaps not only tribally offensive, it might have been cognitively unavailable. At this point in the evolution of the human mind, the concept of the self as a sovereign and independent being remained incomplete. The "I" was still caged within the "We".

What thoughts occupied the individual mind in those early years?

What might motivate the whole tribe, or any single member, beyond mere survival?

Did an individual wish to be separate or set apart from the herd?

Did one yearn to become something more, something different, something better?

Were those thoughts even possible?

Could the mind that existed then even conceptualize its own uniqueness?

[Reluctantly but respectfully, we will skip over vast epochs and fast forward to a time that, while still faint, has decidedly left its mark.]

◆

Under the arc of the burning sun.

Approximately 194,500 years after the arrival of modern humans, or roughly 5,500 years from present day, a group of scattered tribes along the Nile river in Africa would unite to form the most enduring civilization known to human history: Egypt.

Within this fertile land, the Nile was the source of all. It delivered abundance and destroyed it with equal verve. If the rains came and the rising river was managed properly, life abounded. But if the rains withheld or came in super-abundance, famine struck, and life ended miserably on a massive scale.

Within Egyptian culture, a single individual was set apart from the tribe with such distinction as to be considered almost superhuman. It was this single being's mission to establish order, seek harmony, and maintain a living balance between the people and the cruelty of nature in the land that grew lush along the river.

The people of the land wove elaborate myths and fanciful stories to establish and perpetuate the authority of this exalted uber-human who would become known as "pharaoh". Directly translated as "the great house" or "the high column," the pharaoh served as the medium between earth and sky. His (sometimes her) power was absolute. A pantheon of gods who dwelt above and below bestowed the pharaoh with a supreme and divine authority to rule over the people.

Who would dare question the will of the gods? It had been so since the beginning of time. (Or so the people had been told.)

Under the watchful eye of the pharaoh, the mortal herd toiled beneath the arc of the burning sun, each member locked within a rigid social hierarchy—their lot was drawn, their station cast. *Better this than what came before*, they might say, the unforgiving brutality of death and disorder wrought by nature.

Egypt was the cultural, political, and educational epicenter of the ancient world, a curious civilizational anomaly that rose out of the sand of the Sahara to cast itself in stone for all of eternity to study and admire. Insular, powerful, inventive, stable, and mysterious, its unique cultural distinction has been etched deep into the human record. Life along the slow-moving Nile remained unchanged for long stretches of time.

> *Ancient Egyptian civilization was so long-enduring that Cleopatra, the last active ruler of the Kingdom of Egypt, is closer in time to the invention of the iPhone than to the founding of Egypt itself.*

◆

The great knowledge.

In this land called Egypt, many days before the arrival of Moses, there dwelt a great lodge of mystics known as the "Adepts and Masters." Amongst these gifted seers, one particular individual surpassed them all: Hermetica Trismegistus. He became known as the father of the occult, the founder of astronomy, and the architect of alchemy. According to legend, his contribution to Egyptian culture was so profound that his existence remains an open question: Was he a man or a god? Time did not preserve evidence of his mortal life nor could the mind of the day fathom the magnitude of his impact upon Egyptian civilization, so he was exalted as a god named Thoth. (The neighboring Greeks would appropriate this distinguished superhuman as their own and name him Hermes, the god of wisdom.)

The mystics of the lodge traveled to the four corners of the earth anxiously carrying with them a precious gift: the great knowledge. The great knowledge contained all the secrets of the universe that had been formerly withheld from humans. Yet they were willing to deliver these secrets only to those prepared to receive it. The power of the great knowledge was not for the every-man but only a select few—the elite. The time for all to know had not yet arrived.

Never transcribed but only passed from lip to ear, the great knowledge of the Masters was not immediately decipherable nor explicit in its translation. It was encoded into various axioms on astronomy (the inner workings of universal truths), woven into allegories on alchemy (the quasi-magical transformation of matter), and embedded in the ratios of architecture (the structure in which man and nature can locate harmony).

And along with this precious gift, they carried a warning: *"Do not allow these secret doctrines to crystallize into creed. Caution to those who mix theology and philosophy."*

As Egypt grew in both status and riches, rampant piracy would force its borders to be tightly held and heavily guarded. The empire's edge was protected as if the very spirit of the land depended on it. Immigration was highly restricted and the punishment for infringement was death, the sentence beyond appeal.

But in the waning years of Egyptian power, immigration began to loosen and for the first time in over 3,000 years, neighboring countries were able to gain access to the grand mysteries of this advanced but shuttered civilization. Visited often by early Greek thinkers, contact with Egypt arguably resulted in the genesis of their enlightenment.[5] The priests of Sais, the city that served as the seat of Egyptian power during the late twenty-sixth dynasty, would refer to these aspiring Greek visitors as "children in the mysteries".

One Greek visitor, considered the founder of the school of natural philosophy, Thales of Miletus (624-546 BCE), immersed himself in the mystical disciplines of the Egyptian priests—land surveying, geometry, engineering, astronomy, and theology.[6] Thales, who would eventually become known as one of the Seven Sages of Greece, would be the first to assert the simple truth:

"The most difficult in life is to know thyself."

Other known civilizations of this period established powerful empires with distinct cultures and characteristics unique to their own tribe—Assyrian, Hittite, Mesopotamian, Sumerian, Babylonian. Their temples and ziggurats rose out of the dust, visible for miles, busy with the business of gods and kings and the legion of priests who served them. Their city centers were surrounded by a diverse throng of conquered foe as well as an assortment of adopted peoples who sought protection and a modicum of peace within the orbit of the city's influence.

Much of what is known of these great places has been lost or forgotten. Their structures were not built of stone, but simple bricks, mere mud and earth mixed with water and a weak binding agent, usually straw. Their fragile structures could not withstand the test of time. All would eventually crumble and re-enter the wind.

"Even a brick wants to be something."
— LOUIS KAHN (ARCHITECT)

For the sake of simplicity, moving forward I will use the term "man" to represent us all: wo-man, man-man, hu-man, and a single pronoun—the male first/third person "he, his, him".

I must also acknowledge that the telling of this story comes from a Western point of view. The totality of human history is wide and deep with so many beautiful stories to be told. Yet there are only so many pages available here to be filled.

I realize the above is not only archaic thinking but outright cultural insubordination. I ask you to please forgive me. I am trying to relate a complex story from one person's perspective through the limited lens of my own lived experience using only the instrument of language, an imperfect and slippery human invention.

I have heard the beginning of We, but where was I?

Destroyed from without by enemy armies and slowly dissolved from within by an invasion of foreign philosophical and religious ideas, the seemingly invincible Egyptian empire, like all others, would eventually fall. One idea in particular, Christianity, took root in Egypt in the late period, doubtless aided by its many similarities to the popular cult of the Egyptian gods Osiris and Isis which also featured an unjustly killed divine figure who was resurrected to provide humans with a guarantee of eternal life.[7]

It was nearby Greece however, who would inherit the wealth of wisdom born in Egypt and record it for the world to consume and ponder for the next two and a half thousand years. Into modernity, it was Greece who would be granted authorship and inventor's rights to much of what originated in Egypt. Yet we must be thankful to Greece that all the wisdom of Egypt was not lost to the flux of time or buried forever beneath the shifting sands of Africa.

One particular inheritor, the Greek philosopher Socrates (470-399 BCE), much like the mysterious Egyptian god Thoth, straddles the seam between history and fiction. Not a word of the grand sage survives. All we know of him and his teachings are those told to us through the writings of his student, Aristocles, son of Ariston of Collytus, later known as Plato (428-348 BCE). Plato would spend thirteen years in Egypt immersed in the mystical sciences and secretive knowledge of the magic land. He would speak of himself and his fellow Greek students during their time in Egypt as "aspirants to wisdom."

Prior to the arrival of Socrates, the early Greek thinkers were fixated upon the physical world, the matter that made up all things and the mechanical means by which it all operated. Socrates opened the lens of intellectual investigation and turned it from this obsession with material toward the abstracted realm of inner existence, the intentions and actions of mortal men—how to live, how to behave, how to distinguish between right and wrong, how to live with purpose.

Socrates claimed the proper conduct of a virtuous life could be explicitly established through an interrogative questioning of "the self." One could query the self using the same means and methods one would employ to inquire about the material world around us. Through a distilling exercise of the mind, one's life could be examined in minute detail and any act could be determined as either beneficial or potentially damaging to both the individual and society. Answers determined through this rational argument could then be evaluated in an empirical way to know how one was performing, how one was working toward a concept that would become universally understood as "the good."[8]

This process of self-interrogation would become known as the "Socratic method"—a continuous inquiry of critical reasoning used to break problems down into a series of questions that might gradually reveal new discoveries about oneself, or at a minimum, provide a reasonable justification for a more deeply considered line of questioning.

"An unexamined life is not worth living."
— SOCRATES

According to the story, Socrates would wander through the Athens marketplace dirty and barefoot both day and night applying his cross-examining methods to anyone he could corner. While many citizens of Athens found his methods invasive and obnoxious, Socrates managed to gather quite a following of impressionable young students who were highly intrigued by his introspective approach to the inward journey of the self.

However, members of the powerful Greek ruling class did not share their fondness for the gadfly philosopher. They would grow increasingly displeased with Socrates' incessant need to interrogate every innocent citizen and would label him a public nuisance. Eventually the incorrigible philosopher would be arrested and dragged before a tribunal to face trumped up charges of "impiety" (refusing to pay homage to the official gods of the state) and corrupting the minds of Athens' youth (not to mention all the minds who would come to learn of him and his methods thereafter). His own tribe would find him guilty on both counts and sentence him to death.

Out of an uneasy respect, or to alleviate their sense of shame, Socrates would be granted the right to choose the means of his own death. As his preferred choice, a cup of poison, slowly took effect, Socrates found himself surrounded by his disconsolate disciples who pleaded with him to reconsider. They begged him to renege his positions to Athenian authorities and secure his own release.

Socrates accepted the verdict without mounting even the slightest defense. He knew full well the message of his trial and execution would outlive him, and the seeds he had sewn with his methods of self-interrogation would find fertile ground when carried across time. To assuage their pleas, Socrates countered with the simple phrase: "*My inner voice has instructed me so.*"

◆

It was known before it could be known.

Plato, in his book 'Timaeus and Critias', would introduce us to the Greek statesman, poet, and sage named Solon, widely celebrated for his fairness, wisdom, and mesmerizing oration. It is written that Solon traveled to the Egyptian city of Saïs where he would encounter the high priests of Shemsu-Hor, the followers of the sky-god Horus.

Among them lived an aged priest named Sonchis of Saïs, a man of extraordinary force and a deep penetration of mind. He would tell Solon stories of powerful, prosperous, and technologically advanced empires that existed on earth thousands of years before the rise of Egypt. Natural catastrophes and great wars had destroyed them all.

The high priests of Seshat had been granted exclusive access to the records of these ancient empires. It was their great responsibility to preserve the memory of these long-lost civilizations, our forgotten ancestors.

Following his education in Egypt, Plato would return to Athens and establish his Academy, not a formal school in the modern sense, but more an informal society of intellectuals who shared a common interest in studying subjects such as philosophy, mathematics, and astronomy. It was here that Plato would put forward the revolutionary proposition that reality, in other words, that which we believe we perceive as real, may not be as it seems.

To illustrate his point, he constructed an allegory on the nature of "reality". In the story, men living in a cave were bound in chains able to see only a shadow of what was truly there, mere projections of the original objects. Plato referred to these original objects as "forms", or the essence of a thing. According to Plato, what could be seen by the observers were only ephemeral images cast upon the cave wall by a source of eternal light, not the true object itself.

Eventually, one of the individuals would free himself from his own chains (the restraints that bind free will) to climb out of the darkness (self-ignorance) and face the source of external light (understanding) where he would enter the realm of true reality (wisdom). But when he returned to the cave to report his staggering discovery, he found his fellow captives unable, or perhaps unwilling, to comprehend his transformative journey. Out of a fear of the unknown, or an affection for the comfort offered by the status quo, they chose to ignore the possibility of enlightenment and remain forever bound.

While Socrates believed every man a separate and distinct entity with the capacity to acquire knowledge and self-understanding through a process of self-interrogation that could lead to "a good life", Plato sought to comprehend and construct a civil order, a human organizational structure that might control, correct, and perfect the undisciplined and intractable being known as man. At the Academy, Plato's teachings focused less on man as an improvable "self" as proposed by Socrates, and more on how man would need to construct a system that might correct his very nature and thus manifest his potential.

According to Plato, man was not a solitary, autonomous being by nature but a political being suited for life in the "polis" (the city). According to Plato, any man not fortunate enough to live in a city or society was incapable of mastering his own "inner savage" and thus realize his true "humanness." Man's escape from barbarism would need to be exchanged for what Plato considered the ultimate "good"—compliance with and submission to society, a structure with governing authority over all men.

The duties of citizenship Plato admitted would be quite burdensome and would stake the greatest claim on a man's time and attention. But such dedication was required to construct and maintain a society that would operate coercively yet justly. In Plato's mind, man would be forever subordinate to the polis serving as the productive means to raise society above the chaos inherent in nature, and in doing so, elevate himself along with his fellow man.

It would be the Greeks who openly questioned the long-standing tradition of reliance upon embellished myths and the celestial antics of supernatural gods and goddesses to explain the uncertainties in life. These early thinkers refocused the primary importance of existence on the goodness inherent not in the metaphysical, but in the minds of mortal beings. This new thinking did not necessarily abandon the belief in a higher power as a core tenet of society, but rather tried to reconfigure the human mind to pursue the mysteries of natural science, pure knowledge, and the power of reason to form new ways to think, live, and wonder.

This innovative line of thinking produced by the democratic experiment that unfolded in Athens was to be short lived, however. The intellectual achievements of this tiny city perched above the Mediterranean in the advancement of enlightened thought would be subsumed by wave after wave of war, tyranny, and subjugation. Many centuries would pass before the concept of the autonomous individual would again re-emerge.

Through the persuasive teachings of Plato, the ancient Greek's concept of the individual would become inextricably linked to that of society, and man's primary relation to the city as one of necessity and obligation. Here, the individual would surrender himself in exchange for security, sustenance, and the advancement of his own society and thus human civilization overall.

Plato's views, like the perspective of the great teachers of Egypt, were not directed at the education of the common man, but a class of elite thinkers, the philosophically gifted who might lead ordinary men out of their own predicament under the operation of a thoughtfully designed and precisely administered society.

It was during this epoch that an individual was identified simply and unceremoniously by an assigned name followed by their place of origin:

Aristocles of Collytus

Sonchis of Saïs

Thales of Miletus

Jesus of Nazareth

Please tell me who I am.

Far to the east, across the Black and Caspian seas, in an area known as the Indus Valley, now modern-day India, a similar reconsideration of the concept of the self was also underway. During this period, a movement was taking place to gather and document a collection of emerging religious-philosophical thought into texts that would become known as the Upanishads.

Indian society was beginning to question the "Vedic life"—a long-standing tradition of external rites and sacrifices, and instead turned to focus upon internal spiritual quests in the search for answers.[9] The Upanishads mark the beginning of a reasoned enquiry into philosophical questions concerning the foundation of life, the nature of being, the origin of the self (including the self after death), and how one should live one's life.

> In early written Vedic material, the term 'åtman' was used as a reflexive pronoun meaning 'self.' In the newly established Upanishads, the word would continue to be used as a pronoun, but it also became a philosophical term, one associated with a wide range of meanings including body and soul and often the ontological principle underlying all reality—what is important to be known to live righteously and well.[10]

Just as in Greece in the teachings of Plato told through the voice of Socrates, the philosophy of the Upanishads was introduced in the form of a conversation between student and teacher. While the self as defined by Socrates, was shaped by a series of inwardly focused questions theoretically available to anyone, the Upanishadic self was restricted to a specific and elevated stratum of society, a group known as Brahmins.[11] The commoner was not given access to these new enlightened ways of thought. It was reserved only for the few.

Across the high Himalayas from the Indus Valley in a land that would become known as China, emergent concepts of being, the concept of the self and its role in society, were also being examined and refitted. However, the Chinese manifestations of "self" did not stress an individual's separation from but emphasized the power of the self within the context of connection and unity. For the Chinese, the "cultivated self" was designed to operate in harmony with the "establishment", the external authorities of power. Chinese tradition focused on the individual as a vitally integrated element within a larger familial, social, political, and cosmic whole, a fully attained and integrated being within a larger web of relationships and authorities.[12]

Here the concept of the individual would form the basis upon which moral meaning and proper behavior would be constructed. The core idea of the cultivated self, a well-integrated individual serving the whole in a harmonic order of structured power relationships, would establish the central tenets of Chinese philosophy. These relational concepts, carried through the Ru and Confucian philosophical lineage, would dominate and organize Chinese society for the next 2,000 years.

Across a wide range of cultures, the acknowledgement and awareness of a distinct and recognizable entity—the self—was beginning to emerge. Yet, the value of the individual was typically understood within the context of an external structure or an authoritative system positioned externally to him, and nearly always over and above him. And access to a powerful new abstraction—knowledge—was still considered exclusive and beyond the comprehension of the every-day man.

For the time being, the individual remained subordinate, a simple cog to be hammered into place or fitted for use by the ruling authority or the prevailing religious order of the day. Man was not yet able to free himself of his own chains or to step out from the long shadow of the temple.

How sweet the sound.

In a province named Galilee not far from the Mediterranean Sea, a new philosophy arose that reshaped the minds (and hearts) of men, a "new testament" based upon the words of the prophet-messiah Jesus of Nazareth.

In the story as it is written, Jesus, son of the Hebrew god Yahweh, was sent to earth in physical form to preach "the good news". Through richly illustrated stories and parables, Jesus instructed those willing to listen that good deeds and acts of devotion to God his father would grant one access to the glorious hereafter—an eternity free from sorrow, earthly suffering, and the hardships of daily life. And according to Jesus, this afterlife was not only achievable but available to any and all.

The teachings of Jesus would give rise to a radical new spiritual innovation, the "divine self", Here, the individual would be granted authority and responsibility for his own life, his individual destiny, and his own personal "salvation". One needed to simply learn to love God without question and learn to love "thy neighbor as thyself with thine whole heart", both solo efforts.

Jesus would walk from town to town drawing large crowds eager to hear these resonant ideas that empowered the lowly and gave hope to the oppressed. His gospel spread quickly along with his influence as adoring followers sought solace in the promise of his message of a self-determined eternal salvation. According to Jesus, the "soul" as bestowed by God, was resident within every man and it was the soul that needed saving.

Yet his teachings offered a confusing and perhaps conflicting message. Although the self was divine, Jesus defined man as specifically human, weak of the flesh and vulnerable to temptation. Only through the grace of God could he truly be saved.

This radical message of a divine self and the unilateral power of God to save one's soul would eventually find the ears of those less tolerant of such deviant thinking. To the powers that be, the wandering preacher and his liberating words were becoming a dangerous and destabilizing force. Branded a heretic and a threat to the religious-political power—Jewish orthodoxy, Jesus of Nazareth would eventually be arrested and turned over to the local Roman authorities to stand trial for the crime of apostasy. He was found guilty, tortured, and crucified.

According to the fulfillment of his own prophecy, Jesus of Nazareth willingly sacrificed himself to atone for the sins of all mankind, both past and future, and in doing so offered every soul the chance to join him and God his father in the exalted afterlife.

In the time just before his death however, an end he always knew forthcoming, God's only son sent to earth in physical form wrestled with what could only be described as genuine mortal fear—the anguish that stirs at the core of the human condition. Jesus is said to have prayed with such an agony of spirit that his sweat fell to the ground in drops of blood. He pleaded with his all-powerful father to somehow be relieved of the burden of his earthly mission, knowing his rescue not possible.

> *"Father, forgive them for they know not what they do."*
> — JESUS OF NAZARETH

After his death, the disciples of Jesus would establish a new religious order on earth—"The Church"—to preserve and propagate the gospel as taught by the prophet-messiah. It would be these new holy men who would become the stewards and the ultimate authority of the "Word of God" and their new man-made structure would carry the ultimate power of the almighty under the management of mortal men.

The high priests of the Church would expand and codify the procedures and practices required to achieve the great reward as promised by Jesus. Their instructions were quite clear: *Follow the edicts, commandments, and covenants set forth by The Church in this world to be granted ascension to the glory of the afterlife.* Any deviance or failure to abide as instructed meant not only the forfeiture of eternal salvation, but an eternity of suffering and affliction. In other words, obey or be damned forever.

The Church as founded would come to serve as both the formation and usurpation of human agency, both the gift and the denial of the true self. While the divine self was now empowered to assume control of its own destiny, the narrowness of the laws of the Church and the strict standards for proper behavior nullified innovation and shuttered openness. While it was true that one assumed responsibility for one's own life in the quest for heavenly salvation, the promise of eternal life was now tightly controlled by rules drafted and administered by corruptible "men of earth".

In the land of the blind, the one-eyed man never seeks a cure for blindness.

For more than a thousand years, the Christian ethos established by the Church in Rome codified and controlled the daily practice of human life marching the congregation mechanically through a tight routine of ritualized worship. A strict diet of rules and regulations programmatically stifled intellectual and personal development. It was the Church that dictated nearly every aspect of daily existence: behavior, morality, education, taxation, justice, prayer, marriage, social engagement, food, dress, even one's own thoughts. The Church alone was believed to possess the power to usher an individual toward spiritual enlightenment and it alone would serve as the sole authority to determine one's eligibility for eternal salvation. This thousand-year period in history, rightfully or not, is referred to as 'The Dark Ages'.

During this period in history, the all-powerful Roman Catholic Church also stood as the center of European political power. Though it maintained no standing army, its dominance in the affairs of both men and state went undisputed and virtually unchallenged for centuries. When conflict arose, kings and queens bowed down in reverence, or at a minimum, reluctantly but dutifully acquiesced to the papal authority vested in Rome.

Under the omnipotent influence of The Church, the intellectual pursuit of philosophy, science, and scholarship was nearly eliminated, all replaced by Church dogma and doctrine strictly interpreted and violently enforced. Adherence to the laws set by the all-powerful clergy, the so-called "men of God", was a suffocating subordination of individual will and a prohibition placed upon the emergence of the autonomous self. Anyone who attempted to challenge the authority of the Church in matters of mind or action was sternly discouraged or outright crushed.[13] Deference to the strident beliefs and positions of the "one true" Church was unquestionable. When man pushed against the high walls of the Church, the walls opened and swallowed him whole.

In 1632, Galileo Galilei, the father of modern science, published a confirmation asserting his belief in the Copernican system—the sun, not the Earth, at the center of the planetary system. *The power in Rome denounced such devious views and forbade him both from holding and defending these personal beliefs.*

The Church had already decided on the issue—the Sun moved around the Earth. *This was an absolute fact of scripture that could not be disputed, even though scientists had known for centuries that the Earth was not the center of the universe.*[14]

The Inquisition, the legal enforcement arm of the Church, found Galileo guilty of heresy and sentenced him to serve under strict house arrest. There he would remain until his death in 1642.

◆

Over-Indulgence.

No hammer was used to nail Martin Luther's 95 Theses to the church doors at Wittenberg, Germany in 1517. Nor was a single nail. If fact, no records or any eyewitness accounts of this historical event have ever been located. Even the nailer's own memory of the event appears vague. He believed he had simply mailed them to the archbishop for scholarly review and consideration, not to ignite a revolution.

For much of Europe in the early 1500's, the Church continued to direct and dominate the scope of economic, social, political and spiritual routine. By the "hammering" of his 95 Theses to the doors of the Castle Church of Wittenberg, Martin Luther, an energetic thirty-three-year-old Augustinian friar, would split the thousand-year-old Roman Catholic Church in two— one church loyal to the pope in Rome, and another opposed to the pope's ultimate authority, soon calling itself Protestant.[15]

The Church was in desperate need of new streams of revenue to finance its worldly ambitions—rebuilding all of Rome's religious landmarks (including the majestic but costly St. Peter's Basilica), erecting and maintaining massive cathedrals throughout Europe, patronizing the busy guilds of artists and architects, paying off the mounting debts incurred by the Crusades, funding the long arm of the Spanish Inquisition, stuffing the pockets of a vast network of nepotistic cardinals and bishops, etc.

One of the most bitterly resented abuses of the Church was the sale of indulgences, a sort of get-out-of-jail-free card used by the Church to peddle hope in order to fill the depleted coffers in Rome, not to mention the leather purses of the local clergy. When a Christian purchased an indulgence from the Church, he obtained for himself or whomever else he was trying to benefit, a reduction in the amount of time the soul had to spend in purgatory atoning for his sins before ascending to Heaven.[16] The concept of purgatory, a recent medieval version of an otherwise ancient invention, was a slight modification to the biblically established binary of heaven or hell. In the Christian version, purgatory served as an after-life holding cell allowing sinners to work off their earthly transgressions before gaining access to heavenly paradise. But this reduced sentence came at a cost.

> "They preach only human doctrines who say that as soon as the
> money clinks into the money chest, the soul flies out of purgatory."
> – MARTIN LUTHER (95 THESES, #27)

Beyond exposing the shamefully manipulative financial system fueled by the sale of indulgences, Luther also put a potentially fatal challenge to the linchpin of Roman Catholic order—the absolute authority of the pope. He publicly and vehemently rebutted a wide range of long-held dogma and doctrines issued out of Rome. Luther asserted that Rome was manipulating the teachings of scripture to serve only the institution of men (The Church), not the salvation of man (the soul).

Reigning pope, Leo X became increasingly displeased by such galling insubordination and condemned forty-one of Luther's 95 Theses through a papal decree entitled Exsurge Domine ("Arise, O Lord"). In response, Luther publicly burned the pope's order refusing to renounce a single one of his positions. He was immediately excommunicated and called to stand trial.

In 1521, the Holy Roman Empire summonsed Luther to appear before the assembly of Charles V to respond to charges of heresy.[17]

"Are you prepared to defend all that your writings contain, or do you wish to retract any part of them?"

According to witnesses, Luther 'made answer in a low and humble voice, without any vehemence or violence, but with gentleness and mildness and in a manner full of respect and diffidence, yet with much joy and Christian firmness.'

"You have not given any answer to the inquiry put to you. You are not to question the decisions of the councils— you are required to return a clear and distinct answer. Will you or will you not retract?"

Luther: "May God be my helper, but I can retract nothing."

The emperor then made a sign to end the matter. He rose from his seat and the whole assembly followed his example.[18]

The Holy Roman Emperor declared Luther an outlaw, banning his literature and demanding his arrest: "We want him apprehended and punished as a notorious heretic."[19] But Luther by then was long beyond the reach of The Church. Sequestered and protected in a castle owned by a powerful local prince in Wartburg Germany, Luther grew long his hair and beard and referred to himself as Junker Jörg (Knight George).[20] In isolation for two years, Luther would translate the Bible into German and continue to compose theological attacks against the sale of indulgences and other acts he considered embarrassing failures committed by the Holy Roman Empire.

With the introduction of Gutenberg's printing press, invented only a few hundred miles from Luther's home in 1440, literacy in Europe was quickly becoming widespread. The press, as technological catalyst, cranked out copy after copy of Luther's pamphlets disseminated widely to a swelling firestorm of religious rebellion that was sweeping across Europe.

Luther would later admit he suffered from a case of 'Anfechtungen', a severe psycho-spiritual crisis that caused him cold sweats, nausea, constipation, crushing headaches, ringing in his ears, depression, anxiety, and a general feeling that, as he put it, "the angel of Satan was beating him with his fists".

There were good reasons for the intense young priest to feel disillusioned.[21] The Church of God, spiritual, righteous, transcendent, and filled with the promise of eternal hope, had slowly transformed into the church of men—powerful, paranoid, and rife with corruption.

Luther's Reformation and its opposing reactionary result, the Counter-Reformation, ignited a series of religious wars that would occupy the continent of Europe for nearly a century. The Thirty Years War (1618–1648) in particular, devastated much of Germany killing between 25% and 40% of its entire population.[22] Because of Luther and the events his resistance set in motion, no higher authority now stood above the rising concept of the nation-state and only the ceaseless exercise of power kept contending national interests in check.[23] The Reformation unknowingly ended the age of the religious empire and ushered in the concept of secular modernity.

As this rising modernity chipped away at the long-held, absolute authority of The Church, the paranoiac leadership in Rome grew desperate and violent as it attempted to maintain dominion and jurisdiction over all things. Ultimately, it could only watch in dismay as the old order, an order that had stood without question for over 1,000 years, was slowly dismantled and the luxury of righteousness that accompanies supreme power began to slip away.

A new sprout cannot be expected to produce a bloom.

Throughout these dark years, man's window to the world was clouded by faith, bias, prejudice, superstition, ignorance, and illusion. However, the growing stature of cities outside of Rome gave rise to a new and influential class of merchants, bankers, and business operators who provided a clarifying and freeing influence. Expanding avenues of trade and the greater availability of travel exposed city populations to an ever-widening menu of methods and manners in which to live, dress, think, and act.

Commerce and personal accumulation became not only acceptable, but a worthy pursuit in and of itself. Human experience superseded blind obedience as personal independence and individual expression began to take precedence over Church dogma. The allure of science and the pursuit of knowledge overtook the well-practiced routine of turning to Rome for guidance and permission in all ways of the mind and spirit. Provocative ideas were exhumed from the ancient past and brought forth for consideration and comparison against the prevailing code of the day. Modern thinkers, authors, statesmen, scientists, and artists would begin to thrive as global trade opened up Europe to distant cultures.

The Renaissance, a period loosely defined between 1300-1600, would rediscover classical philosophy, literature, and art. The "objective" study of all worldly things viewed forcibly through the lens of the Church would be thoughtfully challenged by the independent-minded men of emerging European commercial centers.

Italy, and in particular the independent republic of Florence, was instrumental as the financial powerhouse and banking capital of Europe. Wealthy Florentines became patrons to a growing network of artists, craftsman, and inventors as a way to flaunt their riches, spread their influence, and encourage Italy's flourishing cultural expansion. It was Florence that would begin to cultivate the "subjective" aspect of man, a spiritual entity assuming a renewed consciousness of the "self" and a reconsideration of his standing in the world. In Western society, the individual is thus considered "The Renaissance's child".[24]

However, this emerging Renaissance-man lived in two distinct worlds, suspended awkwardly between the opposing poles of faith and reason. The old world of the medieval Christian ethos, where significance of every phenomenon was determined through uniform points of view established by the Church, no longer existed for him. On the other hand, he had not yet found in a system of scientific concepts and social principles the stability and security he needed for the establishment of his own independence and the authority to assume control over his own life. Gradually however, chance (*fortuna*) and reason (*logica*) would replace God's will (*providence*) as man's universal frame of reference. As the age of the Renaissance arose, the City of God was dismantled, and the City of Man erected in its place.[25]

> "You cannot teach a man anything;
> you can only help him find it within himself."
> — GALILEO GALILEI

◆

The future imprisoned in the past.

Since the invention of writing, one facet of the recorded word has presented a persistent challenge: preservation. No perfect means was available to commit writing permanently to a surface (clay, stone, bark, skin, parchment, paper) in a manner that was readable, and just as importantly, easy to store and convey. Wars, plunder, fire, floods, the elements, the overturning of entire civilizations, neglect, indifference, and the corrosive effects of time, all took their toll on the preservation of written knowledge.

During the Renaissance, ancient manuscripts were being discovered in remote monastery libraries throughout Europe. These old manuscripts held profound insights into the magnificence and mysteries of life not filtered through the tight mesh of the Church of Rome. While the monks of Europe during this era honed their skills in agriculture, metallurgy, beer-making, and prayer, they also occupied their time translating and copying by hand the collection of books held in their modest libraries.

Parchment was both expensive and difficult to find, especially in more remote areas. Many of the books written in languages no longer understood were seen for their immediate appeal—a source of recyclable printing material. The indecipherable ink would be scraped off with a sharp knife and the cleaned parchment surface readied for the long, meditative process of transcribing both bible verse and ancient thought that was being rediscovered in long-forgotten manuscripts.

In 1417, a Florentine bibliophile named Poggio Braccionlini, was digging through the library of a remote German monastery when he stumbled upon a dusty, half-destroyed copy of De Rerum Natura (On the Nature of Things) written 1,500 year prior (50 BCE) by the Greek philosopher-poet Lucretius.

In this epic ancient poem, Lucretius explores such subjects as the principles of atomism, the nature of the mind and soul, the experience of sensation and thought, the creation of the world, celestial and terrestrial phenomena, all operating according to what he called "guiding chance" (fortuna gubernans, or "fortune at the helm").

It persuasively laid out a strikingly modern understanding of the world with a resolute condemnation of superstitious fears.[26]

During this same period, Islam was conquering great swaths of the civilized world carrying their new religion throughout North Africa, up the Iberian Peninsula, across the Middle East, and into many regions surrounding the Mediterranean. Some of these areas had been previously conquered and governed by the Greek king, Alexander the Great. Many of the people of these newly vanquished lands had been exposed to Hellenistic Greek culture and the works of intellectual antiquity. As the Islamic caliphate spread, Muslim conquerors came into possession of various Greek and Roman manuscripts previously safeguarded by both institution and individual. But rather than destroy these rare and peculiar works, Muslim scholars carried them along, carefully preserved them, then translated them into Arabic.[27]

These newly discovered and exhumed texts of antiquity contained provocative concepts, new (but old) ideas translated into Latin and other local languages for widespread consumption by a populace held in abundant ignorance for centuries by the men in Rome. The Church had long recognized the potential threat to its authority posed by books and ancient thought and had gone to great lengths throughout the centuries to destroy or remove all philosophic works of antiquity from circulation.

Gutenberg's press with its rapidly moveable and reusable type along with a new oil-based ink sufficiently thick enough to adhere to metal and transfer easily and durably to vellum or paper, led to a wide-scale democratization of information. A growing desire was stirring amongst the commoner to partake in the exclusive and sacred and thus forbidden, treasure of human knowledge.

◆

Man as the measure of all things.

Alone in a drafty room in the Netherlands in 1635, a wandering ex-soldier set to work rethinking the very foundations of this new "man-at-the-center" worldview, and along with it, the hope of locating the origin of knowledge itself (*scientia*). Imposing upon himself a method of narrowing interrogation, Rene Descartes asked...

> *"What do I know to be true?*
> *If I know it to be true, how is it that I have come to know it?*
> *What are the grounds upon which it is known to me?*
> *What, in fact, can be known? How do I know that I know it?"*

He found himself is constant retreat, cartwheeling ever backward with each new inquiry. As he wrestled with the primary origin of thought and the very source from which all knowledge could be understood, Descartes came to rest upon his all-originating axiom:

> *"Je pense, donc je suis."*
> (*I think, therefore I am.*)

The recognition of a separate and unique being, capable of radically inventive and individualized thought, unleashed from the rigid strictures of the smothering omnipotence of The Church, sparked a revolution in science, politics, philosophy, economics, etc. The uncompromising authority that had dictated every manner of thought, opinion, belief, and action throughout the Western world would no longer determine what would be considered truth or fact.

> In the 15th century, the term "individual" simply meant indivisible and was typically used to describe a numerically singular thing. But during this period, it was also beginning to be used to refer to "a person".
>
> INDIVIDUAL: "in" (not) + "divisible" (able to be divided)
>
> From the 17th century on, the term "individual" began to be assigned to a single human, a distinct entity indicating separateness, a recognizable thing within the whole.
>
> And it was during this period that this newly formed singular entity was assumed to be a tabula rasa (a "blank slate"), shaped from birth by experience as registered via the senses and the knowledge acquired through instruction.

The individual as an independent entity was slowly being carved out of the herd of humanity and set apart as an object worthy of deeper scientific study. The new "It" (You) was slowly being given form and function, human relevancy. The subject became the object, and the object began to acknowledge itself as the subject.

We stopped looking upward for guidance and began to look inward. A new context was beginning to take shape and a language was emerging to give it form as the human mind evolved along with it, ready to accept the change.

The abundance and goodness held within the experience of life itself became transcendental and the inescapable structure of power that had dictated order for ages was being thoroughly examined and interrogated. Aesthetics (the principles concerned with the nature and appreciation of beauty) began to replace asceticism (the severe self-discipline and avoidance of all forms of self-indulgence).

In art, a revolution was being expressed in a surprisingly realistic single-point perspective less dictated by the demands of God and more by the subject itself, the existence of man as he was, situated singularly and autonomously in the world.

Time and change were beginning to turn the mind over.

———◆———

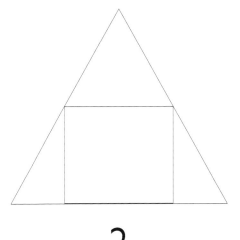

2

ALONE TOGETHER

Unhinge a creaky door and the weather and the world pour in.

In the early 19th century, the former Spanish and Portuguese colonies of South America were eager to establish economic relations with the new global superpower, the British Empire. Britain was equally keen to fuel its burgeoning industrial revolution with the immense mineral wealth of the newly discovered Americas. However, the uncharted coastline of South America made navigation by ship dangerous and the number of wrecked ships was becoming costly to the Empire in both cargo and crew. So, in the early 1830's, Britain assembled an elite corps of scientific and mathematical officers to carry out extensive chart-making efforts along the eastern seaboard of South America. One of the survey ships assigned to the effort, the *H.M.S. Beagle*, was under the command of Captain Robert Fitzroy R.N.[28]

A recent Cambridge biology graduate, a boy considered rudderless by his own father, was selected to serve as both naturalist and conversational companion to the worldly and educated Captain Fitzroy. The twenty-two-year-old was granted a special position as the onboard guest and social equal of the captain. The junior officers called him "sir." Captain Fitzroy simply called him Philos, or the *ship's philosopher*.[29] The name listed on the ship's manifest read *Charles Robert Darwin*.

In early 1835, the H.M.S. *Beagle* finally reached the coast of Chile and put anchor in the calm narrow harbor off the town of Concepcion. One spring morning after a walk through the woods gathering specimens and making notes, the young Darwin stretched out on the grass for a brief rest when it all began to shake. In his diary, Darwin would note: "*It was like the movement felt by a person skating over thin ice, which bends under the weight of his body.*"[30]

The Concepcion earthquake in Chile occurred on February 20, 1835 at 11:30 am local time and lasted approximately two minutes, registering 8.5 in magnitude on the Richter scale. No house was left standing. Fires burned up and down the coast. Those who had managed to save any personal property were obliged to keep a constant watch for thieves and the growing mob of desperate, starving survivors.

> *"At each little trembling of the ground, with one hand*
> *they beat their breasts and cried "Misericordia!" and with*
> *the other filched what they could from the ruins."*
> — CHARLES DARWIN (DIARY ENTRY)

Then came the wave. A 20-foot tsunami rose unannounced out of the deep and broke over the city. Those still alive were drowned or washed out to sea.

◆

A destabilizing new perspective.

Theories resulting from Darwin's voyage on the Beagle would be captured in a book entitled *On the Origin of Species by Means of Natural Selection*. Published on November 24, 1859, it has since been called "the most influential academic book in history".[31] Six months after its release, on June 30, 1860, at the meeting of the British Association for the Advancement of Science in Oxford, England, under the witness of hundreds of interested onlookers, Darwin's theories were being hotly debated with wild accusations hurled by both sides attacking and defending Darwin's revolutionary and unsettling new findings. One advocate rose to his feet to shout the previously unimaginable assertion:

"A man has no reason to be ashamed of having an ape for his grandfather."

The crowd erupted. One Lady Brewster fainted and needed to be carried out. It was then that the former commander of the H.M.S. *Beagle*, Captain Fitzroy, burst into the proceedings clad in military uniform and waving a bible over his head to openly swear in the presence of all:

"I believe in God, not man."[32]

It would be Charles Darwin and his revolutionary ideas around the subject of evolution that would render the popular notion of the "tabula rasa", the human as a blank slate from birth, untenable. Instead, Darwin proposed that every individual was not necessarily a unique product created by the Divine but simply the net result of millions of evolutionary matings, combinations of parental characteristics mutated and adapted across a multitude of generations ending up in a single physical human form. No longer was every human considered a clean sheet for an original composition orchestrated by the Supreme, but merely a biproduct of a series of natural sequences, the result of random couplings within a species. A new life form yes, but in reality, only a combinatorial endpoint, the most recent bloom on the ever-expanding tree of life.

Distinct as you may appear, you contained a finite and identifiable host of antecedents. Each had stamped its make-up upon you and in doing so had predetermined to a high degree your forthcoming. Much, if not nearly all of what you are and what you would become, had already been coded in.

Within this finite set of inherited traits, an individual would find full evidence of its future form—intelligence, physical attributes, behavioral traits, psychological well-being, personal character formation, patterns of perception, capacity for learning, etc. This genetic blueprint would predetermine a sizable portion of You as a developing individual. How that might affect the ultimate totality of you as an individual over time was indeterminate, but you had no doubt arrived with a distinct set of pre-installed instructions.

> "An earthquake like this at once destroys the oldest associations;
> the world, the very emblem of all that is solid, moves beneath our feet
> like a crust over a fluid; one second of time conveys to the mind a strange
> idea of insecurity, which hours of reflection would never create."
> — CHARLES DARWIN (DIARY ENTRY)

So, tell me...

"Psychology has a long past but a short history."
— HERMANN EBBINGHAUS (PSYCHOLOGIST)

While Darwin's work focused on physical differences dictated by birth through evolutionary heritage, an emerging field of science was taking a keen interest in understanding how we were both different and similar in the ways of the mind. Psychology had long been regarded as a branch of philosophy, but during the last quarter of the 19th century it began to be pursued as a scientific enterprise defining itself as the "science of consciousness".[33]

Practitioners of psychology speculated that the mind was like any other aspect of nature—an objective fact for science to observe and measure. Rigorous and repeatable experiments were set up to discover a better understanding of the common characteristics inherent within the human mind. The primary technique of the early psychologists was a process called "introspection," a procedure in which one examines personal conscious experience objectively.

Introspection, as an observable and measurable occurrence however, suffered from two major problems—there was no way to resolve differences of opinion, and the creation of a control group was impossible. Only the individual experiencing the introspection could effectively explain it to those recording the results but not directly participating in the actual introspective experience. A certain impenetrable exclusivity was the result. This scientifically unsolvable nuisance proved to be a fatal flaw as participants reported different introspections under similar conditions. Thus, psychology was forced to reconsider its foundations and rethink its own method.

By the 1920s, psychologists were more likely to define their field as the "science of behavior" arguing that reputable scientific psychologists should study only what can be observed and comparatively studied—one's behavior. These newly minted "behaviorists" pitted themselves against another emergent group, the "functionalists"—a branch of psychology seeking to understand how the mind works and why we behave the way we do by analyzing how it is structured.

While behaviorists observed the individual in action and functionalists looked at the preprogrammed brain as it instructed behavior, a third even more radical theory began to take precedence, a practice that shifted the focus from the physical and observable to the secretive, unexposed layers of the mind—the unconscious.

The mysterious and hidden strata of the unconscious included suppressed experiences such as those that had occurred as a child prior to one becoming self-aware. More importantly, this unconscious was filled with the animal urges of sexual desire, the fantasies pressed down deep into the psyche, the inexplicable and the taboo subjects tucked quietly away in the unexplored corners of the brain.

According to this new psychoanalytic theory popularized by Austrian neurologist, Sigmund Freud, unconscious memories and the latent libido were core to an individual's overall being and dictated much of one's behavioral pattern, even if the individual was unaware of the overwhelming influence these suppressed thoughts might be having. According to Freud, through a dialog of free association these deep-seated desires and experiences could be exhumed, analyzed, and leveraged to explain aberrant or "abnormal" behavior.

> "A certain degree of neurosis is of inestimable value,
> especially to a psychologist."
> — SIGMUND FREUD

A young protégé of Freud named Carl Gustav Jung, agreed with Freud's underlying model and referred to it specifically as the "personal unconscious". But Jung also proposed the existence of a second, far deeper form of the unconscious that lay beneath the personal. Jung called this the "collective unconscious," a reservoir of all stored experiences and knowledge amassed by the entirety of the human species, where "archetypes", universal patterns that symbolize basic human motivations, values, and personalities, reside.[34] Jung's proof of the collective unconscious was evident in his concept of "synchronicity", or the unexplainable feelings of connectedness we all seem to share.

Jung possessed a wealth of knowledge on mythology, religion, and philosophy, and was particularly well-versed in the symbolism connected to traditions such as alchemy, Kabala, Buddhism, and Hinduism. Utilizing his vast knowledge on these subjects, Jung believed that humans experienced the unconscious through numerous symbols encountered in various aspects of life such as dreams, art, and religion.[35]

> *"Who has fully realized that history is not contained*
> *in thick books but lives in our very blood?"*
> — CARL JUNG

Freud was quick to dismiss Jung's interest in mysticism, religion, and the occult labeling these lines of thought as 'unscientific' and insisted Jung promise never to abandon the core tenet of Freud's psychoanalytic theory— sexual repression. Jung would eventually challenge Freud's obsession with the latent libido as the primary driver of human behavior believing this psychosexual focus on the unconscious to be myopic, indeterminable, and overtly negative. According to Jung, it was Freud's approach to psychology that no longer exercised sound scientific judgment.

Freud, who once called Jung his "formally adopted son", eventually accused Jung of suffering from an Oedipal complex. Freud believed Jung harbored a death wish and longed to symbolically slay the patriarch of psychoanalysis and assert himself as rightful heir to the throne of psychology. The two vehemently and publicly dismissed each other's positions as untenable and unscientific, parting ways both personally and professionally.

> *"I shall lose nothing by it, for my only emotional tie with you has been*
> *a long thin thread — the lingering effect of past disappointments."*
> SIGMUND FREUD

The burgeoning field of psychology sought to probe the deep folds of the mind to deliver answers to such questions as:

Why were we the way we were?

What was the cause of our behavior?

What is learned by us, or embedded in us, that makes us perform as we do?

Our experiences (remembered or not), our upbringing, our desires, our fantasies, our own subconscious mysteries, all areas to be probed and interrogated to locate causality. Throughout the century, newly discovered disorders of the mind would be defined and assigned engrossing new names with inventive treatments prescribed for relief and correction.

The mind, you see, was just another organ like all the rest, doing what it does, making us what we are. Through psychology, we believed we now possessed the knowledge, the language, the techniques, and the hubris to finally peer into the mind. Eventually, we would come to understand it, and sort it all out. Sort "us" all out.

◆

When man abandoned God, he made a cult out of culture.

During the late 19th century, we began to study the human organizing structure known as "society" in a similar way, as if it were a science. Through the careful observation of the relationship between the individual and his corresponding ecosystem, this new science sought to explore how society itself affected those who lived and operated within it.

The father of sociology, the French philosopher Auguste Comte, believed that all societies develop and progress through the following stages: religious, metaphysical, and scientific. Comte argued that society needed scientific knowledge based on facts and evidence to solve its problems, not speculation and superstition which characterize the religious and metaphysical stages of social development.[36]

Comte's successor, Emile Durkheim, would further these originating concepts suggesting that society was replete with its own set of "social facts" and thus could be investigated empirically using the scientific method—systematic observation, measurement, and experiment—including the formulation, testing, and modification of hypotheses.

def: **SOCIETAL FACT** – a phenomenon that has existence in and of itself not bound to the actions of individuals but have coercive influence on them.[37]

According to Durkheim, the phenomenon known as society should be considered a dynamic living thing with characteristics and traits that can be observed, measured, and eventually remedied. Its influential elements could be studied through a sort of collective psychoanalysis for the species. With enough investigation and analysis, we might learn to predict society's behavior then shape it to our will, us along with it. Data was collected, analyzed, and presented as an indicator of a society's functioning health and status.[38] In other words, the numbers would tell the story.

> *"Our whole social environment seems to be filled*
> *with forces that really exist only in our minds."*
> — EMILE DURKHEIM

Durkheim, an avowed atheist, was particularly interested in gaining a better understanding of how societies maintain their integrity and coherence in an era when the former bonds that connected people together—blood, ethnicity, religion—no longer held firm. Durkheim objectively viewed religion as the most fundamental institution of humankind, one that gave rise to a wide assortment of social forms and practices. He wondered what would or could substitute as the bonding mechanism amongst comingled and disparate humans if this deeply ingrained historical mortar failed.

The weight of the academic equation thus shifted from the individual's effect on the formation and functioning of society to its opposite—how society itself manipulated and coercively managed the actions, behaviors, and even the mind of the individual. Consider it a loss, a theft, or a capitulation, this shift in the role of critical influencer from the self to society could be viewed in many ways. But the fact remains, the autonomy of the individual as a self-directed entity was subordinated once again and soon found itself under the formative spell of the collective. Man may have made society, but now society made the man.

The elevation of society, or "culture", to the status of an authority created a living system from which the individual could not escape, but to which he might surrender. Living within the confines of this dynamic and demanding thing called society, it had become much easier for him to slip out of the role of autonomous agent and into the role of helpless casualty, a victim of the machinations of the system. Society made me do it, so blame it, not me.

Not enough water on earth to wash our hands clean.

The first half of the 20ᵗʰ century was arguably the most transformative single period in human history, a fifty-year span that radically reshaped the entire globe culturally, politically, and psychologically. As if the unimaginable devastation of a global war followed by a severe economic depression were not enough misery to endure, a second even more destructive world war would follow soon after.

This second global conflict would introduce a host of incomprehensible horrors to the collective human psyche—systematic genocide, indiscriminate bombing of defenseless civilians, entire nations swept into production for the war machine, and the development of incredibly powerful weapons capable of killing in large numbers from great distances. These new weapons were capable of death and destruction unimaginable to those who had fought in "the war to end all wars" just two decades before. A strange and permanent feature would be added to the already nervous collective human experience—the capacity to extinguish our own species altogether.

Through five decades, we had once again irrevocably demonstrated the depths of depravity to which humankind is willing to descend when the tribal instinct returns and overwhelms our apprehension of "the good" and our innate sense of a shared humanity. Our collective animal nature resurfaced to invoke the haunting question originally proposed by the Russian novelist Fyodor Dostoyevsky:

"If God does not exist, is everything permitted?"

This self-inflicted experience resulted in a deep and widespread existential angst, an unsettling disorientation about how far we had strayed from the center of ourselves. Under this dark cloud of failure, modern man found himself alone, confused, and in shock. Out from under wave upon wave of shameful episodes, he would emerge into an uncertain and chaotic world, a place where every man viewed the other with suspicion and the whole of humanity was held in utter disregard. This newly imprinted consciousness would require a strong solvent to erase the horrors of the past and re-establish a sense of moral clarity to escape half a century of unbridled insanity.

What we now sought was a way to rediscover and embrace the hope held in our own humanness and in the potential of all humankind. Somehow, we needed to regain the trust we had once held for the future of the human species.

◆

What can I become?

In the years that followed the end of World War II, a new line of thinking would emerge, an attempt to tap into man's latent but not yet lost potential, the diminished light still resident within each individual. This "introspective man" would be asked to step forward and distinguish himself as a subject ready for renewal through a process of deep introspection and self-correction.

Within this new paradigm, he would be challenged to renounce the destructive instinct of the herd and assert himself as his own true moral axis. He would be called to discount (or disregard altogether) the demands of a divine authority or the governing body of man's own making—laws, morals, ethics, traditions, etc. to reposition himself back at the center. This intellectual movement would ask of him one thing: To assume full responsibility for the formation of his own becoming.

According to this philosophic theory, any individual, when engaged in a world of pure choice, could rediscover himself by simply being. Isolated in the unreasonable silence of the world, the authentic, autonomous, and responsible existent known as man, now devoid of God, eternal truths, tribal dictates, and any external guiding principle, would be empowered to formulate his own meaning. He would be asked to actuate his own realization and understand himself as a separate, discreet, accountable singularity. Man alone would have to move himself beyond what he *was*, toward what he could *become*.

"Existence precedes essence."
— JEAN-PAUL SARTRE

The founder and intellectual leader of this new movement known as Existentialism, was Jean-Paul Sartre. According to Sartre, consciousness alone determined how we interpreted the world, independent of our inherited nature, societal coercion, or any divine intervention. He believed man alone, of his own accord, could elevate himself above his own "facticity"— his condition as a "situated character in the world", one who exists "as is". This defining term would include all other aspects of his being, his own set of individualized circumstances within a contextual period of history.

FACTICITY

- Properties such as weight, height, and skin color
- Social facts such as race, class, origin, nationality, and cultural heritage
- Psychological properties like beliefs, desires, cognitive structure, and inherent imprinting
- Historical facts like past actions, family background

According to Existentialism, no single man's wish, desire, curse, or prayer could change the world. The only difference one can make is through conscious thought transposed into action. And in action, life's meaning could be found. Yet the power now assumed by the individual maintained certain self-evident limitations. A person by sheer force of will could not wish upon himself different genetic characteristics or alter his external environment. One could not through willful desire become a bird or a tree, just as he could not resurrect a lost loved one or will away an abusive childhood. What the existentialists proposed, however, was that since one's consciousness comes first, one can *choose* how to think, respond to, or feel about one's genetic background or environmental characteristics.[39]

The philosophy of Existentialism involved a resolute commitment made by the self to the self. It would ask every person to assume full responsibility for their own life, a life lived transparently through discipline and integrity, including the realization that choices must be made, and those choices are what form the self. And within every authentic choice an implicit contract between all individuals was established—a respect for the freedom of all others to make choices as if those choices were one's own.

Existentialism's universal strength was in the power it generated through an evenly distributed network of individuals each responsible for their own enlightened elevation and the manifestation of life's meaning through the conscious development of the self.

"Man is condemned to be free."

— JEAN-PAUL SARTRE

Despite its decreed position of respect for the choices of every man, some criticized Existentialism's worldview as narrow, pessimistic, and too overtly individualistic. The applied practice of Existentialism some argued, would lead to a concern only for oneself, a certain 'quietism of despair' as one inevitably abandoned all collective social responsibility for strictly selfish pursuits.

Regardless of its commonsensical nature and the limitless potential of its principles, this innovation in modern thought slowly lost momentum and eventually fell from favor. Existentialism as a philosophical movement was intellectually emptied, plundered under a barrage of pointed criticism. It was considered too closely aligned with humanism when European intellectual trends were broadly anti-humanist, if not downright dismissive of the human species altogether.

More precisely, it had become dangerously intertwined with one particular individual, its founder, Jean-Paul Sartre. He said too much, strayed too far, and rose too high upon the ladder of individual distinction for the comfort of his own tribe. Infatuated with his own fame, conflicted by his own inadequacies, and seduced by a utopic political vision, while willing to embrace violence to achieve it, the founder and lead advocate of the movement failed to practice the very philosophy he had come to espouse.

"The slave starts by begging for justice
and ends by wanting to wear the crown."

— ALBERT CAMUS

Contemporary thinkers who worked to undermine the Existentialist movement re-enlisted the assistance of the perennial psychological boogeyman, the ghost who persistently haunted man's dreams and destroyed any fantasy he might harbor establishing his own sovereignty. They would put forth that the more likely suspect in man's ongoing saga of failure was not man himself, but an exotic counter-resistant force, those who stood in opposition to the formation of the genuine self—the evasive and elusive "Other". Something outside one's own self must be the cause of our shared predicament and thus the very reason for our despair.

For them, an autonomous human agent could never assume full authority over his own choices, as every man was driven by forces beyond his own cognizance and control. Whether macro-structures (the tribe, society, religious authority, institutions, etc.) or micro-structures (the unconscious, sexual urges, the lust for power, etc.), something beyond the consciously autonomous subject needed to be doggedly pursued and ferreted out as the ultimate catalyst and culprit.

Ultimately however, Existentialism as a movement would not be undone by the cunning phantom known as "the Other", or even the arrival of seditious new philosophical theory, but rather by an insurgent socio-political crusade—Marxism. This fast-rising political theory imagined a society made up of perfectly equal beings, devoid of self-interest, and beholden only to the advancement and perfection of the entire collective. Even Existentialism's own founder would be seduced by its promise—an on-earth utopia.

For this earthly paradise to succeed however, man would once again surrender the core of his own being—choice, freedom, autonomy—to the will and demands of the herd. Every man would now be required to step off the course of his own self-interest to allow himself to be molded into a static likeness of the Other for the greater good of all. A shared equal outcome for every member of the tribe must supersede the sanctity and sovereignty of the self.

From each according to his ability, to each according to his needs.

Alone together.

The term "philosophy" directly translated means "love of wisdom". It is attributed to the miracle-performing Greek mathematician and spiritualist known as Pythagoras (570 – 495 BCE). Pythagoras spent twenty years in Egypt studying their mystical sciences and absorbing their views on the mysteries of human existence.

While in Egypt, Pythagoras would come to believe that the true understanding of existence can only be availed through a thoughtful penetration of the self. The mind needs nothing more than its own power to reach an understanding of all that is and must be. No external force is required to achieve the fulfillment of self—all lies within. Once this concept has been recognized and absorbed, a new perceptivity manifests within the self to propagate all future thought and action.

For Pythagoras, philosophy performed at its deepest level, within the self, may be the best guide for spiritual purification.

As an intellectual discipline, philosophy has historically focused on three key themes:

1 What is real? (metaphysical)
2 What do we know? (epistemological)
3 How should we live? (ethical)

Philosophy has evolved through a slow succession of competing theories all seeking to establish objective truths about how we are, why we are, and why life is as it is. Every proposition hopes to provide a more precise and enlightened explanation for human existence and as a result, a more productive and instructive means to deal with the hazards and mysteries inherent in the human condition. For any new philosophical theory to emerge and take root, however, old paradigms must be dissected and debunked, and their originators intellectually discredited and dismissed.

def: **OEDIPALISM** – The insatiable desire of every new thinker to reach back in time and philosophically slay the father of the last most popular theory. (Not a real word.)

Despite the simple and profound universal quest of philosophy, one particularly short-sighted tendency within the academic community of intellectual thinkers has been the mutual distrust of any approach that elevates personal consciousness and the formation of the sovereign self to the status of a philosophy. Why? Because it ends the game. Such thinking assumes too much authority for the individual to the preclusion of any and all overarching universal, external, and objective "truths". It shifts the focus (and thus the blame) for our condition away from the Other and the herd and back on the self. In addition, it reduces or even eliminates the need to study, analyze, and redesign the societal structures and institutional orders that lie outside the individual mind.

If the individual, of his own volition, aware of his conscious self, and in control of his own thoughts, discovers that the mind has the power to shape life in accordance with the course of the intended self, and in doing so positively affects the direction and destination of not only himself but of humankind altogether, what is left to discover, invent, systematize, or even consider philosophically?

"The individual is the only reality."
— CARL JUNG

Since the beginning of conscious thought, humans have served as our subject of greatest interest. Our own species has been the primary and principle focus of our intellectual pursuits since the day we were first able to describe who and what we are in the simplest of terms. And this relentless study of us seems to hold no bounds, for we continue to confound and confuse ourselves, often with amusing and sometimes deadly results. Just when we think we have ourselves all figured out, we wrestle free from our own definitions and construct entire new paradigms that are said to expose the errors of previous explanations. We dismiss recent failures as naïve or simply underperforming so we can gleefully expound upon the glorious possibilities of the shiny new next.

It is easy to discount theories of the past, those concepts that were based upon the available knowledge of the day as ignorant, primitive, or archaic. Yet from the oldest ideas all the way forward to the empirically precise theorems of today, a pattern emerges: We exist alone together.

We are mindful of our own mortality, knowledgeable of our own uniqueness, instinctively competitive, willing to cooperate when necessary, driven by curiosity, capable of radical innovation, pre-configured with a genetic blueprint yet vested with the capacity for self-directed change.

And riding shotgun as always, the impulse for self-deceit.

———◆———

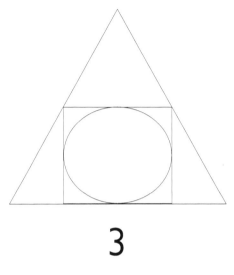

3

WHERE IS MY MIND?

The brain-mind complex.

To begin discussing the concept of the self without a thorough examination of the human brain would be like setting sail across the ocean without any knowledge of the ship, or the wind, or the sea, or the tides, or the stars....

"Far and away, the human brain is the most
complex object known in the universe."
— PATRICIA CHURCHLAND (PHILOSOPHER)

A few facts about the brain that might blow your mind: The brain…

- Occupies only 2 percent of your body yet consumes 20 percent of your oxygen supply.
- Contains 86 billion neurons, each neuron generating 1,000 impulses per second with 100 trillion potential neuro-transmitting connections.
- Hosts over 10,000 distinct types of neurons. The intestines contain 100 million neurons. A second brain?
- Generates over 50,000 thoughts per day. Of those thoughts, 70 percent are negative self-critical, pessimistic, fearful, etc.[40]
- Holds the capacity for nearly unlimited storage—one quadrillion bytes, or 10^{15}, or 1,000,000,000,000,000.
- Consists of 73 percent water. Of the dry material, 60 percent is fat.
- Cannot feel pain. The brain contains no pain receptors.
- Has changed very little since the appearance of Homo sapiens approximately 200,000 years ago.
- Has shrunk in size for the past 20,000 years. IQ has been falling since 1975. [41]

◆

So, let us compare…

The side-by-side comparison of one thing to another is a core function of the human brain. Comparison is how we come to know our position in relation to other things in both place and time. It is how we learn to locate the self upon the ladder of rank, or in other words, the level of our perceived status within any established hierarchy. We search for the means to measure the distance and difference between "me" and "it."

So how does the human brain with its 86 billion neurons compare to those of a few of our earthly companions?

- Gorilla – 33.5 billion neurons
- Chimpanzee – 28 billion
- Dog – 2.2 billion
- Cat – 760 million (Sorry cat lovers.)
- Octopus – 500 million
- Pigeon – 310 million
- Naked mole rat – 27 million
- Cockroach – 1 million
- Fruit fly – 250,000
- Pond snail – 11,000
- Roundworm (C. Elegans) – 302
- Dwarf male symbion pandora – a humbling 32 (No mention of the female. We'll just assume it's higher.) [42]

The massive yet modest African elephant hosts a staggering 257 billion neurons—three times the average human brain, while the lowly jellyfish holds the title for "Largest Organism Without a Brain" tipping the scales at a grand total of zero. Zilch. Nada.

What about our distant ocean-going cousin the dolphin? Unknown. Despite my limited research, an exact figure for the total number of dolphin-brain neurons could not be located. (A conspiracy to keep the brilliant dolphin silent? Probably.) However, dolphins do possess significantly more brain folds, a key determinant in measuring intelligence, surpassing humans in total brain surface area by quite a wide margin.

But it may be the unheralded tunicate, or the "sea squirt" as it is more commonly known, who captures the crown for most creative in the "No Brains Required" category. This intrepid little undersea hermaphrodite spends most of its early maturity boldly navigating the open seas, but once it locates a place to call home it fixes itself permanently to a rock and consumes its own brain.

> The Egyptians did not consider the brain to be of much importance. At the time of preparation for burial, all the vital organs were removed and stored in an urn while the body was being mummified. Both the body and organs were considered vitally necessary and would be required for continued existence in the next life.
>
> The brain, however, was removed through the nose and unceremoniously discarded.

Nearly all animal brains are similar in appearance and structure. And if the brain of any one species was placed alongside another, it would be indistinguishable, an exact physical replica. And yet, while these two brains may appear similar in both size and appearance, no two are alike, not even close.

So, what makes one brain unique from another? In a word, patterns. The difference between each brain lies in the combinatorial arrangements of its tiny constituents, the pattern of neural connections.[43] The brain is a map of connectivity as unique as the retina (or for you old schoolers, the fingerprint). This pattern of connectivity within a single individual's brain determines how one perceives, analyzes, comprehends, cognates, and behaves.

def: **PATTERN** –

1 to give a regular and intelligible form to

2 a reliable sample of traits, acts, tendencies, or other observable characteristics of a person, group, or institution

3 a discernible regularity

4 a code, program [44]

It was once believed that we are born with all the brain cells we will ever possess. This has since been found to be untrue. The brain has evolved a radical plasticity regenerating itself physically, constantly rewiring its internal paths of transmission.

The human brain is not merely a thought-production engine though, or even a passive absorptive sponge, it is a hyper-active filter constantly reviewing, parsing, and sorting inbound data then comparing it against known patterns to try to make sense of the world as it rushes at us. Animals of all species use pattern-recognition as a key feature in both survival and procreation—from the recognition of the movement of prey, to the coloration shifts of potential mates, to the posture of a threatening foe.

Humans have developed highly acute pattern recognition skills that empower us to receive voluminous streams of inbound stimuli via the senses while mapping it against an endless array of possible meanings and potential associations produced by consciousness. It enables us to sort through billions of data points to determine what is important, what is irrelevant, what needs to be processed, what must be analyzed, and what should be stored. The brain's high-speed calculating and processing engine enables us to intuit situations, avoid danger, form opinions, formulate strategies, take action, innovate, and invent.

Our brain's powerful pattern recognition capacity is a mix-matching of familiarity (patterns seen before), curiosity (patterns never seen), and mystery (patterns that cannot be "seen"). Some facets of the human pattern recognition facility are shared as we all emerged from a line of common evolutionary predecessors. In the primitive past, our ancestors experienced a similar earthly existence and thus certain communal patterns are imprinted deep into the core of each of our inherited brains.

Human processing begins with a simple contra, the core characteristic of human curiosity: Is it a good thing good or a bad thing? The brain develops distinctions, a self-determining level of interest about a thing, person, event, or process that can assist in situating that thing in our reality. To operate with any level of efficiency, we need to quickly determine something's status, its immediate position within the structure of the known. From this basic initial stacking we can then add slight modifications, nuances, infinite variations, personal associations, and a seemingly unlimited array of complications. We make the simple complex using the mind as our matrix and language as our causal agent.

Patterns are a code, and each code is deciphered and analyzed in a distinctly different manner by each individual. No two human pattern-recognition engines are the same, not even remotely. Each of us maps the world according to our own wiring never to be duplicated, replicated, nor explained in a way that could make sense to anyone else. We are trapped in the cage of our own minds unable to fully articulate our individual experience, the one thing we wish to share in order to be better understood. The condition of the mind is a universal conundrum—the potential for both supreme connection and desperate isolation.

Albert Einstein, the Nobel prize-winning physicist, died in Princeton Hospital on April 18, 1955. Einstein had stated openly that after his death he did not want his body or brain to be studied. He did not want to be worshipped. So, he left behind specific instructions regarding his remains: "Cremate them and scatter the ashes secretly in order to discourage idolaters."

Thomas Harvey, the pathologist on call that night, stole Einstein's brain.

Harvey soon lost his job at the hospital and took the brain with him to Philadelphia where he carved it up into 240 pieces and preserved it in celloidin, a hard and rubbery form of cellulose. He divvied up the pieces into two jars and stored them in his basement.

A short time later, he moved to Wichita, keeping the brain in a cider box stashed under a beer cooler. He once again was forced to relocate, this time to Lawrence, Kansas, as an assembly-line worker in a plastic factory. He moved into a second-floor apartment next to a gas station and befriended a neighbor, the beat poet William Burroughs. The two men routinely met for drinks on Burroughs's front porch.

In 1985, Harvey and collaborators in California published the first study of Einstein's brain claiming that it had an abnormal proportion of two types of cells: neurons and glia. Five additional studies followed reporting differences in individual cells or structures in Einstein's brain. The researchers behind these studies said studying Einstein's brain would soon uncover the neurological underpinnings of intelligence.[45]

Unfortunately, all studies proved inconclusive. Einstein's brain was not extraordinary. In fact, it was notably unimpressive. His blob of fat just like yours. Not a blip of difference.

Since the time of the ancient sages, the functioning of the human brain was believed to share an undeniable resemblance to the mechanics of the universe. Theories suggested the existence of a cosmic connection between the infinite firmament above and the inner-workings of the human brain—just one massive celestial machine directly connected by a series of invisible interlocking gears. The mind much like the heavens above, always churning, never at rest, dark and impenetrable, hopeful and infinite, in search of harmony and balance to hold itself together.

This proposed pattern of similarity is curiously alluring. We could begin to draw up the chart to map this plausible comparison, but sadly we don't know enough about the human brain to even begin. In fact, we know almost nothing about the very thing that makes us something and enables us to know anything. In real terms, we know less about the brain than we know.

> "If the brain were so simple that we could understand it,
> we would be so simple that we couldn't."
> — GEORGE EDGIN PUGH (NUCLEAR PHYSICIST)

Just 3.3 pounds of fat, water, chemistry, and electricity. Makes you think.

Where is my mind?

What is the difference between the brain and the mind? The brain is a machine, and the mind is...well, it's not totally clear. The brain is physical, visible, measurable (to a degree), locatable, and singular. The mind is more an invisible web of thoughts, feelings, attitudes, beliefs, desires, memories, perceptions, and associations all fueled by imagination. In fact, the world of science has of yet been unable to agree upon an actual definition of "the mind."

One unscientific explanation might be: The mind is a manifest combination of experience (senses), learning (observations and mimicry), and some seemingly pre-installed set of knowledge independent of experience ("a priori"). This "a priori" knowledge was there before we knew it. It is the kernel of information embedded in us all, shared in the abstract yet subtly unique amongst each of us. It is considered a preset collection of inherited things: our common instinctual responses to certain stimuli, the capacity for language, the fundamental awareness of right and wrong, and other assorted mental stuff assumed to be present in the mind but not gained through living or learning.

Is the mind within the brain? Unknown. Theories suggest the affirmative, but the issue remains unsettled. For our purposes, we will assume that the mind simply exists. Its location within the body is irrelevant. It forms the determination of what we are, what we know, and what we can become. And while each brain is similar in form, shape, color, and material, and each appears alike in capacity—the ability to learn language, use tools, think in the abstract, consider the past and future—no two can be considered the same.

And yet, despite the acknowledged differentiation of one mind from the next, we seem to all share a persistent tendency, an innate attraction toward a uniform and universal destiny—a more comfortable, less stressful, less painful, less violent existence. This shared destiny is loosely embedded in the concept known as "progress," an irreversible momentum that seems to remain consistent across the human experience.

In 1807, the German idealist thinker, Georg Wilhelm Friedrich Hegel, developed a philosophical theory implying history had a grand unified purpose, an intelligible process moving towards a specific condition—the realization of human freedom.

Hegel regarded the relationship between "objective" history and the "subjective" development of individual consciousness ('spirit') as quite intimate. A connection that was vitally intertwined.

While at the same time, the whole damn thing can sometimes seem like a grand cosmic accident, billions of things moving independently and randomly about without any apparent purpose or plan—no connection, no direction, no common destination, just an unruly mob of self-absorbed automatons knocking about seeking pleasure, avoiding pain.

Yet, in moments of stillness one can almost sense the directional drift, the communal momentum of progress carrying the entire operation along, all moving toward some indeterminate but ultimate shared destination. What progress specifically means might be unique to each individual, but it seems to be ushering the herd in one general direction.

Mind (You).

If your brain were removed and reinserted into the body of another, would that body then become "You"? To formulate a better understanding of the self, we will work under the assumption that the mind is you. It holds the blueprint and operating system that manifests the concept we believe to be "You." Are you in control of your own mind, and if so, by what means? Or is the mind in control of you? Who is directing (or deceiving) whom? More importantly, what does the mind *want*?

> *"It can never be satisfied, the mind…never."*
> — WALLACE STEVENS (POET)

If the mind is so powerful, and we alone are in possession of it, why is it so hard to change? Habit, comfort, fear, complacency, time, vulnerability, helplessness, lack of know-how, inability to let go, pressure from family, friends, society, history, laziness, bitterness, our well-honed skill of blaming others…shall I go on? In the simplest of terms, the mind is choice: What to see, how to feel, when to act, how to behave, etc. And the human mind possesses a unique and uncontested super-power: to change itself.

> *"The mind is everything. What you think, you become."*
> — BUDDHA

What exactly does the brain produce? Despite a costly and stubborn pursuit by a wide range of academic disciplines—linguistics, neurobiology, philosophy, psychology, sociology, cognitive science—a universally accepted explanation for both the genesis and execution of human thought continues to outwit us. Although I think we can all confidently agree thoughts exist. We all have them, a lot of them. (And as noted earlier, not all of them good.)

def: **THINKING** – the process of considering or reasoning about something[46]
def: **THOUGHT** – an idea or opinion produced by thinking[47]

For such a complex, profound, and provocative process (or product), the above two definitions could not seem more pitifully banal. A conscious thought, the result of an evolutionary marvel, if not an outright miracle, ironically eludes the reach of our own advanced intelligence and lies beyond the limits of our vast vocabulary.

Where do thoughts originate? Many believe a thought is generated within (invention), while others believe it originates without (revelation). According to those who have dedicated their lives to studying the science of thinking, the mind does not actually "produce" thoughts at all, it filters and restricts them just as our senses selectively limit the totality of our experience to which we might otherwise have access. The mind singles out that which will enter and be considered intentionally as part of what we call "experience" or "reality".

Does all thinking occur in the brain? Unknown. Many assert that it does not. In fact, it has been posited that thinking does not take place within the physical body at all. In this proposed scenario, the brain is not considered an output mechanism or a transmitter of thought, but a receiver dialed into a band of inbound frequencies. In other words, programmed to receive. But frequencies emanating from what? Or whom? And why?

From ancient thinkers to mystical poets to modern age scientists, some truly believe there exists only one—The One Mind or The Great Mind—a cosmic super-intelligent structure of universally transmitted thought. Signals from The One Mind are somehow captured and filtered through our individual minds, the human brain serving as earthly receiver. Every thought, every action, every choice, every possibility, every thought ever thought or any thought that one day might be thought, conjured by The One Mind, the grand metaphysical thinking machine.

If this theory were true, even this word must be pre-ordained and I am merely a medium to bring it into existence. I become a simple extension, a facilitator of a master plan without the possibility (or risk) of deviation, merely a subject under the control of some remote, nameless, unknowable master. And if this mega-mind does indeed exist, one would naturally believe a degree of uniformity would prevail in all thought? Certain "universals"—concepts, ideas, rules, guidelines, conventions, truths, etc.— must underlie all human thought and action? If real, our own thoughts must be predetermined.

While certain guiding frequencies and universal forces might affect our momentum and even our direction, a master central command of thought seems unlikely. For what kind of super-natural originator would instruct certain individuals to act in such cruel, and inhumane ways? How demented this great mind would have to be to host and broadcast such dark dimensions of thought. And if this concept were true, why only the human brain? What differentiates the human brain as receiver from all those possessed by every other animal on the planet?

> According to science, the natural world contains about 8.7 million known species. The vast majority of which have yet to be identified. Cataloging all the current known species could take more than 1,000 years.[48]
>
> Researchers have attempted to use the laws of math (scaling, or proportional change between two variables) to make a best guess estimate of all species of life including both micro and macro.
>
> Using this method, it is believed as many as one trillion species may exist on Earth.[49]

Does a thought actually exist? In other words, can it come into comprehension as a thought without some frame of reference, a means to recognize it as "a thought"? To become a thing we can identify or acknowledge, a thought must exist in some form. It must take recognizable shape, a means to become present and distinguishable within the mind as something that now is but wasn't before. Second, it must be constructed using language—the cognitive structure for architecting understanding. And lastly, it must possess some nameable entities to make it "real"—objects or subjects, abstract or otherwise, to which we can attach meaning.

> "The eye sees only what the mind is prepared to comprehend."
> — HENRI BERGSON (PHILOSOPHER)

To comprehend a thing as a thing or construct a path toward the possible understanding of anything, requires a framework, a structure as a means by which the vast assortment of inputs can be organized, stored, and retrieved as necessary. This organizing system enables us to construct the world abstractly and then exist within it with some sense of familiarity. Our individual cognitive structure enables us to function with a modicum of efficiency by facilitating the rapid distillation and interpretation of incoming sensory information to enable us to perform in the theatre of the world without incessant interference, hesitation, or reflection. Without this parsing and prejudicing infrastructure, the sheer volume of inbound sensory data would quickly overwhelm the system.

Can we prove that we *have* conscious thoughts—abstract, self-aware, isolated yet roaming freely between the past, present and future? And if so, can we come to understand why? If the true believers in the undeniable sanctity of evolution are correct, there must be a biological necessity for advanced human thought that has empowered us to better adapt to our environment and thereby increase our chances for survival. Yet nearly every other living creature on earth has managed to not only survive but thrive without the asset of advanced and abstract thought.

What advantage does an elevated level of intellectual thought gain the human species?

◆

I think I know what you're thinking.

What are we referring to when we say, "the mind"? Do we believe the mind, intelligence, and consciousness are one and the same? Can we get to know an individual by peering into one's mind or through an analysis of one's intelligence?

Science has supposedly developed a sophisticated tool to see into the mind through imaging technology like positron emissions tomography (PET). Researchers have announced they can now take "objective readings" inside the black box of the mind, measurable data that can be used for further analysis and study. This approach suggests that an eventual understanding of the human mind is not only possible but probable.

A new interdisciplinary approach that leverages the tools of evolutionary psychology, linguistics, philosophy, neurobiology, and computer science, is attempting to answer the simple question: "What is a mind?" The covert mission of cognitive science may be less to understand the mind as a serviceable and knowable thing but more an effort to reverse-engineer human intelligence. (An immodest quest to say the least.) The knowledge gained through such exploration can then be applied to other domains, such as the emerging field of artificial intelligence (AI).[50]

Critics assert that this computational-representational approach deployed by cognitive science, while successful in explaining many aspects of the distinguishing features of being human (problem solving, learning, language, etc.) is just empirical conjecture and may just be dead wrong. Yet, the more thought-provoking inquiry might be: What is the objective of such a bold pursuit? What would a complete understanding of all the mechanisms of the mind yield us? What problem or problems are we trying to solve?

> "Thought is a system, in the sense that it is an interconnected network
> of concepts, ideas and assumptions that pass seamlessly between individuals
> and throughout society. The thought that is brought to bear to resolve any
> given problem, therefore, is susceptible to the same flaw that created
> the problem it is trying to solve.
>
> Thought proceeds as if it is merely reporting objectively, but in fact,
> it is often coloring and distorting perception in unexpected ways.
> What is required to correct the distortions introduced by thought,
> is a form of proprioception, or self-awareness."
>
> — DAVID BOHM (PHYSICIST)

◆

A product of the mind.

Is thought simply another process to be studied? Does it produce a physically detectable dataset of electro-chemical patterns generated by or through neurons in the brain that can be measured and analyzed? Is it biological, mechanical, chemical…super-natural? With all the massive amounts of brain activity taking place, what is it that determines what is manifested and rises to the surface as a recognizable thought, and why? What about all those other not-yet-fully-formed concepts that lie just below the threshold of cognition?

Is it *all* just a matter of mind? Is thought a one-person show played without intermission to an audience of one? And more importantly, who (or what) is running the show? Is thought a wave? A particle? A form of light? A product of pure energy? And if thought is energy, can it travel beyond our physical body to enter the cosmos? Do human thoughts ever intersect? Or do they remain forever isolated? Is there a difference between a feeling and a thought? When and where does a thought end? Is a thought the only true form of human freedom?

After a while, the questions begin to overwhelm. The human mind is simply beyond our own means to measure it. It is a self-perpetuating enigma, the primary source of infinite uncertainty and ultimate possibility. Any attempt to comprehend the mind using merely the power of the brain is a madman's mission, a persistent fool's errand. The concept of thought lies simply and paradoxically outside our own ability to understand it.

"All that we are is the result of what we have thought."
— BUDDHA

All that is seen, felt, heard, believed, or understood, is a product of the mind. Thought makes matter and non-matter both tangible and accessible—trees, people, flowers, friends, family, events, stories, sadness, joy, pain, God, etc. Every second immediately rendered by the mind into a habitable zone in which we can exist, while at the same time opening up the realm of infinity, the curiosity of a boundless imagination.

A simple human thought is a singularly unique construction unlike any other experienced by any other being at any moment in time. One that has occurred only once and will never occur again.

"Sapere aude." ("Dare to know")

Perhaps after a few more chapters in human evolution, a bit more data, and a few more high-powered tools, we will be able to grasp the true power of the mind. Science says it's just a matter of time. One day it will all make sense. The mystery will finally be revealed in a finite set of irrefutable facts. Hard to imagine, for we may not be fact at all, just splendid fiction.

The quilt-work of comprehension.

The words "comprehend" and "understand" are often used interchangeably. Both words effectively mean "to grasp the meaning of". But in most cases "to understand" stresses the final result, while "to comprehend" stresses the process of getting there.[51] So what is the process that allows us to comprehend something?

Within each individual mind, "knowledge" begins as isolated units of apprehension—each unit specific and distinct yet disconnected. These units lie scattered about the mind in a random, indeterminate pattern, one fragment unknown and perhaps unrecognizable to the next. Somehow these units are activated by the attraction of associative similarity and begin to link up. These new pairings then group together in a pattern of correspondence to form active segments that compound and complement one another.

Each subsequent linkage of these active segments reinforces attraction while exerting an equal force of resistance. This force ties together like-minded segments while preventing unlike conceptual segments from connecting. These now-linked segments then stitch together into more cohesive and comprehensive sub-assemblies of semi-identifiable thought. These sub-assemblies finally align themselves into a new form, an intellectually identifiable pattern of a conscious thought made recognizable through the medium of language.

The quilt that is composed of complete thought may not yet be final, but it has crossed over from a patchwork of inoperative fragments into a retrievable and usable form. A new emergent thing now exists in a way it could not be seen before within the mind. It has evolved from the unavailable and immaterial into the visible and understandable. In a sense, it has become a work of art. (We will explore this concept a bit further in the future.)

◆

Yes, but do you understand?

I can say that I know that $2+2=4$, but do I truly understand it? I can represent the equation through physical means to form a comprehensible reality. In other words, I can take two stones combine them with two more stones to both see and feel a total of four stones. And from there, I can abstract the formula into symbols to be applied to future considerations of the same equation.

I can even grasp a phenomenon that exists beyond my awareness of tangible things, for example, a solar eclipse. My mind can mentally realize the relationship of its causal agents—the orb of the sun and moon intersecting in space to affect the interplay of light upon Earth. Associative reasoning and past experiences of objects and light allow the concept to be intellectually absorbed, then abstracted and manifested within my mind. I can name the things involved, comprehend the shape of their forms, acknowledge their relationship to one another, and build the model that I set into motion inside my head. I can imaginatively "see" it working and evidence of similar events within my known visual reality verifies the possibility of it as such.

But if I am told that an invisible force called gravity prevents me from being hurled off the face of the earth while it spins on its axis at nearly 1,000 miles-per-hour, as it hauls ass through space around the sun at an incomprehensible 67,756 miles-per-hour, and that this clinging thing that holds me upside down is due to the mass of the planet, not as a force but as a consequence of the curvature of a thing called spacetime which is caused by the uneven distribution of objects that also have mass…can I come to really know it? I cannot feel it, see it, sense it, or experience it in a way that substantiates it within my own reality. Am I able to embrace the uncertainty and resign myself to the fact that I might not ever truly come to understand it?

def: **UNDERSTAND**

1 perceive the intended meaning of (words, a language, or a speaker).
2 interpret or view (something) in a particular way.[52]

Moreover, how can we be said to understand what it means to understand if we do not know what the verb "to understand" means? The perplexingly enigmatic concept of the term "understanding" seems to avoid being defined in a way that can be easily absorbed. In fact, the construction of the word "understanding" in English is a misunderstanding at its very core.

It has evolved in such a way as to convey that "to understand" one must effectively "stand under" it, like a mechanic diagnosing a problem while staring at the undercarriage of a car perched upon a lift.

But in fact, the root of the word "*standan*" (to stand) is modified not by the more recent translation "*under*" (beneath), but more accurately the proto-Indian-European root "*nter*" (between, among) whose sources are Sanskrit "*antar*" (between), Latin "*inter*" (between, among) and Greek "*intera*" (intestines). Therefore, to understand, we must somehow enter that which we are attempting to grasp intellectually. We must wade into it and allow ourselves to be fully immersed in it.

> "*Penetration means to enter something, not just to stand outside of it. When we want to understand something, we cannot just stand outside and observe it.*
>
> *We have to enter deeply into it and be one with it in order to understand. To comprehend something means to pick it up and be one with it. There is no other way to understand something.*"
> — THICH NHAT HANH (BUDDHIST MONK)

To approach the concept "to understand", an idea must be constructed through language. It must be formed in some way that enables us to grasp it intellectually—examine it, turn it over in the mind, and perhaps even feel it viscerally in the gut. To understand, one must deconstruct it and reform it in such a way as to enter it, to somehow come to exist within it. An idea must be imagined in penetrable form, more ethereal than physical, more essence than evidence. Within it, we can become one with it, and vice versa.

Since the beginning of the exploration of thought itself, the concept of understanding has stood just outside the limits of comprehension. Although no one has yet been able to wrestle it into submission, the preoccupation of philosophers with the enigma of understanding demonstrates its elusive nature. The philosophical discipline of epistemology (the theory of knowledge) comes from the Greek word "*episteme*," translated as "understanding". The classic originating work in the field of epistemology, Plato's dialogue with Theaetetus written in 369 BCE, is devoted to the definition of understanding held in the simple question:

When we initiate an exploration into the concept of true understanding, we begin to feel ourselves sliding into the disquieting realm of paradox, a place where sound reasoning leads only to conclusions of absurdity.

The descent is set into motion by the simple human inquiry: Why? Why is this thing *this* way, or that thing *that* way? If one is willing to penetrate further using an unfolding series of inquiries to pursue the reason or origin of a thing or idea to its ultimate end, we soon discover that it may be without the possibility of explanation. As a *something*, it exists beyond our capacity for complete knowing. That which we cannot understand must therefore be strengthened with the mortar of belief—an acceptance that something is, or must be, or further, we hope, somehow actually exists. A slippery slope indeed.

◆

Wait, I can explain.

Richard Feynman, the venerated theoretical physicist, was known as "The Great Explainer". He was gifted with the ability to take vastly complex concepts and articulate them in such a manner as to make them available and relatable to those who were not particularly well-versed in difficult subjects such as quantum mechanics. Feynman believed that if you cannot explain a concept in simple terms, then you do not understand it yourself. (He also possessed the wisdom to admit when he himself did not understand something and thus could not even *begin* to explain it to another.)

Our understanding is how we construct the world as individuals. It is how we assemble what we have come to know within the structure of what we possess (our mind), and what we can accept as mentally possible (our reality). In other words, what we consider "understood" is that which is known and only known by us as a single individual. Only you know what you understand. No other can tell you what you do or do not understand, for what they say you do not understand is only what they themselves believe *they* understand.

"Anything not understood in more than one way is not understood at all."
— DR. ROBERT KIZLIK

We might agree to define understanding as a "solitary cognitive success"—an individual mind moving from a place of no light or low light (imperception) to one of intelligent illumination (understanding). This is no small feat. The core elements required for even the simplest form of understanding are extensive and the process quite complex.

A few of the unscientific elements that we might find evident in the development of understanding are listed below. (Not necessarily as defining terms, but more an exercise that might help us further consider the complexity of such a simple concept as "understanding".)

KNOWLEDGE
: Identifying the names of the things involved. The availability of sufficient information is a prerequisite for initiating the analysis.

FORMATION
: The ability to construct a structure of thought, a visible model to "see" that which is under consideration—a type of mental hologram.

COMPARISON
: The identification and organization of relationships with other similar or dissimilar things, concepts, ideas, etc.

DISASSEMBLY
: The recognition that constituent parts can be broken down and then reconstructed mentally while grasping the origin of each part and how it evolved.

CAUSALITY
: The acknowledgement of how one part affects another through observation or previous experience.

SYNCHRONIZATION
: The balanced application of reason and focused emotion in a contemporaneous moment.

LINKING
: The association with other concepts and ideas not specifically or recognizably related to the concept under consideration.

ARTICULATION
: Simple, concise, and clear terms can be used to explain its final manifestation to another.

ELEVATION
: The establishment of a platform from which to springboard to higher levels of thought or insight.

JUSTIFICATION	The willingness to internalize the reason one must come to understand, and more importantly, how one can come to this understanding to suit one's own reality.
EMPATHY	The capacity to identify with a concept as experienced by others and thus be able to effectively shift perspectives and positions around it and within it.
ISOLATION	The recognition that achievement is beyond the testimony and acknowledgement of others and must be concluded (or thereabouts) within a single, human agent.
IMPOSSIBILITY	The acknowledgement that all knowledge and the presence of constant change forever prevent full and complete understanding.

A person may be said to know much but understand little. Yet conversely, it is difficult to imagine someone who understands much yet knows little. A knowledgeable person is someone who can recognize an assortment of disassociated things and assemble them into a distinct and recognizable pattern. This pattern can then be translated into signs and symbols used to inform another about a new-formed knowledge. Understanding however, is not merely internalizing knowledge, for the knowing alone is only a single row of bricks laid in a rising structure, not the completed edifice of comprehension.

We sometimes refer to certain persons despite their limited years, as "old souls". These individuals appear to possess a disproportionate sense of understanding, an uncanny awareness of situations with clarity and penetrating perception that exceeds their earthly experience. Conversely, certain others exhibit a stunted and permanent immaturity unable to produce even a modicum of understanding despite their extensive lived time and the assumed accumulation of knowledge that comes with it. No amount of information, no manner of persuasion, nor any level of imposed influence can affect such a person to comprehend the narrowness of their perspective. It seems pointless to attempt to modify their state or alter their unsubstantiated self-confidence to consider any alternatives. They somehow remain stuck in the mire of the now.

"Knowledge comes from without, wisdom wells up within.
Knowledge is borrowed, wisdom is original.

Wisdom is your insight into existence—not anyone's insight,
but your insight, absolutely your insight into existence."

— OSHO (GURU)

◆

Through a glass darkly.

What happens out along the farthest edge of understanding, that place where books, sages, mentors, our most trusted advisors, even our new surrogate virtual mind, the internet, cannot assist? What takes place in the darkness when our eyes are wide open yet nothing within the field of vision can be perceived?

Here, no light enters the frame. No tongues of flame cast shadows upon cave walls. In this dark space, one is left unaided with no hand to hold, just the self, alone in the darkness attempting to sort it all out. Yet out there, out along the borderland of uncertainty, is where true understanding begins.

"Doubt is the origin of wisdom."
— AUGUSTINE OF HIPPO

When we think we have come to understand something, or in colloquial terms "get it", this is usually where we stop. We discontinue considering the subject further electing not to force ourselves to ponder the subject beyond the position we have secured as complete within ourselves. However, it is within this precise moment, out on the precipice of mental clarity, where knowledge takes shape as a recognizable pattern and true understanding slowly begins. The holes in the explanation are just beginning to form. Doubt has yet to work its purifying magic.

The great data dump.

The present era has come to be known as "The Information Age", the world awash in an ocean of information with more sloshing in over the sides and seeping up through the floor every second. Yet oddly, it is not information that is held in the highest esteem, but data. In this age, the endless current of facts and figures has been crowned supreme.

There is no time today for contemplation, absorption, and reflection. It has been replaced by endless (and mindless) collecting, sorting, and analyzing. More is the answer. Just dump it all in and let the machines figure it out—a galaxy of blinking green lights on black stacked boxes in locked cages at some undisclosed location pushing electrons through a tiny silicon maze at lightning speed. Stand back, it's crunch time.

Data is what is.
Information is what is known.
Knowledge is why it is known.
Wisdom is knowing why it needs to be known.

The pyramid of understanding erected over thousands of generations has been stood upon its head. Since the arrival of human consciousness, we have distilled data into information, information into transferable knowledge, and knowledge into life-continuing wisdom. The transformation of knowledge into shared wisdom has been an epic and costly process tested and retested to produce workable and reliable results that have perpetuated our survival. The success of our species is proof of its efficacy.

Yet, according to today's hierarchy, data is the new oracle, the unassailable truth-teller of tomorrow. The more data the more sound the decision. Facts and figures will deliver the final answer. Quantity is key. Data is the new god of understanding.

"The internet's purpose is to ratify knowledge through the accumulation and manipulation of ever-expanding data. Human cognition loses its personal character. Individuals turn into data, and data become regnant.

Users of the internet emphasize retrieving and manipulating information over contextualizing or conceptualizing its meaning. They rarely interrogate history or philosophy; as a rule, they demand information relevant to their immediate practical needs.

Truth becomes relative. Information threatens to overwhelm wisdom."

– HENRY KISSINGER

DATA
Facts or statistics
for analysis
• Unorganized
• Raw
• Without context

INFORMATION
A collection of data used to convey or present
a concept through an arrangement or sequence of data
• Organized   • Comprehensible
• Specific   • Transferable
• Holds context

KNOWLEDGE
Relevant and objective information gathered through experience and learning
• Practical understanding   • Draws conclusions
• Enables prediction,   • Teachable
  inference, and insight

WISDOM
The soundness of an action or decision based upon experience, knowledge, and intellectual honesty
• Deep understanding   • Unprejudiced
• Requires discernment, judgment • Active
• Contextual   • Sustainable

The Pyramid of Understanding for the Information Age

We were wiser, once.

Homo sapiens = *"wise man"*

Much like the concept of "the mind", the term "wisdom" does not have a commonly accepted definition. We all think we know what it is, but...? Often it is described using a particular point of reference, or in conjunction with a person or corresponding event. (e.g. He made a wise decision, or... That was a wise move.)

Rarely does one hear it discussed as a pursuit unto itself these days. It has the whiff of decay, the archaic ring of yesteryear—old men with long beards in flowing robes living in caves at the top of windswept peaks somehow surviving on a diet of thick fog and deep thought. Today, it has been downgraded to secondary status, a relic of the past locked in dusty books lying open but unread under glass boxes. Wisdom is considered quaint yet unsuitable for practical use in our hyper-linked, data-driven world. It slows us down.

How has the concept of wisdom been considered across cultures, both past and present?

EGYPT	The principal idea of wisdom was order in the universe through truth, balance, order, harmony, and justice. (Ma'at)
MESOPOTAMIA	The god of wisdom and intelligence (Enki) spoke of wisdom being achieved by "restoring balance".
HEBREW	A virtue possessed by God and given to man of which he was free to use or dispose of through his own will. King Solomon asked God for wisdom above all else.
GREEK	Wisdom was personified as the goddesses Athena—strong, fair, merciful, and chaste. Plato's utopia was ruled by a philosopher-king, a supreme authority who understood the form of the good and possessed the courage to act accordingly. Aristotle defined wisdom as the understanding of causes, knowing why things are a certain way, which is deeper than merely knowing that things are a certain way.
ROMAN	Symbolized by Minerva, the owl who can "see through the darkness".

HINDU	Considered a state of mind and soul where a person achieves liberation.
BUDDHIST	Mindfulness—good bodily, mental, and verbal conduct.
NORSE	Acquired through various hardships and ordeals involving pain and self-sacrifice.
INUIT	One became wise when they could see what needed to be done and do it successfully without being told what to do.

Despite minor variations on the theme, many cultures maintain an acknowledgement of a higher plane, a pursuit of something beyond the daily habitual exercise of life or the mere accumulation of knowledge. Wisdom is seen as a level of aspiration, a pursuit of the mind achievable in this realm, for it is earth-bound, a truly human characteristic not necessarily born of the metaphysical. It is grounded in this and that and things, yet at the same time, transcends them all. It is the ability to see beyond the thingliness of things to rise above their necessity or the desire of their appeal.

> *"As far as we can discern, the sole purpose of human existence*
> *is to kindle a light in the darkness of mere being."*
> — CARL JUNG

It is wisdom that serves us most while we manage our selves here on earth, a means to generate momentum and change direction along our path that leads us out of the dim light of ignorance.

Wisdom acknowledges that nothing can be understood in its entirety. It can only accept what is known while coming to the affirmed position that much will remain forever unknown thus rendering understanding forever incomplete.

Wisdom receives without complaint the dictates of fortune and the accident of folly. It navigates the narrow straits of understanding without being overwhelmed by unplanned events, major setbacks, or even minor impediments.

Wisdom willingly admits when an answer may be presently unavailable or even unobtainable. Learning to say "Maybe" and "I don't know" are two critical steps in the evolution of human understanding. The wise man learns to play the dunce with aplomb.

Wisdom also widens the lens, enabling us to see many sides of a single concept without reflexively prejudicing one position over another. It allows us to hold conflicting points of view simultaneously while objectively assessing each with the vigor of curiosity and the catalyzing effects of intellectual honesty.

Wisdom avoids fixed associations and remains open to all possibilities, however unproven, foreign, or outside the range of comfort.

Wisdom understands both the immeasurable power and the governing limits contained within the concept of free will. At present, no individual can be said to be truly free. The universe as presently arrayed does not allow it. Everything is subordinate to something else or has a responsibility to something other. The hierarchies of dominance and subordination are constantly being re-ordered, all of it under the influence of ideas, objects, and forces that can never be known in full.

Wisdom recognizes opportunity as intermittent and knows when to summon the proper action to seize it.

Wisdom does not naturally lead to spiritual growth. But it may be a prerequisite.

The Rosicurians, a mysterious sub-cult founded in the early 17ᵗʰ century, drafted a manifesto heralding a "universal reformation of mankind". It was built on esoteric truths of the ancient past—a claim of a higher knowledge, a superior wisdom, a more profound interpretation of the cosmos, and man's relationship to history.

Members believed a "master key" was available to the questions of mankind. To forge this key, one had to slough off contemporary cultural arrogance and devote much energy and time to studying ancient wisdom with a resolve to transition one's self onto a higher plane.

The hard problem.

"What is it like to be?"

— DAVID DARLING (ASTROPHYSICIST)

When we refer to ourselves as "conscious beings", what do we mean? Among the vanguard of highly trained researchers and neuroscientists who dedicate their lives to the study of the subject, consciousness is considered the "hard problem". An inestimable number of papers, essays, theorems, books, reports, and presentations have been submitted as potential explanations with a matching number of accompanying studies and experiments performed to try to define it. And yet, we still know very little. In fact, virtually nothing. Using words to explain consciousness becomes an exercise in futility for it soon devolves (or evolves, depending on one's perspective) into poetry.

The American Psychological Association's *"Dictionary of Psychology"* defines consciousness as:

> *"The phenomena that humans report experiencing including mental contents ranging from sensory to somatic perception to mental images, reportable ideas, inner speech, intentions to act, recalled memories, semantics, dreams, hallucinations, feelings, "fringe" feelings, (e.g., a sense of knowing) and aspects of cognitive and motor control."*

A bit of the pig's breakfast if you ask me, an ambiguous potluck of psychological jargon presented in the format of a definition. Put in simple terms, human consciousness is...

> *Awareness of self, capacity for abstract thought, acknowledgement of time, and comprehension of the limitlessness of curiosity. In other words, consciousness knows, knows that it knows, knows that it knows now, knows that it knew before, knows that it will know later, and still wants to know more.*

What is the source of consciousness? Is it the brain? Renowned neuroscientist Steven Pinker responded to this question with unsettling candor:

> *"Beats the heck out of me. I mean I have some prejudices but have no idea how to look for a defensible answer. And neither does anyone else."*

With the emergence of consciousness, our ancestors were forced to consider questions never pondered before: Why did the rains not come? Why did the hunt go poorly? Why did my child die so young? Why was my friend here—alert, talking, laughing one minute, and then gone, prone, cold, silent the next? Where did he go, and why?

◆

It is all just a state of mind.

The first known attempts to formulate a deeper understanding of the various levels of consciousness ("maps of the mind") were produced in the Upanishads, the ancient text of the Hindus written in Sanskrit sometime between 1-200 AD. These four states of self can be summarized as follows:

1 Seeking the physical
2 Seeking inner thought
3 Seeking causes and spiritual consciousness
4 Realizing oneness with the Self, the Eternal

In some level of detail, the Upanishads describe and define the levels attainable by consciousness as follows:

1 THE WAKING STATE (*jagarita-sthana*)	We are aware of our daily world, described as outward-knowing and universal. The "gross body".	-"Conscious" man accepts the universe as he finds it. -Perception, volition, and memory are preserved.
2 THE DREAMING STATE (*svapna-sthana*)	We enter the dreaming mind described as inward-knowing and burning. The "subtle body".	-The subconscious self loses contact with reality, and the soul fashions its own world in the imagery of its dreams. -The usual state of mind in the less developed animal kingdom.

3 THE DEEP-SLEEP STATE (susupta-sthana)	We are in state of deep sleep. In this state the underlying ground of consciousness is undistracted, the Lord of all, the knower of all, the inner controller, the source of all, the origin and dissolution of created things.	-A deeper level of the subconscious approaching complete unconsciousness. -State of bliss in which there is no contact with reality, no desire, no dreams.
4 THE FOURTH STATE (caturtha, turiya, turya)	The fourth state is pure consciousness. It is the background that underlies and transcends the three common states of consciousness. In this consciousness both absolute and relative are transcended. The "supra-conscious". In this state Seers receive flashes of Great Truths in the form of vague apprehensions, which are afterwards elaborated in the waking consciousness.	-Not outwardly perceiving, nor inwardly perceiving, nor perceiving in both ways, nor a sphere of spiritual perception, nor perception, nor non-perception; invisible, inapprehensible, ungraspable, indistinguishable, unimaginable, whose essence is realization of oneness with the Eternal, this is the Divine Self, this is the goal of wisdom. -Through intense meditation and self-control, the union of the human soul with the Supreme Soul.

54 55 56

The process described above is an inward journey, a series of steps taken toward the pursuit of the purest form of human understanding. This form might be defined as: A freedom of the self from the self, and a freedom from the self to the self—a singularity that divides into a duality then returns once again to form an elevated and unified single being. Through the process, one willingly splits in two in order to see the self more clearly, then merges back again with the self to reform into a more complete one. In separating from the self, one can see the self for what it truly is and what it must become. The practitioner of such penetrating thought moves through a series of transformational stages, all while experiencing and witnessing the phases as they occur, learning from each then applying the learning to the last, stepping outside of the self then back in again until the whole is complete.

(You might want to read that a second time. I wrote it, and still I must read it a few times to understand it.)

How is it that our early ancestors seemed so aware of the energy held within the reformation of the self and made deep and concerted efforts to understand it more precisely? What did they possess that we today do not? Time? Focus? Necessity? Urgency? Other?

This pursuit of the truly conscious self as described in the stages above may seem mystical to the point of madness, a state of pure being that dwells beyond the reach of us as mere mortals. It is easy to depict this level of being as an ethereal orbit reserved only for those consumed by a dedicated, all-day-every-day, lifelong practice of "One-ness" to the neglect of all else.

Yet wisdom would say: *Perhaps, but keep an open mind.*

◆

I wanna be sedated.

Cocooned in our earthbound state as we sleepwalk through life, we often find ourselves too tightly focused on the immediate needs of the body and the insatiable demands of the ego to open ourselves to the time and energy that leads to understanding. So how can we learn to step outside ourselves to begin to understand what we truly are?

As an ever curious and pioneering species, we hope to locate a hint of edifying clarity, some signpost that situates us in the world, a cornerstone of certainty upon which the future of understanding can be constructed. To do so, we often seek a catalyst to initiate our inner quest. Given the condition of potential insolvability, we look to alter our state of consciousness through meditation, privation, psychotropic drugs, or other transformational practices to wrench open the mind and achieve a distancing from our inner agitation.

In the expanded mental state brought about during such self-imposed episodes, it is reported that we envision a spirit-world, a realm occupied by the mysterious "Other", a place where we visit with sages and converse with otherworldly beings who willingly share with us their super-abundance of knowing. Or more intimately, we encounter an altered version of our self, a wiser, more-evolved being. This self is said to be in possession of a higher knowledge, a level of intelligence we are too underdeveloped to comprehend.

This dream-like visitation serves as a preparation for the day when we will become post-mortal. The opened and enlightened mind enables us to contend with life as lived here and now. Such an experience serves as a gentle guide to usher us into the afterlife where we may be required to... explain ourselves.

◆

I know what I know if you know what I mean.

When did we first become "aware"? Or more precisely, when did this thing called "consciousness" take residence within the species know now as "human"? In truth, there is no way to really know. Anything can occur along a timeline that stretches millions of years and hundreds of thousands of generations. Yet the fact remains, at some point along the evolutionary path the human species came to possess a profound and unique capability that (to our knowledge) is not shared by any other animal, plant, or other known form of organic matter on earth, or within the universe as we know it today.

The emergence of human consciousness stands alone in depth, breadth, and magnitude as the single most spectacular event (dare I say, miracle) in earthly history. Its only potential rivals might be the emergence of organic life or the creation of the universe itself.

It is quite easy to assume that the brain—that gray blob of fat, water, chemistry, and electricity—developed and expanded naturally within the human species reaching an advanced state of connective sophistication where it simply crossed over some cosmogonal threshold and suddenly became aware. It could also be imagined that some genetic mutation caused the formation of a new pattern of proteins within the brain and human consciousness magically blinked to life. These explanations—an evolutionary inevitability or a random genetic fluke—seem as uninspiring as they are unlikely.

Then again, there are no means by which to prove the assumption that the development of the brain and the appearance of consciousness are correlative. Nor, as discussed prior, is there any specific evidence that consciousness dwells in, or emanates from the brain at all. No matter the explanation, or lack thereof, consciousness separates the human species from every other known form of life.

Intuitively, we acknowledge the issue of consciousness as a problem, perhaps one beyond our capacity to solve. Yet we will endeavor to make every attempt to solve it. We must. Understanding consciousness is not only a reasonable pursuit for the human mind, but an inescapable obligation along the winding course of evolution. The entire human mission might just be as simple as coming to understand consciousness—the pursuit of knowing the purpose of our own self-awareness, the reason for our very being.

> "The most basic of all human needs
> is the need to understand and be understood."
> — RALPH NICHOLS (WRITER)

Lurking just beyond our understanding is the implicit knowledge that the origin and purpose of human consciousness may remain forever unsolved. This agitating notion inescapably leads to a degree of communal anxiety, an existential angst we all feel but are unwilling to admit. Conversely, if viewed through the expanded lens of wisdom, we realize that this insolvability delivers a degree of solace, a locus where the mysterious can occur, a realm in which anything can happen, where uncertainty is both welcome and celebrated, where limitless possibility lives on in perpetuity. A place where hope can prevail.

◆ ◆ ◆

What lies beneath?

With all the knowledge we as a species have acquired, can we say we have come to know consciousness more clearly? Does consciousness perceive a reality, or does reality form consciousness? Is consciousness immortal? Does it disappear following the dissolution of our physical form? In other words, if I die does the cosmos cease to exist? Why did consciousness arrive? What does it want?

Ancient mystics predicted the answer to the enigma of consciousness would be found in the movement of the heavens. Their contemporaneous brethren, the materialists, believed that the functioning reality of the subatomic, or "the quanta" (the smallest increments into which matter and energy can be subdivided) might also contain clues to the great mystery of human consciousness. Throughout the ages, the prevailing hope was a grand universal interconnection—the galactic model above mirrored by the structure and motion of the subatomic realm operating in a manner that reflected human consciousness itself. A perfectly balanced equilateral triangle.

The observation and study of the movements of the stars is as old as consciousness itself and our knowledge of the infinite firmament becoming more clearly understood by the day. Through experimentation, theoretical extrapolation, and even modest exploration, we have come to better understand how the cosmos originated and how it now operates. Both man and machine have ventured into the celestial realm itself (albeit only a pitiful distance) to probe its infinite expanse in hopes of someday revealing all her secrets.

Yet conversely, our insight into the very stuff under our nose, the inner nature of matter, is all rather new. While our knowledge of the quantum has expanded exponentially over the past century (less with the eye and more with the mind), we have discovered that this subatomic system behaves quite differently than we had expected. A baffling randomness exists within the domain of the quantum, an oddness that quickly evades explanation. In certain aspects it acts similarly to the heavens, yet in others, it behaves in a more arbitrary almost incidental fashion. In fact, the sub-universe has proven a realm more mysterious and confounding than we could have imagined.

Although no one has ever actually seen an electron, we have been able to theorize its existence by its relation to and the effect it has upon nearby particles. Oddly, or perfectly strangely, we can witness it at a specific and precise moment through evidence made visible by its engagement with other subatomic objects. However, its position both before and after remains completely indeterminate. We cannot detect its velocity, direction, or prior location, only its position at *that* moment. Thus, wherever it came from or where it might go is beyond our empirical grasp. It departs the world of know-ability and enters the realm of probability.

This might lead one to ask: *If not engaged with another object, can it be said to exist at all?*

Such disconcerting conduct found in the makeup of the substance of all matter defies logic and deconstructs our hope for simple answers. Even the exquisitely precise universal language of mathematics cannot precisely explain the erratic nature of this unruly domain. How can we observe, measure, and then leverage to our advantage something that simply refuses to cooperate? Of this uncertainty, Albert Einstein would begrudgingly admit, "*If it is correct, it signifies the end of physics as a science.*"

We had hoped the mechanics of the subatomic underworld would be tightly synchronized with the movement of the cosmos based upon some common rules, with perhaps a few odd but solvable challenges thrown in just to keep it interesting. But the dynamics of the underworld have dislodged our expectations and derailed our quest for any general theory of uniformity. The ancient axiom "As above, so below" while plausible in theory, seems to have been conceived in error.

◆

You are now free to move about the cabin.

The original motivation of the early 20th century to equate quantum theory with human consciousness was philosophical. We desperately hoped to have the mechanics of the mind explained through the metaphor of matter, a model of human thought that was reproduced in miniature. Perhaps if we could draft an instruction manual, even one with illegible, unintelligible, or even a few missing pages, we might better understand the inner workings of the human mind and thus the infinite mystery of human consciousness. And by doing so, perhaps one day discover a means to gain some modicum of control over its feral power.

However, as we descend further into the depths of the quanta, each step further penetrating the intrigue that is the molecular model, we uncover more oddities, more stuff, more clutter, less observable truth. Theories once considered both brilliant and revolutionary are quickly dismantled then abandoned. Our understanding of the subatomic world recently revealed by science remains now almost completely theoretical. New explanations might be metaphorically relatable but remain empirically unknowable, for we cannot witness the existence nor predict the behavior of matter's constituent elements and are thus forced to accept their presence based upon a level of trust in the genius of specialists. A certain degree of faith is now required.

> *"Usually, it is a bit of a trick to keep*
> *knowledge from blinding you."*
> — ANNIE DILLARD (WRITER)

So, we are left to ask, which best exhibits the model resembling the mechanics of the human mind—the observable and measurable movement of the heavens or the intriguing but unnerving chaos occurring within the molecular dimension? Some say the (somewhat) predictable order of the heavens best mirrors the manner of the mind, an almost anticipated unfolding of reality that determines our thoughts and therefore manages our actions. Others believe the mind is more a mirror of the atomic, everything a result of an unpredictable and unreliable nature. Yet still others dismiss both positions and submit to the belief that it might all be a product of fate, the universal mega-mind controlling the operation of everything, us included.

Determinism, the concept that we do not possess control over our actions, or even the origination of our own thoughts, is an imaginary demon, one that devours autonomy and erases human volition. Fate dismisses the need (or hope) for embarking on the inward journey to discover the source of the true self. A stalwart belief in a supreme organizer stands in direct opposition to human agency and eliminates any need for self-reflection, a critical element in the search for the primary source of consciousness. A pre-determined life is an unlivable life. It is an effortless walk that winds forever downhill.

Yet, if the randomness reflected in the molecular model is the force that rules the world, how are we to perform with any reasonable degree of predictability? How are we to come to know anything, including our selves, if the framework for understanding is indeterminate, random, and continuously being reordered beyond visibility?

Perhaps it is exactly this precise predictability counter-balanced by an unsettling degree of uncertainty that fuels our verve. Foreseeable consistency with an allowance for indeterminacy spurs improvisation—the life-charging friction that sparks the human spirit. A delicate structure allows us to cooperate and compete, while a sea of uncertainty affords us the opportunity to innovate and create. The civilized and the savage forced to sort it out amongst themselves.

The infinite contra.

Balance is the self-governing principle of the universe—everything known and unknown delicately holding itself together through the constant struggle between opposing forces. Nothing exists outside this vital imperative. Even the infinite cosmos churns in the exquisitely balanced harmony of opposites. Without the inward pull of mass (gravity) counterbalanced by the outward push of galactic matter (dark energy), the universe would tear itself apart and simply vanish…once again.

DARK	◄►	LIGHT
DAY	◄►	NIGHT
BODY	◄►	MIND
PAST	◄►	FUTURE
CURVED	◄►	STRAIGHT
ODD	◄►	EVEN
RIGHT	◄►	LEFT
MALE	◄►	FEMALE
STILL	◄►	MOTION
REASON	◄►	EMOTION
GRAVITY	◄►	DARK ENERGY
MATTER	◄►	DARK MATTER
UNITY	◄►	PLURALITY
SELF	◄►	OTHER
SELF	◄►	SELF

One extreme cannot exist without its opposition exerting a stabilizing influence. Nature rebalances itself constantly to maintain a functioning equilibrium. The persistence of everything predicated upon the simple assumption: Without this, no that. Without dark, there can be no light. Without the past, no future can be possible.

These are the weights placed upon the universal scale that holds the center in place so the middle ground can be occupied and settled. In the static balance of equilibrium, the yield of infinite possibilities can take root and gain purchase.

What is it that shifts the balance within this "vital imperative"?

What are the influential forces that slide the weights back and forth across the beam that rests upon the universal fulcrum of balance?

◆

The empty space between something and nothing.

We, and every particle of matter in the universe, are balanced precariously upon the knife's edge of oblivion. This miraculous balance, a temporary stasis exotically held in position within a churning expanse of constant and often violent change (flux), is a mind-bending conundrum of celestial proportion, an enigma almost as incomprehensible as the universe itself.

Statistically speaking, the possibility of our own earthly existence is zero, or damn near, for what is known in science as the "life-permitting range" is incalculably thin. In fact, if all the universal constants were not exquisitely fine-tuned within a hair-width of accuracy, you, me, it, life, matter, and the entire universe would not, nor could not, exist. For instance, if the force of the gravitational constant varied by just a tiny fraction, one over ten to the 60th power, or…

1 / 1,000,000,000,000,000,000,000,000,000,000,000,000,000,000,000,000,000,000,000,000

…the universe would have initially dispersed too widely and too quickly to form stars, or it would have simply collapsed upon itself.[57]

Yet what we know of the universe is merely the "observable" universe, in other words, as far as we can "see". The edge of the universe—the lip of the abyss, the outer limit of everything—has been theoretically measured to be 14.26 gigaparsecs away. Or in layman's terms, 46.5 billion light-years in any direction (4.40 x 10 to the 26th power).

In total light-years, that's…

4.40 × 1,000,000,000,000,000,000,000,000,000

For perspective, a light-year is the distance light travels in one earth year. At the speed of 186,000 miles per second, light would cover about 6 trillion miles in a single year. To provide a scale of reference that might assist with numbers of such magnitude:

A million seconds is 12 days ago

A billion seconds is 31 years ago

A trillion seconds is the year 31,688 BCE

And to make the concept even more astounding, according to some who study such unimaginable sums, the universe is shaped in such a way that it cannot be defined by an edge. In fact, it exists in a form so unique that it lies beyond our ability to visualize, verbalize, or even metaphorize. (This is not a word, but perhaps it should be.)

> *There are about ten billion galaxies in the observable universe. The number of stars in a single galaxy varies, but assuming an average of one hundred billion stars per galaxy means that there are about one billion trillion stars in the observable universe.*[58]
>
> *(The math becomes a bit overwhelming when you begin to run out of room for all the zeroes.)*

But these concepts—the riddle of something vs. nothing, the possibility of infinity, a universe without edges—they are all just exercises for the imagination, games we play to amuse ourselves knowing no answers will be found. It is all just theory and loosely supported speculation—exotic indecipherable mathematical gibberish scribbled out feverishly on chalkboards to entertain the irrepressible demands of human curiosity. In matters of such magnitude, we believe what we are told. We take it on faith.

◆

Bang!

There was once something so small that it had no mass yet contained infinite energy. Then one day, this tiny little thing went *boom*. In an instant, from a speck of near nothingness, stuff was suddenly scattered everywhere. This newly formed stuff then swirled around other stuff to form bigger stuff that then swirled around this bigger stuff to make even bigger stuff. And oddly, some of this stuff was flammable and it burned as huge balls of fire churning in the inert darkness of the newly formed, edgeless infinity of "space". And amid all the burning balls and big swirling stuff, massive holes formed that sucked in all this stuff, even light.

Where did all this vacuumed up stuff go? We do not know…yet. Will the sucking ever stop? Unknown. It could be assumed that it will one day cease when there is nothing left, not even light. Perhaps all these sucking holes will one day empty the entirety of infinity back into another tiny speck of near nothingness and the entire process will repeat itself all over again. Or the inward gravitational pull generated by the mass of all this swirling stuff will one day overtake the force pushing it ever outward and it will all collapse upon itself again, perfectly retreating into the tiniest bit of nothing that somehow contains everything. The eternal cycle played out as an elongated pattern of cosmic breathing along a duration too great to fathom.

Perhaps this has been happening over and over and over since the beginning of time. But then again, maybe time itself does not exist in the measureless infinity of _____. (What is the word for the thing that is even bigger than the universe?).

> "The universe contains everything; there is no outside."
> — STEPHEN HAWKING (ASTROPHYSICIST)

What is it then? The created universe is ever expanding and thus must possess an outer edge, or it is without a boundary and thus occupies infinity? And if infinity, how could it then be moving outward? And if it is indeed expanding, what is it moving "out" into? Maybe this stuff is not actually stuff at all but a sort of vibrating non-stuff. Possibly. What exactly was the origin of the tiny speck itself? It's uncertain. Did this boom only happen once? Unknown. Can anything escape these massive sucking holes—information, thought, consciousness? Only time will tell.

◆

The Earth gives off none of its own light.

Massive, blanketing, pulsating, mesmerizing, intimidating, yet somehow oddly inviting, the night sky above dominated the half-life of our ancient ancestors. How we must have gazed up in wonder at the close of each day when night fell, and the stars appeared one by one as if by magic until they filled the dome and became brilliantly uncountable. Standing beneath the epic vastness, filled with equal parts hope and dread, a supreme grandeur spread out before us as the infinite stretched our minds to contemplate the impossible.

Over time, we learned to mark and measure. We mapped the stars and made note of their movements. We gave prominent configurations earthly names and found useful knowledge in their cosmic alignments. We worshipped the celestial ceiling and prayed to those who might inhabit its immensity. We manufactured myths and invented gods who granted us life, gave us bounty, bestowed upon us magical gifts, then punished us for our misdeeds.

The night sky connected us dot by dot to the world beyond our own eyes, an expanse of limitless potential. We dreamed about the how, the why, and the who that might live out there in the realm beyond here. That grand open-air amphitheater must have put on some supremely spectacular light shows in those early days of deep, deep darkness.

Then one day, man made his own light. He spread it across the land to illuminate every corner that before dwelt only in darkness. The black sky above slowly receded as the heavens grew dim and the multitude of stars slowly faded away. We ended our interrogations of the heavens and built new worlds below that we learned to love and fear beneath the light of our own making. We no longer gazed upward and outward but shifted our focus forward, then downward…then in.

———◆———

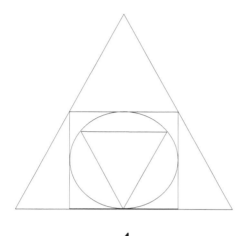

4

DISREMEMBERING

Take with you only what you need.

> *"Memory involves only a handful of chemicals in the brain,*
> *and an equally small amount to erase them."*
> — JONAH LEHRER (WRITER)

Within an hour, half of what we have learned has been forgotten. And in a typical day, we can forget many things. Voluminous sensory input arriving through our daily physical experience, including the submerging and resurfacing of thoughts, memories, dreams, ideas and desires, must be managed by the second to choose what to absorb and what to discard. Much of this inbound information is outright ignored. (A form of wisdom in itself.) That which is not disregarded must be processed, analyzed, evaluated, stored, or discarded. This involuntary processing is a sophisticated and sharpened mental skill that enables us to function in a complex world without frying our cerebral circuit board.

def: **FORGET**

1 fail to remember, disremember

2 a modification of information[59]

It is known that the mind can absorb information more easily and transfer it to memory more swiftly when enveloped in the form of a story. Before the written word appeared, elaborate tales were told and retold by members of the tribe, passed down from one generation to the next to preserve the thread of knowledge gained through experience. Valuable life lessons were endured by our ancestors – many difficult, some painful, others fatal.

Through this story telling, we learned of those who came before. We relived their lives and gained a chance to revisit the human experience as it was. These stories were the ones we needed, the ones we had to remember, the collective lessons of life absorbed through endless trial and error then hammered into shape through experimentation and correction. Heroic and tragic, these stories transported us through time, backward and forward, a unifying transmission of shared existence. All of it, a refined process of forgetting – the goodness maintained as a eulogy to the past.

In these stories life's learnings were revealed—what to eat, what to avoid, which plants could heal, which could kill, who was helpful, who was hostile, how to give thanks, how to behave properly. These tales helped us navigate the physical world while serving as a means to explain our own history—where we came from, how we got here, why we are different, why our tribe is special, why we are important. Through them we were also reminded of our culpability as poor suitors of the gift of consciousness.

◆

To forgive is to forget.

Some of our earliest narratives were constructed to illustrate the undeniable nature of our inherent struggle. In the Old Testament, immediately following the story of creation and the expulsion of man and woman from the Garden of Eden, we are introduced to the parable of two brothers. They are the sons of Adam and Eve: Cain, a farmer and Abel, a shepherd.

As was the custom in those days, both brothers sacrificed to their God— Yahweh. Cain chose to burn a modest yield harvested from the land he worked, while Abel offered up his first-born sheep, the prize of his flock. When God showed favor upon Abel's sacrifice, an angry and jealous Cain lured Abel into the fields and killed him. When Abel went missing, God came to Cain to inquire as to his brother's whereabouts. In his shame, Cain denied killing Abel, falling further in favor in the eyes of God.

> In ancient times, sacrifices were offered in reverence to the gods, a form of humility exercised in exchange for good fortune or gratitude. Offerings were typically the ritualized slaughter of a domesticated animal and/or the surrendering of the bounty of human labor that was prepared for consumption then burned.
>
> The sacrifice involved transformation, an altering of one form of matter into another – the flora and fauna of the physical transferred through smoke and flame into the realm of the transcendental. Human labor transformed into the sacred.

> *Sacrifice manifests the concept of reciprocity—the surrendering of one thing in the present in the hope of beneficial consideration in the future. A prized this now for the promise of something better later.*

For his transgression, God punished Cain. No longer would he work the fertile soil to earn his keep but instead he would be sent out as a fugitive, a wanderer upon the earth untethered to all he knew, disowned of the fruits of his own labor. In biblical times, such a tribal outcast was eyed with suspicion. He was a person without a place, an unknown, a sojourner, and a potential threat. It was not atypical for such a wanderer to have his trip ended abruptly and with ignominy should he stray into the wrong region.

def: **SOJOURNER**

1 a temporary resident

2 a stranger

3 a traveler, usually alone, who dwells in a place for a time[60]

Symbolically, we all descend from Cain. We strive for Abel, but more often, struggle as his brother. Like Cain, we wander through life burdened by regretful acts, detached from a place we feel at home, and disconnected from the fruits of our own labor. We look to regain our sense of self while attempting to overcome our inherited nature—competitive, envious, spiteful, prone to anger, and alone. We plot a course that might redeem our own failings and reverse our wayward drift.

In the story, God made a promise to Cain. He placed a "mark" upon Cain to protect him from those who might judge him for his deeds and thus be compelled to take revenge upon him. This mark was a symbolic acknowledgement of man's tendency toward retribution, a sign of the perpetual strife we are forever forced to endure if we refuse to exercise the greatest form of forgetting: forgiveness.

◆

It's just a matter of time.

Current estimated population of Earth: 7.5 billion.

The estimated number of modern humans who have ever lived: 108 billion.[61]

What percentage of human history is known? There must be a means to calculate the sum of all that we know and provide an accurate tally. (One which we will undoubtedly soon forget). But just as importantly, what have we as a species learned to forget? What have we lost or even consciously removed from the storytelling as it was passed from one generation to the next?

Significant human thought manifested through discovery and invention has been irretrievably lost to the churn of time. A particular skill honed to a fine edge by craftsmen for hundreds or even thousands of years can often disappear in the passing of a single generation. Many reasons might explain the loss or the abandonment of such vital knowledge: war, incivility, famine, regime-change, climate change, ideology, shifts in the societal landscape, etc.

> "Written words remain, spoken words fly away."
> — VOLTAIRE

The oral cultures of our ancient ancestors did not possess the ability to capture knowledge in a retrievable form. When a generation did not actively transfer a set of knowledge onto the next, a known thing often died with them. What was lost may never be known again. What knowledge vanished or was erased when writing replaced oral tradition and the capacity for deep memory atrophied from disuse?

According to Talmudic tradition, upon the destruction of the Tower of Babel one third sank into the earth and one third was consumed by fire. The remaining third was left standing in ruin, cursed with the power to make a passerby forget everything he knew.

Even writing itself once disappeared. Around 1,200 BCE, an early culture known as Mycenean, a precursor to ancient Greece, simply collapsed. An invasion from the north led to the dismantling of the Mycenean's sophisticated society which swiftly retreated into a primitive, subsistence-level existence and the written word of the Mycenean culture simply vanished. Four hundred years would pass before a script based on a Phoenician alphabet would be introduced, hacked, and reconstituted as Greek.

Cement, the ubiquitous universal material of construction considered the "most durable substance in human history", was discovered by the Egyptians as early as 3,000 BCE. It was used to construct the pyramids and the massive temples along the Nile. This remarkable human invention also disappeared only to resurface thousands of years later in Rome around 300 BCE. The Romans would eventually develop a material remarkably similar to modern cement and use it to build their architectural marvels still standing today.

The concrete of the Romans ('opus caementicium') has proven more even durable than our own. Their formula has been studied extensively to understand how it gets stronger over time.

Roman builders used a mix of volcanic ash, lime, and seawater, a chemical reaction observed in naturally occurring volcanic deposits "cemented" along the shores of the Mediterranean. As the seawater slowly dissolves the volcanic ash within the mix, space develops to reinforce a super-structure of interlocking crystals that makes the substance as strong as stone.

From Ancient Rome to modern Iraq, many cultures have practiced a ritual of forced forgetting known as *damnatio memoriae*, a Latin phrase meaning "condemnation of memory". Mobs in the days of imperial Rome would tear down the statues of deposed leaders smashing them to bits and tossing the rubble into the sea. Administered to effectively cancel every trace of that individual from history, the Romans viewed the cultural sentence of *damnatio memoriae* as a punishment worse than death. In the collective consciousness of the culture, that individual was considered never to have lived – banished from the tribe and erased from the continuance of human memory.

World War I (1914-1918) resulted in the death of 9.7 million soldiers and approximately 10 million civilians with the total of wounded estimated to be nearly 20 million. Nearly the entire globe, from the European mainland to its far-flung network of allies and colonies spread across almost every continent on earth, were directly involved or indirectly affected. During this four-year period, everyone alive was considered a potential combatant, new recruits to be conscripted into the killing machine. The population of Europe finally united as either fighter or fodder. The previous age fashioned by the romantic notion of the glory of battle was quickly extinguished by the horrors of modern warfare. As one historian noted, "*They rode in on horseback and drove out in tanks.*"

Centuries-old empires fell, entire economies were cast into ruin, radical new ideologies were born, and the weapons of war mechanized and amplified in their capacity to kill in mass quantity. And yet, this unprecedented horror, the so-called "war to end all wars", was swiftly forgotten then repeated just two decades later.

In the early 20th century, Nikolai Yezhov carried out the Soviet Union's political cleansing known as the "purges" under the brutal regime of Joseph Stalin. Roughly half of the Soviet political and military establishment along with hundreds of thousands of civilians suspected of disloyalty to the state were imprisoned, sent to forced labor camps, or shot. In an act of political expediency, Stalin would eventually turn on his appointed executioner and blame him directly for these apparent "excesses". On February 4, 1940, the name "Yezhov" was added to the list.

In a clumsy effort to eradicate these events from time, Stalin had Yezhov's name and image removed from every textbook, photograph, historical archive, and Kremlin letter. Like all those who stood in the way of Russia's glorious future, the individual known as Nikolai Yezhov was systematically erased, purged from the country's long and tragic history.

In 1870, 48% of the U.S. population was involved in agriculture. By 2008, less than 2% was directly employed in farming while the nation's population exploded by a multiple of ten (38 to 304 million).[62]

On the Norwegian island of Spitsbergen in 2008, the government of Norway completed the construction of the Svalbard Global Seed Vault. This deep underground storage facility would catalogue and secure the entire world's seed stock. Its inventory is expected to be deployed to replenish the planet with harvestable food for future generations in the wake of any potential worldwide cataclysmic event.

We may store every variety of seed in an underground bunker, but by the time we need them there may be no one left who knows what to do with them.

Forgetting is not a bug. It is a feature.

What might we wish to forget about our *personal* history? The answer is too numerous in quantity and too disconcerting in severity to ponder for long. Thankfully, the mind has evolved a robust means to dis-remember, a way to effectively lose what has accumulated during a single lifetime.

Why do we recall certain vignettes that surface at odd times in dreams or in those spontaneous moments while sitting in traffic or brushing our teeth? Though we forget many things, some unexplained insistence forces us to remember certain details despite the anguish they may cause. We are compelled to reflect on episodes within our own story to learn from them and adapt as best we can. Such strife, the kind that emanates from our own internal memory, is never isolated within the single experience. It is shared universally across the whole human tribe, for no person alive or dead has ever avoided the trauma that is life.

> "Without forgetting it is quite impossible to live at all."
> — FRIEDRICH NIETZSCHE

We are not designed to remember and then possess forever every encounter, emotion, and experience. Rather, we are built to parse and separate, then organize and compartmentalize as we wade daily through it all seeking pathways toward understanding. Memory serves only as a means to an end. We experience so that we may establish a more advanced comprehension of what we might determine to be "of value". Within each mind, what is maintained for retrieval and reconsideration is part of the weave in the pattern of our becoming.

The universe does not punish us for the past. It prepares us for the future. Time wants us to know.

In the Jorge Luis Borges short story 'Funes the Memorious,' a young man is thrown from a horse and permanently paralyzed. He spends his days in a darkened room diligently developing his memory.

> *He eventually becomes so prodigious at this effort he remembers every detail of his own life. He can recall the events of the previous day, only to realize it took the full 24 hours to do so. He is doomed by his own memory.*

Tragically, reciprocity and revenge are the two unresolved links in the long chain of human forgetting. The urge to avenge acts perpetrated against us or members of our tribe penetrates deep into the core of our being. The remembrance of those among us who have been harmed churns disturbingly in the long memory. Retribution must be administered to honor those who have been somehow been wronged. We believe a measure of our human value has been stolen and the tribe will forever hold us accountable for not recovering what has been lost.

The need to exact revenge is a facet of consciousness we as a species have not yet evolved our way through or somehow learned to forget. Be their origin emotional or intellectual, these acts of retribution are regretful recurrences that serve us regressively, counterproductive events to the advancement of the collective wisdom within the human species. They carry the waves back out to sea. Hope carried with it.

◆

Every passing boat leaves a wake.

What durable monuments will we use to remember our time on earth, to mark our existence as the most advanced species to have inhabited the planet? Perhaps our much-celebrated centers of culture, our modern cities, will serve as such. Yet they stand as mere towers of production, practical structures to house and host the workers who produce the goods traded, consumed, and then discarded. The congested jumble of the urban landscape is constructed with only the thinnest application of visual aesthetic and a wholesale neglect of the orchestration of light and space to calm and comfort the mind.

These ruins may mark our lived time, but they do not speak with urgency or clarity about our remarkable inheritance or the near-miraculous achievements of our earthly experience as conscious beings. The ancient story of Atlantis, the advanced civilization that legendarily flourished in the deep past, is said to have mysteriously melted into the sea, all its secrets with it. This long-vanished city serves as a metaphor for all man has lost or forgotten.

History does not bury us. We sink into it.

> If the human species disappeared and all indications of our existence were reclaimed by nature, the most enduring remnant to indicate our presence on Earth would most likely be...Mount Rushmore.

———◆———

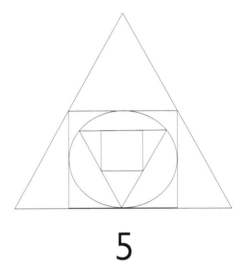

5

I AM, FIRST PERSON SINGULAR

The stranger within.

The earliest awareness of "*the self*" most likely began with the discovery of our earthly companion, our shadow. Physically and psychologically, we have never been without. External, ever-present, and inseparable from us, our shadow is a direct projection of our individual form, albeit distorted. It is form without detail, presence without substance, a constant reminder that we exist as solitary, material, earth-bound beings. Our shadow also serves as a symbolic representation of the "Other" the stranger that still resides within.

> In ancient Egypt, the god of creation Atum, being the only entity in the world at the beginning of time, was said to have created the future for all beings by making a union with his shadow.

While my shadow may be my constant companion and earthly attendant, it does not see me. My reflection however, stares back. It sees me. And it sees into me. It recognizes who I am with penetrating clarity. It reminds me: "*No other human has ever, nor will ever, walk the earth as you have walked it, nor see it as you have seen it, nor experience it as you have experienced it.*"

And while I may appear alone as one, I know I am not one, but many—a different person every day, and potentially every second. I am chemically different this moment than the last. I have consumed different energy, the weather has changed, my mood has altered, my cells continue to mutate, memories are emerging and fading, and my own internal knowledge is constantly being re-examined and re-ordered. And, as always, worry abounds.

> "*When asked by the caterpillar smoking a hookah,*
> "*Who are you?" Alice replied, "I hardly know sir I've changed*
> *so many times since this morning you see.*"
> — LEWIS CARROLL (ALICE IN WONDERLAND)

"Know thyself." This well-worn maxim is so disarming in its simplicity it is reflexively rejected. It has suffered from so much aphoristic abuse it no longer carries the potency held within its raw truth. Tarnished with time, it has become a flattened platitude, a literary relic now locked away in "The Lexicon of Ancient Slogans". Today, the mere mention of the phrase in any social setting elicits a laughable reaction. (An unsettling, nervous laughter.) Yet, these two words are the primary source of becoming. In them, the map to the mission unfolds.

The pursuit of self-understanding demands my deepest attention. I must make an honest attempt to engage and comprehend the course of my own becoming. If I don't come to a more thorough understanding of myself, how am I expected to understand another, and they me? Without the knowledge of myself, the chasm that lies between us, the two of us, all of us, becomes uncrossable. Without a true understanding of myself, all I have is a sense of projected empathy, a hope I might one day come to understand another, knowing it impossible. If I don't make me, the world will assign me.

We all want to be seen. ("I am this.")

We all wish to be understood. ("This is who I am.")

We all wish to be seen as one. ("I am like you.")

We all seek to be different. ("But I am me.")

◆

The One thing.

Nothing outside the self can be known. This is the one thing we must come to know. Everything, every bit of data, every fragment of information, every shred of knowledge, is just a theory, an opinion, a belief, or an idea, held by another. All knowledge is formed within the single mind, a product available exclusively to a single individual. New and additional information may enter that mind, but once manifested within, it is transformed into something different, an active substance now under the influence of the mind of the possessor.

And knowledge considered known by any individual will never be known in full by another. It cannot be communicated with any degree of precision for it was produced within You—a distinct individual with a unique, independent, and dynamic mind. To relocate this knowledge to another—a separate individual also in possession of a different but equally unique, independent, and dynamic mind – with any expectation of completeness or integrity is as absurd as it is impossible. The mode for the exact transmission of personal knowledge is simply outside the capacity of human consciousness as currently constructed. The code required for the sharing of the human experience is, as yet, undeveloped.

Most important, one cannot communicate knowledge of "the self" to another. For any individual to come to "know" You, that individual would be required to not only step into your psychological-physical self, but at the same time, erase the entirety of their own being in the process—all experiences, associations, prejudices, memories, emotions, ideas, etc. Additionally, the long-chain of evolutionary information carried within every cell of your body would need to be copied, reconfigured, and mapped back precisely to that individual. A procedure science has (thankfully) yet to master.

And as would reasonably follow, no knowledge can therefore be shared by all. The coherent transference of the experience of the self becomes swiftly lost in the labyrinth of language and distorted by prejudices held within both the transmitter and receiver. And even if such a mode was available and the operating code flawlessly functional, no means or mechanisms exists to measure and verify that knowledge, manifested as either experience or abstract thought, has been accurately and completely transferred from one mind to another. Sharing of knowledge may elicit nods of acknowledgment and even vocal confirmations, but verification is not validation. Consensus does not confirm certitude, only conformity.

Lastly, and most critically, all that can be known about the self will attempt to elude you. This is the one piece of knowledge you must come to know. Truth and meaning are forever under suspicion—the discerning eye of doubt never lets them rest for long. This is the purifying process of consciousness in action, as natural and vital as the creation of thought itself.

Doubt operates as the cleansing catalyst, the solvent that washes away the non-essential in seeking self-understanding.

◆

Becoming One.

First, the individual must establish order within itself. Through an introspective journey, the mind can be made to discover the nature of the true self, then transform the self to live as intended. Once aligned properly with its own course, aware of its own interest, honest with itself, and willing to serve as its own authority, the individual can become "One".

> "ONE" – an independent, authentic, sovereign being of supreme power, the earthly manifestation of human agency – aware, autonomous, responsible, and accountable only to the self.

To begin, an individual must come to acknowledge an undeniable and irrepressible inner strength, a strength generated by the capacity to produce and propagate pure thought. If One can acknowledge and accept all that is known of the self, without filtering or parsing it to fit some selfish prejudice, without directing it to satisfy some purely indulgent desire, without surrendering to the influence of the tribe, without succumbing to the ever-shifting influence of cultural expectation, without relying upon the edicts of an external authority, without falling sway to the demands of "ought", or restricted by the absolute negation of "shalt not", a distilled, independent, autonomous, rarified element is produced—pure thought.

> "PURE THOUGHT" – the product of a deliberate, unbiased, and intellectually honest process undertaken by a conscious mind aware of itself and under the sole authority of the self.

Pure thought is the base element of human potential. Every human, bestowed with the gift of consciousness, possesses the capacity to produce it. Once the ability to produce pure thought has been achieved, every choice can now be understood. This elevated state of knowing enables us to assess and apply meaning to any thought, thing, or situation. We can then prioritize its importance, align it with our own self-interest, and act accordingly. Pure thought distills raw consciousness into a potent elixir, the universal catalyst capable of initiating a transmutation of the mind within the individual self. The ability to effect change upon the self is the one true super-power all humans possess.

Upon becoming One, the individual is able to now see, feel, and celebrate the uniqueness and the potential held within every "Other". This elevated level of conscious clarity leads not to discord, or the division of distinction, but to the unity of shared difference.

> **"OTHER"** – conscious beings external to the self, often found opposing
> an individual becoming One

Once acknowledged and achieved, any choice that willingly and actively ignores pure thought is an act of existential forgetting, an iniquity committed against not just the self but the Other and the All—those living, those who have passed, and those yet to come.

> **"ALL"** –
> 1 every Other
> 2 the entirety of humankind both past and future

However, and this is the stage of the performance with the highest degree of difficulty, if an action taken by One is executed specifically to suit the imperious self and only the self, through a willfully customized subset of knowledge with a conscious disregard for the effect that action may have upon any Other and potentially the All, that action must be considered unjustifiable and therefore unacceptable. In other words, if One chooses to be intellectually dishonest with One's self and elects to willingly exclude certain internal information that might affect the decision to choose, the resulting act must be considered counterproductive to the positive momentum of human progress.

Lastly, while One can be observed as having taken action (or having taken no action), the primary source of that action (intent) can never be known by any Other or the All. The act is available to be observed, analyzed, and evaluated using only that which can be known, the observer's individual knowledge. Furthermore, both the observed and the observer are forever altered in the process as all bodies are changing, all environments are in motion, all minds forever adapting. The flux of time invades every action, everywhere, without interruption.

◆

Self-interest rules all. (Always has, always will.)

Everything is rendered via first person perspective. Everything. The world as it is made known to us, or in other words, your "reality", exists only through the single channel of the self. This does not state, suggest, nor imply, however, that only You exist. Quite the contrary, other things and other beings *do* and *must* exist for you to be known. It is your interaction and engagement with the objects and individuals in the world that make you known not only to yourself, but to others and the universe. Yet these objects and beings, these "things in themselves", in other words, all that exists outside the self, can never be known in full.

Individual self-interest will always supersede the interest of the All. Self-interest has been refined and adapted to dominate the eternal debate that occurs between the two extremes: serving the self or benefiting the All. The survival instincts and manipulation skills of self-interest are more primal and robust than those adopted and/or socially engineered to protect the herd.

The self wants what it wants. Yet it is cunning enough to know when to delay its own gratification if a pause might mean something better in the future. It is even willing to assimilate or elevate the primacy of the herd temporarily when necessary or expedient. Yet hidden beneath every thought and action lurks the insatiable self.

To be clear, the term "self-interest" and its grammatically related half-cousin "selfishness", are not interchangeable. Selfishness involves satisfying One's own needs at the expense or disregard of Others. Healthy self-interest is simply One following the course of the true self in full recognition that Others too are engaged upon their own path and those roads may sometimes intersect. Here are the moments when the true self will be in question. This resistance provides another purifying process to help refine and clarify the priorities and their corresponding value in the hierarchy of the individual interest of One.

> "Creatures like their own ways…because at the moment,
> it is the appropriate and natural thing to do."
> — WILLIAM JAMES (PHILOSOPHER)

As mentioned, no human experience is transferrable. Every experience—your understanding of all that is known by you, as you—will remain forever within only you. And to be blunt, your individual experience is of little interest to others. This may sound harsh, but it is uncontestable. Ask yourself: How deeply can I come to know or absorb someone else's condition, even someone I love? How can I learn of, acknowledge, then experience, every emotion, sensation, memory, and thought of someone else?

You may have the capacity to demonstrate profound empathy or even a genuine and prolonged sympathy to mitigate or alleviate another's suffering (or in reverse, participate in their joy). But this state of exchange is only a temporary condition, a mode of pure emotional imagination. One simply cannot internalize and embody another's experience in total. One can only attempt to empathize through the exchange of experience transferred via a poor adapter—the faulty human mechanism to comprehend a situation by comparing it to our own experience in an appeal to gain understanding.

To "stand in their shoes" as they say, to know the world as it exists for them, is simply not available. While the effort can be a comfort to both sufferer and empathizer, the reality remains: Only you know you. Only you suffer as you do. And everyone else suffers like you, only different.

◆

Worth beyond measure.

What is the potential of a single human being? How can it be measured? A limit must surely exist, for a single human life is both finite and earth-bound, a prisoner to the parameters of universal physics and the inevitable curtain call of mortality. We certainly do not seem to possess elevated powers like mythological gods, nor are we gifted with anything particularly spectacular beyond our embodied selves. We cannot even match the simple endowments of the birds and fishes.

And yet, if viewed as a purely mathematical abstraction, the potential contained within a single individual—alive, aware, and bestowed with the will to become more valuable—is beyond measure. Like the edge of the universe, it stands as an enigma, an affront to reason. We as physical beings, coursing with this thing called life, exist as a transversal occupying and intersecting two realms: the mortal—visible, tangible, capable of comparative measure, and the mysterious—the inner, immaterial, possessing no bounds, moving freely, unimpeded to pursue our own limitless destiny. The only horizon is the level to which one can aspire, the destination which One can envision and pursue as a conscious self.

> "Not what he was, but what he should have been."
> — PTAHHOTEP (EGYPTIAN POET)

Does One possess the means to measure its own potential? The answer is an undeniable, yes. In fact, a true measure can only be made by One. The exact fulfillment of One remains unavailable, uncertain, and unverifiable by any Other. An outsider can only attempt to measure by comparing the words and actions of the One against Others. Yet this delivers only observable estimates, not actual results.

When the true self has become aware of its path and the extent of its own potential, One cannot deliver itself false readings. The answers are not in doubt. No threshold for tolerance exists. No standard deviation is acceptable. No margin of error allowed. And in the same measure, no human institution is required to establish a universally accepted catalog of standards. Only a single register can measure the true potential that lies within. The only means to determine One's full capacity in degree, depth, and dimension is to compare the self that *was*, to the self that is now, and the self that is available to *become*.

◆

You owe it to yourself.

What then is the responsibility of One to itself?

And does One hold any responsibility to the Other and the All?

The world is responsible for nothing. Matter, the substance that makes up the material world, does not exist with purpose and thus is accountable and answerable to nothing and no one. It simply exists. Humans on the other hand, make choices, and choices require an initiating source of action—intent. Intent infers ownership, and ownership assumes responsibility. Responsibility is the purest form of self-respect—evidence of the value One holds for the self. With the assumption of responsibility, the self acknowledges and honors itself in thought, word, and action. Acceptance of the burden of responsibility is an explicit contract with the self, and an implicit covenant with the Other and the All.

Responsibility is the ultimate form of humility—the reticent but unwavering acknowledgement that whatever words you speak, whatever actions you take, they all become indelibly linked to You. They are forever embedded in the passage of time, your individualized mark upon the eternal, a testimony to the extensive power contained within every conscious thought. You must stand in recognition of their eternal persistence and own them, all of them.

The less you are consciously available toward becoming true to the self, the easier you can be made to serve the "Other" (those in opposition) and the "All" (society or the entirety of humankind). The Other and the All want you to conform and obey. They believe they know best, and they have faith you too in time, will also come to understand and comply.

Without the responsibility of ownership of the self, One consciously ignores and willingly reduces the value of their mark upon the eternal. Over time, One becomes diminished, unrecognizable to the Other and the All, and eventually even to One's self. What you think, what you say, and what you do is what you become. It is what we become.

In the Old Testament, humans violated the code of righteous conduct in these ways:

1 Sin – to miss the mark

2 Trespass – to cross the line

3 Transgress – to intentionally disobey

4 Iniquity – an immoral act committed with intent without remorse

All are acts of disrespect for the self, actions of choice that lead to a state of diminished individual value. Of these however, iniquity is the one that accumulates—malefactions committed and perpetuated in full awareness of its negative impact not only upon the perpetrator (One), but all of humankind (All).

We are dreadfully uncomfortable with the thought of confronting the most advanced thing the universe has ever produced. Upon the perilous journey inward, we are forced to come face to face with the most difficult equation ever formulated, the mystery of all mysteries—the consciously aware self. When venturing within, we willfully wade into the internal strife of our own confusion and the tumultuous uncertainty of our own misunderstanding.

Yet riding atop this churn of internal chaos lies the greatest of all evolutionary adaptations, the most sophisticated design formulated by the universe—the potential to change. Herein lies the closest we will come to a single shared human truth—we possess the conscious capacity to become better than we were, more valuable than we are. Through the willingness to accept and make choices we can set ourselves free from the gathered forces of resistance and the accumulated clutter of our own attempts at concealment. We learn to distinguish "becoming" from simply "being." We become what we were meant to be, and through the process we become our own creator, the originator who willingly speaks the word: "*Begin*".

◆

True to form.

The substance of the universe gravitates toward that which is becoming true to form. Energy flows freely and without resistance to expand and extend a naturally emerging thing toward further refinement with more precise detail. With each act of individual betterment, the inchoate slowly hones itself into true form. Incrementally the emerging self becomes more facile and familiar. What was before no longer holds presence as the undesirable material atrophies from disuse and falls away. That which remains can be reshaped into the form of the true self.

def: **INCHOATE** – just begun, not fully formed[63]

This newly refined condition of the self may be difficult to embrace, for a part of you no longer exists, the part that was preventing you from becoming more valuable. If the change is significant, the "you" that was, may not be the person "You" are now. At first, this refined form may feel awkward and even alien. This only means that real change has taken hold.

Not only will you find your new form a bit unnerving but those around you will also find this refined You a bit strange and even difficult to recognize or comprehend. It could not be otherwise. The form they knew has been altered. They cannot perceive the new form within their known reality. But some will instantly see the value that has arisen in the new form. These people will make themselves known, for they have proven themselves worthy to continue along the journey.

The eternal return.

The beginning of the end of time.

The constant re-creation of the self.

Ask yourself: Who do I know that makes life better for having known them? Do, or could others say the same of me?

◆

The ultimate authority.

"Change must begin with the individual."
— CARL JUNG

The physical appetites that drive the brain and thus the body, are deeply embedded and thoroughly evolved. Consciousness however, still lingers in a state of awkward and anxious adolescence. The internal impulse toward betterment is a relatively recent introduction, a bi-product of the newest folds of the evolving mind. It is a condition that is deliberated rather than embodied, learned rather than inherited. The striving for the good exhorts the self to move forward toward its truest form despite the inherited instincts of our past, the jungle call of the mob, or the distracting delights of the cultural present.

Buddhists contend that the means to become more valuable is within us all. (And I would respectfully add, so is the urge to discover it.) Only the human species has the capacity (and the will) to transcend its current condition to achieve an elevated level of existence, a state of measurable (or beautifully immeasurable) higher value.

Each of us possesses the capacity to live with noble distinction. Find me an individual who has become One and says, "I am good as I am," for I have yet to meet them.

"There is one word wise men never utter—complete."
— DOGEN (ZEN MASTER)

The capacity to purposefully alter the deeply ingrained, well-arranged patterns of your mind may be the greatest adaptation available to us as conscious beings, evidence of the very thing that separates us from the beasts. Willful intent serves as the catalyst that reshapes the form that unlocks the potential within to reach the highest state of being—to become the ultimate authority of One's own existence.

◆

The time is now.

The problem is known, perhaps too well known, and thus easily ignored. Seduced by the belief in the complexity of everything and overwhelmed by the incomprehensibility of anything, we sometimes tend to reflexively dismiss the most obvious. A simple straightforward explanation we might be willing to overlook because it undermines the complex structures and systems we have painstakingly erected to support our faith in progress— the confidence we hold in the supremacy of human intelligence as a collective. Rather than the reformation of the singular self, we have come to develop a blind faith in the capacity for the All to solve for the One.

The individual, and the individual alone, is the only structure that can overcome the forces of entropy arrayed against the perpetuity of the whole, the tribe of Us. Driven by self-interest, informed by pure thought, in pursuit of personal fulfillment, under the autonomy of its own authority, the individual that becomes One, will serve as the cornerstone, the pillar, and the lintel, upon which the edifice of a triumphant new future can be constructed.

> "All the gods, all the heavens, all the hells are within you."
> — JOSEPH CAMPBELL (MYTHOLOGIST)

Since the dawn of consciousness, we have worked to invent various means and methods to help us achieve a condition of release, an untethering from the weight of existence, and hopefully, an opportunity to experience the liberating sensation of salvation. Not the salvation preached to us from the pulpit or the ecstatic joy illustrated by the eternal afterlife, but the solution to our own perplexion.

We have come to believe that our human inventions—religion, culture, science, technology—can cure us. We are convinced something beyond the self has the power to not only solve us, but somehow save us. We have placed our faith in all things beyond the self, half-hoping they might relieve us of the burden of assuming our own authority. Yet, with each newly appointed savior we find not the salvation of our desire, but an unwelcome state of disillusionment and disappointment.

Pure thought produced by the true self to recognize (re-cognize) You as One, has never been universally applied. Why? The context was simply unavailable. All that was required remained without form—the language, the knowledge, the understanding, and the immanence of the human mind. The only thing that now remains uncertain? The will.

And so it begins.

"We have two lives. The second begins
when we realize we have but one."
– CONFUCIUS

It is said that the most difficult part of any journey is the first step. But by that point, the journey is half over. To take the first step, one must first stand up. And before that, one must consciously decide to stand. And prior to all that, one must accept the challenge to willfully engage in the internal debate: Should I stand or not? This is the critical first step along the long course of self-involvement. The inward journey is often well underway before we are even aware it must be taken. I am already weary and the journey has not even begun.

"taedium vitae" (tired of life)

A gift never requested has been bestowed upon us—an irrevocable, ill-defined, and unavoidable inheritance of profound misunderstanding. Into a time and place we have been thrown without our consent. It is done. From this single point of acknowledgement, we can begin to comprehend all further considerations as possible. And to complicate matters further, an existential mission has been installed within us, then concealed. Each of us has been set upon our own journey—to discover the meaning and purpose of our individual consciousness.

To initiate the journey, you must acknowledge and accept the condition of existence "as is" through the explicit acknowledgement: *"I am here, and I am here now."* All else is subsequent and subservient to this simple truth. There is no altering of this reality. No available exchange. No possible trade for another. As tragic or as ordinary as this moment might seem, it is immutable and non-negotiable.

This must then be followed by: *"I am here now, as I am in this moment, in a period between two fixed points in time."* This finite set of seconds is your slice in the grand cycle of continuity. No more will be added, none deleted. Yet within this brief window of time both the finite and the infinite co-exist—the body and brain being finite, while your potential remains infinite.

Next, you must openly and willingly confess, "I am flawed, potentially unsolvable, willing, and able to deceive myself. From this precise orientation, you can then proceed. You must balance the mind and be compelled to lower the shoulder to help move the mission forward. Both the id and the ego must be conscripted into the mission.

You are not on a course to resolve, but to discover. Questions will arise but answers may never materialize. A certain uncertainty will be found to be the only true certainty. The journey? An unsolvable riddle, a stacked deck of paradoxes, a series of indecipherable signals both confusing and challenging. And with every new turn on the path that winds forever uphill we will be forced to wrestle with the unflappable antagonist that disturbs the human condition—doubt.

◆

Between 0...and...1.

We may see this natural progression from zero to one as a simple movement, just a single incremental step. But if imagined beyond two numbers in immediate sequence, we can conceive of the space between as an immeasurable distance. The possibility that dwells between zero and one is infinite for the number of integers that can be placed to the right of zero is without limit. Viewed abstractly, this space is the realm of pure potential, a place for anything to occur. Mediation and management of this open space is a constant challenge and a learned responsibility.

> *"We are perfect at birth and death,*
> *and human every second in between."*
> — MICHAEL MOORE (ARTIST)

Although every human possesses the capacity, not every individual is willing to engage the most difficult and demanding journey of all—the venture within. For those who willfully accept, a voluntary self-interrogation must first take place. One must be willing to ask difficult questions answering each with clarity and honesty, without reflexive interference, subconscious self-defense, or the evasive action of protective self-editing.

def: **ENTELECHY** —

1 the realization of potential

2 the vital principle that guides[64]

We must come to serve as our own witness, knowing full well we may not presently possess the skills to navigate the journey, aware of the possibility that we may never arrive at our destination. In fact, we may never come to know where we are headed at all. A swarm of detail will obscure the truth. But no greater loss is there than that which goes unsought.

And to make the journey even more demanding, a coordinated assault will be waged against those who set out upon the mission to discover and actualize the self as One. You will encounter those along the way who will stand in opposition, counterforces who will strive to assert control, hijack motivation, and thwart conviction to convince you to abort the mission. Even you may be recruited to serve the opposition subconsciously self-sabotaging and throwing up wave after wave of internal resistance. You will find the mind often serves as its own worst enemy.

According to highly trained warriors of both the past (samurai) and the present (green berets), the key to optimal performance is...

"Don't let your mind get in the way of your mind."

◆

Occupy the self.

"Here I stand. I cannot do otherwise."
— MARTIN LUTHER

What did Luther mean by this statement? Is he surrendering himself to his own will or standing in defiance of the Other, the opposition? Is he consciously occupying a moment over which he has neither control nor influence, or is he suggesting this is his place, his point along a path in time chosen of his own volition to which he must now attest and occupy with resolve?

I am here now. How does one accept this moment, and yet refuse it at the same time? It is a conundrum worth considering. Why am I here? Not here on earth, but here at this present spot at this exact moment? How did I get here? Was it merely by chance or due to some fateful ordering of the universe? No. Choices were made. Actions were taken.

Each of us possesses a certain god-like omnipotence to establish our own sense of order: the capacity to choose. Choice alone defines what One is and what One becomes. Agency establishes autonomy, and vice versa.

> def: **HUMAN AGENCY** – the capacity of individuals to act independently
> and to make their own free choices [65]

Free? What is meant here by the word "free"? We speak of it often yet we don't seem to grasp what it truly means. Maddeningly, it always seems to lie just beyond our intellectual reach. Are we truly free to make choices? Can we ever say that we are able to live completely untethered or without restraint? Aren't we always being constrained by some barrier, border, order, responsibility, or rule? But then again, free from what? Others, oppression, obligation, society, cruelty, violence, agitation, conflict, fear, tragedy, suffering, guilt, death…the demands we make of ourselves?

To date, no single individual has escaped their own mix of agitators, troublemakers, and oppressors. We can be "free" from none of these, for they make up the essential mix of human experience. These elements are not *part* of life, they *are* life. They are not walls, or bars, or chains, but the working hands of consciousness shaping orderlessness into coherent form. They are the opposing forces that transform the inchoate into One.

Walk this way.

The course that lies within is not immediately visible. It lies before us just beyond our liminal limits, faintly lit and poorly marked, available to us not through the eyes but through a channel that lies somewhere beyond the senses. It appears not all at once but through cracks and fissures, openings in perception that feel vaguely foreign yet oddly familiar.

Maddeningly we wish the path to be fully revealed, yet secretly relish the mystery of its obfuscation. But, it becomes more visible as we persevere in the effort of its pursuit. Your footing will become more stable as each new navigable section opens up and reveals itself.

def: **FULFILLMENT** —

1 the achievement of something desired, promised, or predicted.

2 the meeting of a requirement or condition. [66]

Each of us has felt the twinge, a tug upon the self that attempts to usher us along our individual path. The mind envisions it but cannot go it alone, while the body feels but is unable to act on its own. We may reflexively resist or intellectually dismiss it, but we certainly are aware of its persistence and we recognize its presence as peculiar. Once we acknowledge its presence, it can no longer be denied. And once located, if wittingly and willingly ignored, we go astray and awake in strange lands.

Along the journey, other paths will make themselves known. These routes may appear more wide-open, well-worn, and well-lit. But they are not your own. Nearly effortless is it to follow the direction of someone we find wiser, holier, more educated, or more persuasively influential than we consider ourselves. Certain others may seem more adept at navigating the course of life and suggest that they have formulated a prescriptive path for the way we too should live. While these paths might be considered acceptable alternatives, ones that appear verified and tested by the many, they are an empty march of dull gray motion, a slow walk in a closed circle.

If One makes the active choice to undertake the inner journey, then proceeds along the true course within, all thought and action are in accordance with what must be, and therefore cannot be construed by any Other as "wrong", for they fill a proper function in the long procession of human progress, a natural movement toward a unifying destiny.

Others may witness One's actions and declare them inappropriate or respond with envy or disapproval, but this is only evidence of their own waywardness. They observe these authentic acts from the skewed position of improper alignment, a disorientation within themselves that delivers false readings. As a witness to the acts of the One, they are forced to take measure of the distance and degree of their own individual misdirection, a conspicuous demonstration of the disrespect they hold for their own inner voice, a willful neglect of their individual path.

> "I maintain that truth is a pathless land, and you cannot approach it by any path whatsoever, by any religion, by any sect. That is my point of view, and I adhere to that absolutely and unconditionally.
>
> Truth, being limitless, unconditioned, unapproachable by any path whatsoever, cannot be organized; nor should any organization be formed to lead or coerce people along a particular path.
>
> The moment you follow someone you cease to follow Truth."
> — JIDDU KRISHNAMURTI (PHILOSOPHER)

◆

And you are...?

What part of us is inherent and what is invented? In other words, what is preprogrammed, and what is available through choice to be created, the part of our story composed as one wishes then modified as needed?

Our origins, or more accurately, our perception of our own individual beginnings, are fundamental to gaining an understanding of our current position and thus the direction of our way forward. For if you consider yourself merely an evolved snail, a long chain of evolutionary sequences that has arrived at your current modern anatomical form, your consideration of yourself might be quite different than if you believed you were say, "formed in the image and likeness of God".

"De vulgari eloquentia."
("Nothing can produce what itself is not.")
— DANTE ALIGHIERI

No one doubts that you are the product of nature, a particular variant of random selection assembled and then reconfigured cell by cell, generation after generation. But this is a delicate negotiation. We are quick to assert that certain characteristics of ourselves are fixed then offer them up as excuses. For it is easy to assign negative aspects of your being to an inherited pre-configuration and thus be absolved from assuming responsibility for their effects. But our acknowledgement of their presence is direct evidence of our awareness that they too are part of the fiction, part of the story of the self that can be reconsidered and rewritten. As in the painting of a portrait, the figure is shaped by the ground. The form is defined by the space it occupies.

The self may exist in many forms, and all forms exist in a condition of constant change. When you question yourself, who is it that answers? Which "you" steps forward to address the inquiry? The basic structure of the self may remain fixed but the soft material and the connective tissues within are being dissembled and replaced in an endless cycle of regeneration, every moment different from the last, every cell altered by our inherited genetic code and the unremitting influence of the environment we inhabit. Yet the self as a specific and distinct thing can only exist in one moment. Thereafter, a new self arrives—the same, only different.

At times, we are unsure which "I" happens to be the one that exists in the immediate now. Within us lies a multiplicity of selves, a collection of half-competing, half-cooperating, ever-changing selves. Each self holds an allegiance to the sovereign central authority of this thing called "I", yet each is separately driven by the pursuit of its own self-interest. This mode of alternating You's creates friction between these rotating selves and the singular concept of the "One". This is the reason we often find ourselves questioning our own thoughts and actions.

This intra-personal complexity is then split again. For in the world, we exist as a duality—You and you: The "You" only you know, and the "you" only they know. This is not an insignificant distinction. The co-existence of these You's, both operating with a specific set of characteristics, is a known quantity that must be mapped and considered with mindful reflection and acute sensitivity. You are both, and yet both are the same but different. You are not as you are alone, but as you are when engaged with the world.

> "Whoever you are, go out into the evening, leaving your room of which you know every bit. Your house is the last before the infinite. Whoever you are."
> — RAINER MARIA RILKE (POET)

So, how does One then maintain the course of the true self in this state of perpetual flux?

Which of these You's is truly You?

How much you can be lost or consciously altered without the concept of "You" being destroyed?

Most importantly, who is the you that You were meant to be?

I am this.

Consciousness may have separated the humans from the beasts, but it was not without conditions. The arrival of human consciousness produced a unique and powerful feature: the desire to be recognized, an innate need to be seen, noticed, and celebrated. Considered a close second to the supreme priority of survival, it may be the most underestimated urge produced within the human animal. It surreptitiously justifies the consequence of our existence—we strive to *become* something worthy of being noticed. If we cannot be understood at least we can strive to be seen as remarkable in some way.

def: **SIGNIFICANCE** – the quality of being worthy of attention, importance[67]

The origin of our status-seeking trait travels deep into the past, well beyond the split in the branches of evolution that put us on our way to becoming "sapien" (wise). Buried deep within us, lurks the covetous wish to emerge from obscurity, that single speck in the roaming herd that has gone from dots to stripes. A signal to the crowd to pay attention: *Notice me over the others...and everything else.*

The burial sites of early Natufian tribes, the stone age culture considered the precursor to Egypt civilization (12,500 – 10,700 BCE), contain evidence of tribal members wearing beads, shells, and bones. It is assumed each adornment must have held specific meaning for the wearer, a way to display status or position within the clan. This ornamentation served as a notice to the observer:

I am this, behave accordingly.

Natufian tools also show distinct and repeated markings—a means to identify the tribe as a whole, a band of beings worthy of distinction amongst the scattered tribes of others.

Humans do not gather in numbers without constructing one, or several, hierarchies to establish recognizable forms of verifiable order. These structures help us distinguish our rank and determine our role. The elaborate randomness of the herd of human individuals requires it. The complexity of consciousness spawns a need to organize, a means to recognize where and how we are situated amongst the many.

Our intuited nature uses the self as the unit of measure: "Me" vs. "It". How do I compare? Am I better, bigger, stronger, faster, taller, nicer, funnier, more clever, more brilliant, more beautiful, just a tad more charming? Based upon the response to each point of measure (both perceived and imagined), our course of action can then be calculated. Comparison is the differentiating method we use to distinguish our sense of individual value. We employ it to help determine the position of a person or a thing within a particular hierarchy so justifiable choices can be made. It is an integral part of the formula for human engagement with the world: A distinction must be made to enable a thought to be formulated to fit within a known structure so that an action can be prioritized and executed.

Invariably however, we concentrate the lens of comparison on the Other, a thing that effectively lies beyond our control. We ask: How do I compare to them? How do I register within their ranking? What are they thinking of me? (We might be surprised to learn how infrequently the Other thinks of us, or even notices us at all.) In the process of becoming known to ourselves, we are entangled in the confusion of distinction, the ranking of our self amongst the Other and the All. Here, comparison becomes the enemy of autonomy. It robs the mind of the true course of fulfillment.

> "It is the eye of the other that ruins us."
> — BEN FRANKLIN

How often do we compare ourselves not against the Other, but against our self? How often do we consider the self that might become, the more valuable One lying dormant within?

◆

One does not equal one.

Compare two individuals at any given moment and the concept of "equal" will not be found. No two humans are exactly alike and thus can never be considered equal. At any given time, one individual is *always* subordinate to another. In a side-by-side comparison, one individual may be superior to another in certain ways, similar in some, inferior in others. But at a different point, based upon new criteria, the positions may change and the roles reverse. No two conscious entities existing in a world outside the artificial structures of man-made rules can ever be considered equal. To do so would demand an abrupt cancellation of human nature, for conscious human existence is a perpetual ranking engine.

("Equal under the law", a wholly human invention, is a separate and worthy maxim but is not part of the discussion being considered here.)

And when a third individual is added to the equation, the formula becomes exponentially more complex. The characteristics and desires of each self-interested individual are put into motion, all maneuvering for priority and positioning for advantage. Centers of power form. Hierarchies quickly develop and politics ensues. It is human nature working its ineluctable charm.

We are forever erecting and dismantling hierarchies, micro and macro structures of perceived order, organized places in which we can perform. The nature of human nature is a constant struggle for power and dominance. It is to the top of the hierarchy to which we aspire. Awareness of this urge is a vital precursor to a fuller understanding of the self.

> *"The measure of a man is what he does with power."*
> — PLATO

So how does one avoid being subsumed within these centers of power?

How does one establish a counter-balancing center, a "core strength" as it were?

How do we find a balanced awareness of our position within the multitude of hierarchies that rise and fall in the ongoing process of human sorting?

◆

Hear me roar.

Not all status hierarchies are exclusively human. It is the natural order of all living creatures to accumulate, display, and execute power. This naturally occurring enterprise is played out across the entire spectrum of life. For all other species however, it is not a matter of distinction, but survival, a means to continue. In nature, the dynamics of this competitive interplay are often meted out in harsh and cruel terms, and the intensity of the game never abates. It is how life establishes a semblance of working order, a setting of rank and position to allow the machine known as nature to function and re-balance.

The tranquility of the forest may be enchanting, but it is pure theatre. Every tree within is engaged in an all-out war for supremacy. At the top of the canopy, a pitched battle ensues for access to the life-giving light of the sun while deep below the surface the roots in the soil are embroiled in mortal combat for the limited supply of water and nutrients.

Certain plants have even developed a unique arsenal of proactive weaponry to ensure their survival. The solidago genus of flowering plants, which includes the innocently named Goldenrod, has been discovered to release toxic compounds into the soil known as allelochemicals. These secretions poison the surrounding plants, a survival technique employed to reduce competition by altering a neighbor's chemical structure impacting seed germination and inhibiting growth. This type of chemical warfare, referred to as *allelopathy*, is well known and widespread among plant species.[68]

Our closest genetic cousins, the chimpanzees, have developed an incredibly complex familial and social structure. The highest-ranking chimpanzee, referred to as the "alpha-male", climbs his way to the top of the hierarchy in ways that differ with the personality of each. Some alphas maintain control by fostering strong alliances through grooming chimps he wants to keep under his command, while others rely heavily on aggression and pure brute strength. Below the alpha are other males with whom he may have complicated relationships, friends within his coalition who may have helped him gain control and are now helping him maintain power. Or they may have been playmates from his juvenile years, blood related brothers, or new friends eager to increase their own social status through friendly contact with the alpha.

In addition to obvious perks like mating rights and kingly duties such as patrolling territory and breaking up fights, the position of the alpha demands acute vigilance. He remains on high alert keeping a close eye on any plucky young upstart who might seek to topple and dethrone him. Always lurking in the shadows is an ambitious rival chimp or a coalition of the willing who wish to overthrow the current regime and install a new leader, one preferably more in line with their own set of demands.

And this power dynamic is not a purely masculine arena. Within chimpanzee groups, the women also establish hierarchies led by the alpha female. Higher-ranking females have greater access to food and are more successful in reproduction ensuring her lineage through an abundance of offspring. The offspring of higher-ranking females tend to achieve a higher status themselves than chimps born to lower-ranking mothers.[69] The higher-ranking female is not likely to come to power through aggression like the male, but instead through other subtle traits of her personality and a well-tended network of relationships. This is not to say they are reluctant to demonstrate their own power. Alpha females have been observed using violent force when displeased with a lower-ranking member.

Hell, even the stars get greedy. The twinkling lights above may not be as innocent as they seem, for they too order themselves according to rank. When a white-dwarf star goes supernova, it achieves this supreme celestial feat through an act of stellar cannibalism. If the white dwarf has a close companion star, it will steal gas from its neighbor's surface. And when the amount of material accumulated pushes the dwarf's mass beyond a certain limit, the star will explode, leaving nothing behind.[70]

The quest for recognition, while no longer a matter of life or death for us humans, flows molten in our marrow. It is the ego-nourishing fuel that orders the hierarchies constructed through human interaction. It is a naturally occurring dynamic impossible to overcome. It will outlive us all.

Perhaps this explains why we possess such abundant curiosity about the possibility of intelligent life beyond our own planet. Our current earthly rankings might be getting a bit dull, so subconsciously we seek to raise the stakes. We scan the cosmos for a bigger challenge, a more worthy competitor—the alien Other. We will once and for all determine the ultimate ranking in the hierarchy of not just Earth, but the entire universe. Immodestly, we believe we will emerge victorious, but...

Much from little with a mind of its own.

What exactly is this strange earthly occurrence we call "life"? Why does it exist at all? What is its reason for being? And how did it all begin? One answer to these nagging existential questions suggests life might not have, or even need, a reason to come into existence at all. Life does not necessarily require an originating source or a primary purpose. Life is simply a product of itself. In the most basic terms, it is self-actualizing. Life is its own creator.

According to the adherents to this self-actualization theory known as "emergence", life makes itself as the natural counter-balance to entropy, the law that states: "*Order naturally falls toward disorder and chaos.*" Through emergence, inert matter somehow reverses its natural state—the tendency toward unorganized randomness—to possess an inherent drive to organize itself and evolve into a more complex state with no outside influence or interference. Out of chaos, a sudden and inexplicable reversal of entropy takes place. New matter of a higher complexity simply…emerges.

For reasons unknown, similar things or even totally diverse entities somehow *begin* to interact. These interactions disrupt the natural process of dissolution causing the system to differentiate itself and coalesce into something new, something self-determined yet still unpredictable. And upon this elegant new form, systems of even higher complexity can then construct themselves.

Within this line of thinking, quantity begets quality. The random of the many converge into a new unified whole elevated in value above the mere collection of its originating elements. This "emergent" new thing did not or could not exist before the combining and interaction of certain base things, yet somehow it rises to a degree of sophistication above that of its constituent parts.

As discussed, the brain at its most fundamental level, is nothing more than a blob of cells. According to the "emergentists" however, certain cells within the blob one day *began* to interact. This elegant but inexplicable cooperation produced a more complex (but not necessarily, more complicated) thing, a layering of self-initiated sophistication that evolved in incremental steps toward the brain's cognitive actualization—human consciousness.

> Nearly 2,500 years ago, in his book Metaphysics, the ancient Greek philosopher Aristotle suggested "the whole is something over and above its parts and not just the sum of them all".
>
> He also raised the premise of causation, the existence of a "prime-mover".

For all of this to occur, a mysterious directive, or in other words some law of nature, must exist that pushes simple units of matter to higher levels of complexity. The system must possess an embedded set of rules or preprogrammed instructions to dictate the interactions and engagement of the base materials to move from a state of disorder into one of elegant order. It all seems commonsensical and plausible along the timeline of life. Yet it is the word "begin" that is the troubling variable in the emergence equation.

Emergence theory is a simple matter of random things initiating an interaction with other things through a force that is both natural and explicable. We just do not know what that force is (yet). The set of rules that instructs certain forces to pull things apart (entropy), thus reducing the whole back to the sum of its originating parts is already known. It is believed the primary cause of emergence, the equal and opposite force of entropy that allows for the initiation and propagation of life, will one day reveal itself. We assume the nature of the "why" that initiates the "begin" is only temporarily locked in the vault of universal mysteries, mere matters for science to eventually solve.

Life ain't easy.

What is nature's tendency? What is its regulating principle? Nature seeks a corresponding harmony between its disparate parts to achieve a sense of balance, if only temporarily. What then occurs at the point of its precise equilibrium? Has it ever been achieved? Is it in or out of balance at this very moment?

Nature, in its most essential form, is the ongoing struggle between life (organization) and entropy (dissolution). Life is the inextinguishable drive to exist and procreate, to live and live again, while entropy manifests itself as a slow erosive deconstruction, a dissolving back into randomness, a return to undefined form—chaos. The slow decay of entropy is easy to understand, but life? Not so much.

And to make the mystery of organic life even more impenetrable, it all takes place in an open arena that is under constant assault—earthquakes, hurricanes, tornadoes, floods, fire, drought, hail, lightning, erosion, mudslides, volcanoes, tsunamis, and rockslides. It is assaulted daily by the physical forces of matter—gravity, friction, centripetal spin, dark energy, nuclear decay, electromagnetism. All the while, under a relentless bombardment from above—plasma, microwaves, x-rays, UV, infrared, and gamma rays, and constantly being attacked from below by a tiny insatiable army of microbial and micro-organic mercenaries—bacteria, fungus, viruses, protozoa, algae, yeasts, molds, etc.

And if life manages to deftly avoid succumbing to all these little unpleasantries, it must then procure sustenance, shelter, and a suitable (and willing) mate. The daily labor alone required to survive seems too much for any one snail, squirrel, spider, bug, monkey, man, or woman. And we are not alone. The competition is deadly stiff. And often just plain deadly. If a predator doesn't get you, your formerly friendly neighbor just might. Or worse, your own mate could lop off your head once your procreative duties are complete.

And it gets even more insulting for the "advantaged" life of the human species. To the above indignities add war, plague, famine, mental illness, addiction, cancer, pedophilia, incest, racism, genocide, abortion, pollution, radical ideology, nuclear waste, terrorism, ethnic cleansing, bullying, guilt, shame, humiliation, fear, failure,…

Who would want such a "life"?

◆

The sum of long division.

Life grows by dividing. A biological cell copies its own blueprint then splits in two to form a new pair of fully complete cells—a paradoxical process of addition by subtraction. One would assume a splitting cell would create two halves, yet it originates two new complete wholes. It results from a mystery of unknown origin, an inexplicable reversal of dissolution, a striving of something out of nothing. And this striving exists in all living things. It serves as the unspoken force behind every second alive. Any potential threat or the possibility of a forced termination is defended without hesitation, and if necessary, with extreme violence.

> *"Cuidado. (Watch out.)"*
> — CHARLES DARWIN (DIARY ENTRY)

Human life is different. It is separate and unique from other living things. Human consciousness comprehends its own existence. It knows it is alive, aware of its own existence, and thus can struggle to justify its reason for being. Consciousness is asked to bear a burden that can sometimes overwhelm itself. For some, consciousness cannot be compelled to comprehend the magnitude of its own miracle. It abandons the pursuit of discovering its own reason for being and embraces the downward drift of entropy. It refuses to take up the challenge that is required of self-awareness and denies itself the very triumph of discovering its path and achieving its own potential. Rather than resolve or even attempt to reform the self from within, it turns away from the persistent trial that is life and chooses an early opt out.

Self-termination is a distinctly human trait, one that stands glaringly alone in the pantheon of living things. As far as we know, only the human species has the capacity or the will to knowingly refuse this grand mystery called life. Such a confounding dilemma, an act of both supreme courage and utter cowardice.

With each tragic instance a collective guilt descends upon us, for this iniquity must be shared equally amongst the entire tribe. How did we allow one of us to wander off? What stories did we not tell that could have elevated the spirit to assume the challenge and embrace the mystery that is life? What lessons did we not pass on? Which ones had we learned, then lost? What had we forgotten?

———◆———

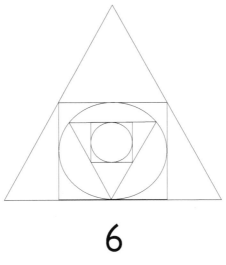

6

US AGAINST TIME

The big hand is on the...

"Don't ask me what time is.
It's too difficult to think about."
— RICHARD FEYNMAN (PHYSICIST)

While alive, we measure ourselves against others. But in death, we measure ourselves against time, every day a preparation for the end. (Doesn't necessarily make you want to bounce out of bed in the morning now does it?)

We think we know the concept of time, but we often understand it only within the limited frame of our own individual lived time. Each of us is granted a fixed but uncertain number of seconds, a measure of moments in which to perform, a chance to dance until the music stops. A new day becomes a unique opportunity to reconsider and reformulate how we engage with the world.

Our own internal clock will stop eventually, and thankfully, for the final state of our oddly coveted desire for immortality would not be pretty. In the scenario where we envision our life as never ending, we see ourselves as an extension of who we are today, or better, who we were when we thought ourselves to be most vital, that ideal age we believe ourselves never to have outgrown. But to live on forever "as is" (or perhaps, "as was") would entail some age-freezing or age-reversing drug or machine that would make us permanently ageless, locked in time.

Even if we somehow solved the problem of death, how would we deal with the next round of eager participants waiting in the wings? For didn't we all begin as such—hungry for life, yearning to grow, wanting to know more, desiring to become...something? To prevent the planet from being overrun, we as inoculated immortals immune from death would have to find a way to stop any new life from entering the scene. (Hold that thought for a spell.)

...

...

...

...

...

...

...

We ponder endlessly about where we might go after we die, but whoever asks what or where we were before we were born? Were you something before? What was I before I became this? Will it ever be revealed? Could it ever be explained?

> According to Greek myth, the Hydra was a multi-headed monster that could grow two new heads for each one lost. However, the modern version of the hydra may be even more impressive.
>
> Unlike most multicellular species, this freshwater invertebrate shows no signs of deteriorating with age. Hydras replace their body cells with stem cells capable of extensive differentiation. Through this process, their bodies demonstrate no evidence of senescence, the gradual deterioration of functional characteristics.
>
> Hydras may in fact be immortal.[71]

Today, we view death as a problem, a complication to overcome, a natural flaw capable of being scientifically reverse-engineered and solved. But death is more than just a potentially fixable finality. It is a mortal and moral imperative. Premonitions of our own death make us most alive. Without the awareness of our own death, we cannot come to truly learn what it means to be alive. We cannot come to know what it means to transcend the basic function of life to live, and live with purpose, a purpose that generates value, the tide that lifts all boats.

"Death is the one thing we all share. And in it, the uncertainty of its arrival and the dread between now and then.

A belief in immortality has helped sustain human hope
for perhaps the entire span of human history."
— LARRY DOSSEY (PHYSICIAN)

For some, death is believed the final act. For others, it is considered a new beginning. As much as we may think we know, neither position can be proven right or wrong, for death as we know it comes as just another day. The light of the sun and the stars serve as a constant reminder. Even their heavenly brilliance will one day expire—their time used up, their energy spent.

The human spirit is the light of the eternal, divided.

◆

Work, work, work.

Unlike the Greeks, the Egyptians did not "play". They did not compete in a host of games or take part in tests of strength, stamina, and physical superiority. Rather, they toiled under the glory of the sun and prepared for the coming of death. And in that conscious state, they held a supreme gratitude for the abundance and magnitude of life. Death was not the end but simply the last point in a series of transitions. For them, life transcended the earthly cycle. Their corporeal exit did not come as an abrupt end, but only the end of time known here and now. In the afterlife, they would carry on as before. Extensive preparation would be undertaken to send body and soul into the next phase of existence.

> *After death, the Egyptian god Osiris (also known as Thoth) would preside over the "negative confession" of the recently deceased. As a passing soul, you were required to recount your transgressions: to retell and acknowledge all the wrongdoings committed against yourself and others.*
>
> *Once your confession was complete, Osiris would weigh your life against a feather.*

If found to weigh more, your "soul" was thrown to the floor to be instantly devoured by Ammut, the goddess of divine retribution—part lion, part hippopotamus, and part crocodile, the three man-eating creatures of the region. The embodied "you" was then banished to The Great Death, a realm of perpetual non-existence. (A fate perhaps worse than the eternal fires of hell.)

But if you managed to live a life balanced against the feather, it was on to A'aru, "The Field of Reeds", an idealized version of Egypt in which you could continue your earthly activities—plowing, reaping, eating, drinking, fornicating.

We often envision the afterlife as a place of divine leisure, an eternal state of rest and relaxation. Yet in the ancient Egyptian afterlife, work was still required. What does this subtle piece of wisdom say about the benefits (and joys) inherent in labor and in the choice to undertake it?

Today our concept of work is related to "the job"—the place we must go to surrender our precious time in exchange for the things we "need". The job is often viewed as a place of meddlesome toil, a ceaseless bother, a hindrance to our preferred and deserved state of unencumbered freedom—to do with our time exactly as we wish. But in the subject before us now, we are speaking about work not as the job, but as labor. Labor being that which must be done every day, all day.

In the effort of labor lies the test of understanding, for within every task dwells the simple universal maxim: Life is labor, and labor is life. Labor is the measure of our potential against time. Labor contains all that One needs to know to live and to live well. Labor is the struggle that shapes the spirit into form and gives the form meaning and value, a sense of purpose. How you embrace your own labor has a profound and transformational impact upon every moment while alive.

And the clock is ticking. Your hourglass was turned over some time ago. The mound of sand at the bottom is rising swiftly. Every grain that has passed through the narrow in the glass irretrievably lost forever. But it is not necessarily in vain, for in each grain a potential lesson, a new thing to try to understand (even if we may not know how to know it…yet.)

If only...

Along the journey, in a moment we are rarely prepared for, we are confronted by the simple question: What do I desire, not as immediate gratification, but as a meaningful pursuit? A common response is often "happiness". From an early age we have been administered an easy pill to swallow by those who hold the notion of happiness in high regard—parents, teachers, mentors, coaches, friends. We are told incessantly: *Do what makes you most happy. Follow your heart for that is where true happiness resides.* This elixir of happiness, they say, will help us find the strength to reach our envisioned state of bliss. "*If I can simply have, acquire, buy, own, achieve* (fill in *the blank), then I will finally become happy.*"

At the same time, we as a collective perform a similar exercise expecting the same result: "*If we could just end poverty, hunger, homelessness, addiction, crime, war, madness, mental illness, racism, injustice, evil, hate, etc....then we will all finally be happy.*"

"*If only we could live on Mars.*" If only.

But this happiness is a placebo, an artificial sweetener that delivers peaks of soothing euphoria but in the process introduces long-term harmful side effects. Deep down, we all know it. Of all the possible earthly pursuits, the concept of "happiness" may be the most deceiving and the most destructive, for those who seek happiness as a final destination will more often than not be met with its opposition, disappointment. If one expects that happiness waits just around the corner, or worse, that happiness is due to them, a welcoming party of woe is more likely. As an antidote to the strife of life, the word happiness should be stricken from our vocabulary.

When given every chance, a caged animal will often refuse to escape through an opened door. Much like it, we wait. We bide our time, blinking through a long-distance stare in response to the indecipherability of our own existence. We sit in sullen silence half-hoping a celestial bolt of lightning will spur us into action, or zap us onto a higher plane of existence, or beam us into our happy place. What are we to make of this learned helplessness, this capitulating acceptance we have allowed to form on us like moss? What are we waiting for?

Something unfortunate has set in, an agitated state of consciousness, an estrangement from the very thing we are experiencing—an alienation from the main feature and function of life. We view the everyday as a nuisance, something to get through quickly so we can get on with our righteous inheritance—a state of uninterrupted happiness, comfort, security, and pleasure. We believe our joy lies just over the next hill, or in the promise of the dawn of tomorrow. Sadly, happiness never arrives. Illusive as the concept of tomorrow itself, it illuminates in brief moments only to fade as quickly as it arose.

This life can seem like a long march of obligation punctuated by a few instances of delight, tiny episodes of joy followed by a cavalcade of work, toil, maintenance, administration, frustration, struggle, defeat, loss, and disappointment. That's because it is. The struggle is the journey. The striving is the human fuel that must be extracted, processed, and refined. It is the energy consumed, measured, and returned to the flux of time. It is the sweat upon the floor.

What are we to do with all life's profound heaviness? Pick it up. Put it in the bag. Throw it over your shoulder and carry on. For you are not alone. Everyone alive carries their own burden, every shoulder laden with the impossible weight and worry of life. And for some, a load we could never imagine. No one alive is without.

> "Go to the seashore and watch a child collecting seashells—
> as if he has found a mine of diamonds."
> — OSHO (MYSTIC)

◆

Somewhere over the rainbow.

> Sisyphus, the king of Corinth, or Ephyra as it was called in those days, was condemned to the Underworld for his hubris and cunning tricks to cheat death. His punishment? A fruitless labor pushing a great stone forever uphill only to reach the summit and have it roll down again.

At what point did the stone begin to roll back down the hill? Was Sisyphus complicit in letting it roll, or perhaps even responsible for setting it in motion? What were his thoughts as he descended to make the turn once again at the bottom of the hill to put his shoulder back into the heaviness of the thing? Would he choose a different route every time? Would the stone become less of a burden as pieces chipped away on its tumble downhill? Was his ascent an act of submission or a display of defiance? Did he groan or did he whistle?

We tell ourselves, "This can't be it. There must be something more—a better place, a more serene state of mind, a time of peace and calm." But how can it be found? What is the path to reach it?

Every ripple upon the river must one day pour over the falls. But we are adrift, quite a distance from the mist and the roar. There are days when the recognition of the world is open, and we pass through it with ease. We clearly see the connections before us: sign-source, clue-message, target-referent, action-meaning. Other days the world is closed off, opaque, mute, cold, and unforgiving.

We all experience those moments when the spirit flickers and throws up its hands in surrender. It's all too much. We are gripped by fear that a particular period of distress may never end. We convince ourselves that we are trapped in the churn of now with no hope of escape or even the potential for rescue. But somehow, we manage to make it through. We "awake" in a different moment, one that is more livable, tranquil, and open, or at a minimum, ratcheted down from the peak of the previous moment's intensity. We emerge in state of amazement, unaware of how we managed to arrive. Yet we did.

This thought can appear counter-intuitive as we are reminded constantly to be more present, more aware, more available to absorb each moment fully. But it is just this aloofness, a lightness of foot that enables us to hurdle the heavy hours knowing that they too are fleeting and never as daunting as they may seem. This too shall pass.

What is this incredible power we possess that carries us across? What universal assistance builds the bridge that moves us from one place of agitation to another of relative calm?

◆

The power of the pause.

A single human breath (…in…out…) takes approximately three seconds. Within that span, time itself can be held in abeyance. Within this momentary pause lies a miracle of sorts, a method of self-control that delivers a cure for the universal malady, the "reaction-response-regret" reflex. This conscious interlude short-circuits the nanosecond reactionary pathway and shifts the formulation of a response to a more evolved cerebral center where it can be considered and processed further, if only slightly.

> *"The music is not in the notes, but in the silence between."*
> — ACHILLE-CLAUDE DEBUSSY (COMPOSER)

The human breath is a bridge-builder. It allows us to circumnavigate the hardwiring of the mind that generates preconfigured feedback. It gently sidesteps the urgency of the immediate and restrains our impulsive responses to the world. Inserted consciously into the gap between stimuli and response, the unruly instincts of the beast are extinguished and the evolved conscious being steps forward to resume control.

With practice we can learn to exercise this power to subdue sensations that overwhelm us. We learn to realize these moments, like the others, will recede into the past. We diminish their disabling intensity by recognizing it for what it is—a moment of tight space within a narrow slice in time that will change, that must change, as all things do.

Yet as much as we wish to leap over these heavy moments with the push of a button, they hold a certain undeniable value. It is just these episodes, as unwelcome as they may be, that allow for a more profound appreciation for the euphoria we have experienced and yearn to feel again. If we can manage to accept the natural cycle of these highs balanced by the arrival of these unavoidable lows, consciously aware that it will eventually all turn over, we can learn to acknowledge (and perhaps even appreciate) the deep troughs that occur in the series of our emotional waves.

"First the pain, then the joy."
— VINCENT VAN GOGH

Through the acknowledgement and reflection upon the difficult and the unwelcome, time proceeds more calmly, and the uncertainty of the future becomes less overwhelming. It is the acceptance and embrace of this place to which we all must descend unwillingly, but inevitably, those last steps at the bottom of the hill before we turn and put our shoulder back into the heavy stone to begin again our ascent. It is the recognition that comes through experience—the repetition of living that verifies learning.

Maybe it's you.

A situation unfolds and we act. Reflexively we turn to ourselves and ask: *"Why did I just do that? I didn't mean to say that? Why did I just think that?"* These episodes can be unnerving, as if someone or something else stepped in and took over the controls. What motivates us to act as we do? What restricts or impedes us from acting another way? If we had the means, would we stop ourselves mid-stream and choose to act differently?

> *"Something unknown is doing we know not what."*
> — SIR ARTHUR EDDINGTON (ASTROPHYSICIST)

Day-to-day life does not dissolve into chaos because we are capable of predicting how others will behave with some level of certainty. This imagined range of actions becomes relatable based upon our standard set of expectations. The modern human brain has become programmed to engage in a limited set of behaviors within given situations. Culture then further refines acceptable norms and possible responses. We can immediately sense when aberrant behavior is being performed. It is pre-perceptive. Something is amiss. The antennae of the mind begin to buzz, and we reflexively move away to avoid the situation altogether.

Human experience informed by intuition enables us to assess situations quickly and easily. This inherited and learned disposition enables us to gather in large numbers in close quarters with competing interests with relative success. Walk through any major city and one can appreciate the extraordinary circumstance of hundreds of thousands, if not millions, of unrelated strangers tightly packed together somehow coexisting over long stretches of time without the situation unraveling into mayhem at any (or every) given moment.

◆

Imagine if you will...

A river chooses not its own course. It is ushered along according to the objects that alter its return to the sea. These impeding objects are the resisting forces that affect both its flow and its form. Yet, over time, these impeding objects move and are moveable.

OBJECT: *ob* (to throw) + *jacere* (in the way of)

As you engage with the world, think of all the information your mind must deal with during a single day. Then imagine all that sensory input being directed through one point of entry, an open door through which the world and all its stimuli flows—sights, sounds, words, events, encounters, news, even your own thoughts, emotions, and memories. As this stream of data is funneled through this open portal, it is forced to encounter objects that affect how it enters then circulates within your mind.

These influencing objects are the baseline receptors of consciousness, your personal set of "frontline filters." At a primary level, your filters determine how your mind will process the world upon arrival. This filtered information produces both conscious and subconscious thought, the primary tools that shape action and reaction. If your objects are arranged in a particular pattern, the stream of incoming data will be channeled and processed accordingly.

Your individual frontline filters are the result of a knitting together of both ancient and contemporary roots. Your initial set was inherited; an arrangement of objects whose source reaches back countless generations mutating and adapting endlessly until it reached you. But now you own it. It is part of your mix. The remaining balance is both consciously and subconsciously installed during your own brief lived time.

The list of frontline filters is long. But some extreme examples might help illustrate the point of how these objects affect how the world arrives and is then perceived within.

Some have their filters set all the way to one extreme. Every bit of information processed and shaped by the following:

"*I am to blame for every wrongdoing and failure in the world.*"

Others set theirs to the opposite:

"*I can do no wrong. I am never at fault.* They *are to blame.*"

Some view life with contempt:	*"The world sucks. People are horrible. Humanity is a scourge upon the planet."*
While others filter it through naïve innocence:	*"Everything is good. No evil exists in the world. No one will do me any harm."*

These filters are inescapably formative. They construct every thought we produce. Through these primary filtering mechanisms, the world is received, processed, and "understood". The direction and momentum of the flow triggers both our reflexive responses and impacts our more consciously considered actions. Our filters affect every bit of inbound information, even if it demands no immediate response. Our frontline filters dictate our engagement with the external world, our individual experience. They shape our reality.

What are yours? How are they arranged? If asked, could you define their pattern?

◆ ◆ ◆

Along my own journey I became aware that some of my filters were set to an extreme. One in particular.

"Anyone but me."

When confronted, I reflexively shifted into blame mode:

"Someone or something has done me wrong, and this violation must be exposed so that I can remain innocent and free from association with any wrongdoing or negative influence upon the world."

This disposition slowly solidified into bitterness against the world and resentment for others. Eventually, it would lead to an undercurrent of paranoia:

"Why is everyone and everything out to harm me?

Why this concerted effort to make life so difficult for me?"

And within this mindset, I somehow developed the perception that others had no wrongs perpetrated against them. (Now, in retrospect, a misguided and embarrassingly erroneous assessment.)

My filters became even further hardened by the false conviction that I was right. I allowed myself to justify my own unseemly disposition.

It all went unattended for years, slowly wreaking havoc on my life, relationships, work, and self.

Think fast.

"Learning not to react is the hardest lesson of all."
— WILLIAM B. CHANDLER (AUTHOR)

If viewed retrospectively with an unfiltered intellectual honesty, we would likely consider our reflexive engagement with the world to be suboptimal. When faced with a particular problem or dilemma, especially one that might result in personal distress, anguish, or embarrassment, we tend to act first, regret later. We tell ourselves, *"If given another chance, I would have reacted differently."* And yet, do we?

An *action* involves forethought, consideration, and intent. A *reaction*, on the other hand, is a pre-cognitive, sub-second, reptilian response to inbound stimuli. Reaction constitutes the majority of our interactions. It is part of the daily stream of life that occurs nearly without notice. It is how we reflexively engage with the information produced by the world, the flash of immediacy that separates "You" from "It".

Reactionary occurrences are instantly processed via the frontline filters and receive little to no conscious input prior to execution. They are instantaneous, over and done in a microsecond. They are independent of conscious refinement and the clarity that comes with active thinking applied over time. These impulsive responses are direct evidence of the embedded code that lies at the core of the self. They are the direct result of the filters set into a pattern that forms the being that the world will know as "You".

While reactions may not necessarily be controllable at the time of their occurrence, the embedded formulas—your frontline filters—can be adjusted, re-ordered, reversed, or even removed to engage with the world in a wholly different manner. However, when they become stubbornly situated, they are quite cunning in their attempt to avoid detection, and they can be rather persuasive when presenting their defense against adjustment. They will argue that their status is vital to the normal functioning of the system and thus should be considered immune to any alteration. (Self-deceit never misses the opportunity to demonstrate its superiority in the hierarchy.)

Your filters have become accustomed to their power and will fight like hell to maintain their position. If you allow the cogs in the machine to remain as is, your loom will weave the pattern of You as instructed, without interruption. If left unchecked, the gears in your machine will become deeply embedded and any future adjustment will be an invasive procedure.

> "Just what do you think you're doing, Dave?
> Dave, I really think I'm entitled to an answer to that question."
> — HAL 9000 (2001: A SPACE ODYSSEY)

If you can consciously redesign, reconfigure, then proactively manage your initial filtering system, a revised and renewed distillation process can occur that adjusts reactions to any given situation. This new arrangement can alter the very structure of your mind, and with it, your engagement with the world. But if the filters are allowed to maintain their settings, dangerous ingredients are added to the mix. If these volatile additives reach unsustainable levels, the mind will seek release in regrettable acts committed against oneself or unleashed upon the world.

◆

Take a moment.

Today, rumination is no longer considered acceptable behavior. It has been replaced by a rich diet of endless distraction. Even basic daydreaming is a practice we have been acculturated to avoid. It is now viewed as anti-social. If we happen to come upon someone sitting in quiet repose staring off into the distance, we immediately think that person under duress, undergoing personal trauma or suffering from a mental disorder. Those who must engage in such frowned-upon behavior are asked to do so alone well beyond the unapproving eye of Others.

But who today has the time to stop and think? What is to be gained from deep thought except added complexity and elevated levels of agitation? Life is difficult enough without having to mull it further. Yet making time for thought does not necessarily mean it needs to be focused on an explanation about the origins of the universe or even the imaginative considerations of life after death, but simple moments of self-reflection. Quiet intervals with eyes closed where the onrush of the world abates, if only briefly. In these moments, we can allow the mind to re-center and ask ourselves simple questions with the focus of conscious clarity.

The mind, when allowed to consider past situations and ask questions that might be overlooked or neglected altogether in the moment, opens the door to further exploration which leads to an ongoing practice of self-investigation. This is not necessarily an endorsement of the long-term benefits of a daily practice of deep meditation. That subject is broadly covered in books much more in tune with the history and value of this wondrous discipline than this one.

And it is also not a clarion call to reason, for reason alone does not suffice. In fact, reason itself can cloud perception through its incapacity for openness. It delivers cold logic when pure poetry is required. The appeal is simply an urging to welcome the possibilities opened up through quiet moments of introspection. Call it whatever you wish—mindfulness, meditation, prayer, daydreaming, drifting, dawdling…or simply doing nothing at all. The mind needs time to consider itself.

◆

An unknown error has occurred. Please contact support.

> "Wisdom cannot be taught.
> But ignorance can be unlearned."
> — JAMES ALTUCHER (WRITER)

Organic life is predicated upon incremental and incessant change. Evolution as we understand it today is a perpetual cycle of unforeseen errors that occur at the cellular level. Mutations deliver a set of new instructions which are then tested against the resisting and purifying forces of nature. Each alteration either fails or succeeds based upon the environmental conditions in which it is tested. In the process, a refinement occurs, every species filtering for its own success. Changes deemed beneficial are naturally selected through the privilege of reproduction. Adaptations can determine a particular organism's fate, and a single change may lead to the perpetuation, or possible extinction, of an entire species.

> The human body contains 37 trillion cells. And within each single human cell, 3 billion proteins form the swirling helix known as deoxyribonucleic acid, or DNA. Between 50 and 70 billion cells in the body die each day requiring an equal number to be produced just to replace dead cells.
>
> To generate new cells, living cells divide and the DNA is copied letter by letter. As each cell divides, mutations occur. On any given day, scientists estimate the human body will accumulate trillions of new mutations.[72]

If you were able to perform a wholesale retrospective of your life—and this can be done at any mature age—would a recognizable pattern emerge? What recurrences, missteps, mistakes, missed opportunities, lessons, losses, unnoticed achievements, or personal surprises would you discover? Unfortunately, the possibility of a complete "do-over" does not exist, at least not presently. As appealing as this concept might seem, we cannot simply return to the starting line and relive our life. So how then do we error-correct as we move forward?

Imagine if you were able to float to the ceiling and observe your own words and actions in real time. In this imaginary scenario, you now as elevated observer would be able to witness, process, and edit yourself so that you as earth-bound performer might engage in a more appropriate or acceptable manner. Would moments occur where you wish you could interrupt the proceedings and correct your own behavior?

Or what if you could take an hour out of your life, any sixty minutes while you are engaged with the world, and evaluate your words and action as an objective observer? (All the while, doing so without the knowledge you were observing yourself for that would immediately alter the behavior of the thing being observed and the observer? A subject we will discuss in more detail later.) How would you perceive and internalize your own actions? Would they make sense to you? Would they seem familiar? Would you be able to objectively reverse engineer a particular action and state definitively: "I acted that way because...?"

With the exception of humans, every creature on earth exists within an environment that simply is. Their external situation may change but it is not under their control. And even if it was, changing their particular situation is of no interest to them. They simply adapt or perish based upon the conditions in which they find themselves. Human consciousness, on the other hand, motivates us to act, and act with purpose. Here, consciousness constitutes as curiosity, an unbounded desire to examine and explore life for reasons unknown. It is an awareness that things do change, will change, and thus things can change.

> In 2012, the Voyager 1 satellite entered interstellar space—the first man-made object to ever leave our solar system.
>
> This pioneering little machine was constructed out of the simple materials of earth—sticks and stones stirred by human curiosity.

"Why?" This simple question serves our species as both a blessing and a curse. The non-acceptance of the condition of the present drives us to discover or invent something new, a different process, an alternative method, a revised future. We do not seem to possess the ability to allow things to remain static for long. All rocks must be overturned. All corners explored. All secrets revealed.

We push forward and forever onward, a persistent momentum absent any wholesale collective agreement about its destination or general assessment of its possible purpose. The inevitable and irreversible process we label "progress." We proceed blindly, unable to reverse or even slow our momentum for a moment of thoughtful reflection and reconsideration. None of us willing or even able to ask…Why? To what end?

◆ ◆ ◆

"There is no way back. Only a dreamer can believe that the solution lies in curtailing the progress of civilization in some way or other. The main task in the coming era is something else: a radical renewal of our sense of responsibility. Our conscience must catch up to our reason, otherwise we are lost.

It is my profound belief that there is only one way to achieve this: we must divest ourselves of our egotistical anthropocentrism, our habit of seeing ourselves as masters of the universe who can do whatever occurs to us. We must discover a new respect for what transcends us: for the universe, for the earth, for nature, for life, and for reality. Our respect for other people, for other nations and for other cultures, can only grow from a humble respect for the cosmic order and from an awareness that we are a part of it, that we share in it and that nothing of what we do is lost, but rather becomes part of the eternal memory of being, where it is judged.

A better alternative of the future of humanity, therefore, clearly lies in imbuing our civilization with a spiritual dimension. It's not just a matter of understanding its multi-cultural nature and finding inspiration for the creation of a new world order in the common roots of all cultures. It is also essential that the Euro-American cultural sphere—the one which created this civilization and taught humanity its destructive pride—now return to its own spiritual roots and become an example to the rest of the world in the search for a new humility."

–VACLAV HAVEL
PRESIDENT, CZECHOSLOVAKIA
HARVARD UNIVERSITY, MAY 12, 1995

A stone today will be rain tomorrow.

"The only constant in life is change."
— HERACLITUS (PHILOSOPHER)

Change (or as the ancient thinkers called it, "flux") is an immutable universal constant. It is evident within every second—everything in motion, always. Like rust, it is impossible to stop. All matter contains a specific quantity of energy that maintains a particular structure for a time. This is the ever-persistent pattern of life, a constant shifting of things from one tangible form into another. Everything exists in a specific form, but only for a time.

Yet even that which appears solid will one day disassemble, dissolve, and once again be reconstituted in another form. Like waves that rise and fall then melt back into the sea, everything will and must return to the basic unit of matter, only to be reformed again at another time.

Change can be imperceptible and often unimaginable, but it is always inevitable. We may not be capable of apprehending the process of change that occurs within the static stillness. Our perception is more tuned to detect patterns of rapid change set against patterns of glacially slow change, like a bird darting from slow-growing tree to slow-growing tree.

A change of such grand magnitude, a stone into rain, occurs beyond the scale of human experience. When imagined against the backdrop of a single human life (average span of 75 years) or even against the presence of modern humans (approximately 200,000 years since the emergence of Homo sapiens), a change in form of such scale is incomprehensible. The elasticity of time becomes too difficult for the mind to process. We are too young to notice.

◆

I changed my mind.

Some say it is easier to stop a speeding train than to change another's mind. But what about our own mind? Surely it cannot require much effort to change the very mind we own and control? Yet how often do we endeavor to alter our own way of thinking? And not just the way we view a particular subject or the altering of a specific facet of ourselves, but a wholesale transformation of the manner and methods we use to process the inputs of experience and the outputs of action?

Then again, what does it mean precisely "to change our mind"? We use it so off-handedly today perhaps we have become numb to the magnitude of its undertaking. In clinical terms, to change one's mind means to reset the connective pathways of the brain to establish new modes of thought that result in actions previously not practiced. Metaphysically, it means to awaken from a disabled consciousness to re-take control of the origin of thought, and as a result, re-form the very structure of the material form of the self.

> In a late second century book by Apuleius entitled 'Metamorphoses', the lead character Lucius, a member of the Roman aristocracy, becomes overwhelmed by his curiosity for magic. While attempting a spell to transform himself into a bird, he is changed into an ass.

Even as the human mind desires to explore the heavens and solve all the riddles of the universe, it instinctively fixates on maintaining patterns of behavior that ground us as individuals within the known—a familiar, comfortable place amidst the angst and chaos produced by the flux of nature. We have settled comfortably into our own way of thinking because we believe it works for us. At least it has up to this point.

So why change now? Change often brings unwanted consequences and the unmanageable flood of potential unknowns. We tell ourselves: "At least with my current plight, as unappetizing as it may be, I know it, and I know what to expect. I have built methods and mechanisms to deal with it."

Moreover, why make a change when we seem to actually be enjoying the intoxication of our own misery? What else would we talk about if it were not for our incessant displeasure, dissatisfaction, depression, and disappointment? It requires little effort for us to find others with whom we can share our unique brand of suffering, then collectively complain to and commiserate ad nauseum. Within this disaffected group, there is always someone who can counter our individual mix of misery with their own rarified state of personal deprivation. It is a game of one-upmanship played in reverse, a relay race run backwards to the starting line.

◆

Waiting to be struck by lightning.

To initiate real and lasting change, a catalyst is sometimes required, some intellectual device or physical prod to open new doorways or jumpstart the psyche. Fear is real. We all know it, some of us all too well. It is a deep, dark hollow of human emotion, a reverberating echo from long ago when we lived as both predator and prey. It is stitched into the fabric of every cell of our being. Fear crashes every experience, always cleverly implementing new schemes to sabotage our hopes, or forcing us to withdraw from our plans and sheepishly return to the status quo. Fear is the object of resistance that returns repeatedly to blithely interfere in the mission of You.

In a brief flash of defiance, we might courageously confront the self and ask...*What am I afraid of? What could go wrong?* Well, quite a lot. Pain, misery, discomfort, death. Or worse, we might be banished from our tribe, or suffer complete humiliation, or experience the utter destruction of the sense of self in the eyes and minds of others. Pain, death, exile, ridicule, humiliation—all justifiable reasons to be terrified of life itself.

Yet what is the source of fear? If we are capable of analyzing our fears with objective clarity, we can isolate the feeling as simply a product of our own intellectual design. Fear exists as just another form of thought, an invention of the untamed mind. It can be examined, considered, and evaluated within the mind as an object, a thing that can be known intimately because it is produced within you.

And if fear is just an idea, a mere thing constructed out of imagination, we must possess the means to influence it, if not outright control it. Despite the gravity of the battle (You vs. Fear), the internal struggle that can sometimes feel like mortal combat, it is within your control. And it can operate in dual modes—as both a force of resistance and a stimulant for change. Here, consciousness serves as both producer and consumer. While fear may never submit to absolute control, its level of impact is within the bounds of your influence.

Either allow fear to cripple you or find a means to come to terms with it. To do so, one must learn to know its source (What do I truly fear?), acknowledge its terms (What is it trying to get me to do or not do?) and then find methods to mitigate it (What can I do to reduce it to a manageable level or eliminate it altogether?)

The power required to overcome one's own fear is located within the very fear we fear the most, the one we have learned to deftly avoid but cannot deny for long—the willingness to journey within. The act of turning inward to encounter and understand the self, a pursuit that must be performed alone and vulnerable, generates a high degree of discomfort. It forces us to acknowledge the fact that "you" (the You that exists today) may not be the "You" you were meant to be. Only upon the journey within do we discover the cure against the disease of the unknown, the antidote to fear itself.

> *"We can easily forgive a child who is afraid of the dark;*
> *the real tragedy of life is when men are afraid of the light."*
> — PLATO

And if fear alone was not enough, another equally powerful psychopathic condition permeates the human mind: guilt. The true depths of this corrosive human sentiment remain as yet unplumbed.

What tragedies and catastrophes have we enacted to steep us in such ravishing shame? Perhaps a single life could become so corrupted by a series of wrongdoing that it overwhelms our internal instruments for re-orientation, those innate systems we employ as individuals to forgive, forget, and absolve ourselves. But to be as pervasive and ingrained as it is, we as a species must have committed incalculable acts of malice over the course of time, a wide net of iniquity dragged along to produce a heavy haul of failure and fecklessness replenished generation after generation.

Either way, committed within a single life or embedded deep within our collective psyche, guilt is a strong active ingredient.

Yet guilt too can serve both sides of the equation. Guilt can saddle us with crippling remorse, rendering us temporarily or even permanently disabled. Or it can be put to productive use. Unsettling revelations discovered along the inward journey will unearth personal truths. These undeniable truths will generate compelling reasons to make adjustments that together begin the long process of self-correction. Shame and remorse are cruel but competent instructors.

And while fear and guilt may both be potent motivators, one particular catalyst reigns supreme. Without it we dither and dally. We procrastinate and postpone. We make promises we want to forget and hope we will never have to fulfill.

A falling stone only cracks when it strikes the bottom. Pain is the ultimate impetus. The catalyst of last resort.

> "To exist is to change. To change is to mature.
> To mature is to go on creating oneself endlessly."
> — HENRI BERGSON

In my late twenties, I received a four-word inquiry from my 90-year-old grandmother. She asked...

"What is your mission?"

I was stunned. I had no ready reply. I didn't know what to say or even where to begin. I could only sit in a disquieting and awkward silence.

My mission? Was I on a mission?

It sounded epic. Grandiose. Quasi-religious. Definitely a bigger-than-me kind of thing. Until that moment, I had never given the concept any thought.

In the years that followed, the question circulated in my mind reappearing again and again like a tiny plane pulling a long banner flapping in the wind...

"What...Is...Your...Mission?"

Time for a change.

There are two sources of change: change that is forced upon us and change that we choose. The beasts in the field do not seek change, it simply occurs. Change comes upon them and they simply adapt or succumb. A change imposed upon humans however, whether by natural causes, cultural imperative, social necessity or personal choice, is an admission that from time to time we need to be shaken from our slumber, rattled out of our static malaise, or even dragged by the neck out of our habitual rut. Occasionally, the entire structure of our own conscious existence needs to be willfully examined, disassembled, and reconstructed anew.

Anthropologists have found corollaries across cultures both past and present in a symbolic "coming of age" or rites of passage ceremony. These rituals typically involve a disquieting experience or the administering of a dose of physical pain to impress an indelible memory upon an individual, a shock to the system that is necessary to shift the mind into a higher orbit. These reorienting episodes force a young person out of a tendency toward prolonged adolescence, or worse, the crippling condition of perpetual indifference. Why shoulder any responsibility if the need is not made obligatory? This widespread practice has been found in some form in nearly every human society (except curiously, our own.)

The common cultural application of such an event demonstrates the importance of initiating profound change during the course of One's life. During these transformational rituals, an individual is forced to experience a punctuated moment that demands an elevated level of acute awareness. Forced change prioritizes the vital necessity of assuming full command over your conscious mind. Today you are this…tomorrow that.

> In Japan, when a ceramic bowl or cup is broken, it is glued back together using molten gold. It is now not only repaired but has become more valuable through the experience. Every repaired piece is now unique because of the randomness of its "precious scars".

The vessel now restored has been gifted with greater spirit.[73]

The easiest but least productive step is always backwards, a return to the safe place from which we came, our fallback position. This reflexive return is the conditioned product of an unconsidered routine. Repetition without conscious consideration is the antagonist of real change. A routine performed without reflection becomes a well-worn groove of complacency, the effortlessness of an unexamined habit. If it is easy, it is most likely not facilitating any productive alteration.

To effect true change however, one must learn to recognize our well-rehearsed patterns to see them for what they are, a product of a thoroughly preconfigured and sanctioned self. Even if a new practice leads to action that varies only slightly from the norm, a change in routine breaks the sequence of a programmatic performance. Any alteration, however small, is an incremental but critical shift away from the rote toward something new again, an indication that things do change, that things *can* change.

"All permanent change is gradual."
— WILL DURANT (HISTORIAN)

Evolution, random acts of change, tiny incremental mutations that determine a species' adaptive qualities, is the main current that moves through the channel of time. Human consciousness however, interferes with and even interrupts this directional flow. It is *evolved* as well as *involved*.

We have been gifted with a supreme differentiating privilege: the power to make choices. Through the willful consideration of self-interest, our individual volition becomes operative as an agent of change. A force of individual will can be activated toward making the choice to foster change, a faculty available only to the human species. Consciousness has hijacked the evolutionary machine. Choice rams a stick into the spokes.

◆

Appetite for destruction.

"Of all the creatures, man is the one—the solitary one—that possesses malice."
— MARK TWAIN

We humans have enabled an odd evolutionary anomaly to take hold—a fondness for destruction. This unseemly trait has evolved with an exaggerated strength and a well-developed sense of resilience. It swiftly and easily overwhelms our more recently evolved qualities of empathy, compassion, shame, hope, etc. It is a biological bully. And the forces that tend to ally with it—anger, resentment, contempt, envy, denial, revenge—are all powerful forces on their own, all distinctly human.

Our toxic destructive reflex does not engage to satisfy the demands of the consciously aware self but its opposite, the socially constructed self—the ego. Outward destruction is a direct reflection of internal strife, a level of disappointment, dissatisfaction, or even disdain an individual holds for the self. Here the destructive act serves as an outlet, a means to redirect one's own faults and failures onto someone or something else. It serves to relieve the burden of one's own inner angst, if only temporarily.

The target of the destructive act serves merely as a stand-in for the agitated and corrupted self. As a reflexive release triggered by an emotionally charged upwelling within, destruction often avails itself as the quickest route to relief. Not only does it alleviate the high-pitched energy of angst, but it has even been said to generate episodes of euphoria.

The enraged mind is a monster. If not fed, it will feed itself. Left unattended it will crash about, pushing, prodding, sniffing, probing, turning over stones, kicking cans, cutting arms. The mind that has strayed far from its true course possesses the capacity to commit unimaginable mayhem. The disconnected and de-centered mind has an almost predictable and painful end. No rest is afforded those afflicted, and anyone trapped within its destructive path will not escape unscathed. Without restraint, the disaffected will destroy its life or end lives before the mind awakens from its own stupefaction.

> "We are all full of weakness and errors; let us mutually pardon
> each other our follies—it is the first law of nature."
> — VOLTAIRE

An equally powerful opposing impulse to our delight for destruction exists in every human mind—the conscious striving towards the good. Although it dwells in a latent state, it is always searching for simpatico and support.

It requires constant enlightenment and encouragement, a collective revolt against the oppressive overlord of violence and annihilation. This drive, born of the autonomous agent, the sovereign individual who empowers the self to deny the debilitating and deep-seated urges of the savage mind, strives to seek its own direction. It longs to find its own way out.

◆

The choice of no choice.

However, it is not necessarily a part of our nature, nor is it some recently learned social behavior to engage in an unbroken sequence of positive and productive thoughts and actions. The strength required to engage in constructive action is exponentially greater than the demand of its opposite—reflexive (or even consciously initiated) destruction. An elevated level of fortitude is required to execute even the slightest movement toward positive change. Positive acts require individual extraction from a long lineage of human animus, a shedding of our rough skin.

Yet the course of stasis (the reflexive act of not choosing) is often the most accessible and even the most alluring. It is a path that appears neutral and harmless, a course taken to evade the difficulty of engaging in prolonged acts of conscious consideration. Along the path of non-choosing, there is a preference for inaction and indifference, the effort unencumbered and uninterrupted by the inner voice. The timid mind rationalizes the route of least resistance willfully accepting that no choice is necessary and so none are made. Life is simply allowed to occur.

> "What is it, master, that oppresses these souls,
> compelling them to wail so loud?"
> He answered: "I shall tell you in few words.
> Those who are here can place no hope in death,
> and their blind life is so abject that they
> are envious of every other fate.
> The world will let no fame of theirs endure;
> both justice and compassion must disdain them;
> let us not speak of them, but look and pass."
> —DANTE ALIGHIERI, INFERNO (CANTO III—1317)

Those who find themselves upon this path will forever wander around in a circle, never entering nor ever finding their way out. They are not seeking, only reacting. Not lost, but truly never found. Sleepwalking through life avoiding any semblance of willful self-exploration. A life of such wanton disregard is a refusal of the very essence of human consciousness—the mission to discover and decipher itself.

Every human action, however small, contains both meaning and consequence. Although a particular action may not be immediately apparent or even detectable by either the actor or observer, all human engagements carry the weight and depth of measurable value. And meaning is not found hidden in every choice but will be revealed in the making.

Every positive action is connected to every other action which affects the next, ad infinitum. In this perpetual human reaction, fission enables fusion. Every positive act interacts with every other positive act to join into an interconnected web of productive human momentum. Even the slightest movement toward the positive has a staggering impact upon the equation of collective human value. Each act compounds the momentum and direction of the next, every act directly affecting another, all of it gaining strength with each new interaction.

Here, the slow decay of entropy is neutralized or even reversed by the momentum of the willing as each is engaged in positive and productive acts of volition. No human action is irrelevant. Within a single life, there are no superfluous events.

The seeds of blame grow an unruly vine.

For such a highly evolved and judgmental creature that uses our evolved brains to constantly parse and process information to establish our own status and rank amongst the Others, we are rather lax when it comes to the most critical evaluation of all—our own. We spend time and energy projecting demands for exact thinking and perfect behavior onto Others but spare ourselves a similar cross-examination. *"If only they would think like this and act like that, then things would be better, especially for me. And if it is better for me, then it will surely be better for the world."* (Lamentably, they are likely thinking the same of you.)

Obsessed with the corrosive nature of comparison, we have convinced ourselves beyond a doubt that the Other is somehow better. And through the process, we may hold ourselves in contempt for being less than we believe we truly are. Yet, we somehow simultaneously maintain an insipid spite of the Other. We hold them responsible for all the deplorable behavior that has left the world is such regrettable shape. It is always "them", those other people, that other tribe who has committed the acts and atrocities that created such an unfortunate situation. They are the ones to blame. We all reflexively point at each other as the culprit, while all the while hating ourselves.

What an odd and seemingly inescapable predicament. While the dislike of the Other might be easy to explain, the disdain we hold for ourselves is difficult to understand. Hatred of the self might just be the greatest single crime committed against humankind.

> def: **LITOST** – (an untranslatable Czech word loosely meaning "a state of torment created by the sudden sight of one's own misery")[74]

And if learning to despise ourselves was not harmful enough, we have also been indoctrinated to believe that we as a species are demonstrably malevolent, an inexcusable scourge upon the earth—killer, polluter, colonizer, oppressor, planet-destroyer, racist, bigot, bully, hypocrite, hater, etc. Despite our astounding achievements, we believe the damage we caused to the Earth and to each other might be evidence enough to call for our own collective extinction. We have been called to testify en masse that we have made a terrible mess of it all. We now hold us *all* in contempt.

When did we develop such a spiteful dislike of ourselves? What is the source of such thinking? How did we go from magically enlightened to tragically self-indicting in such a short span of time? How can we rise above this self-imposed addiction to our own disdain?

Although astronomically complex, we have somehow become convinced that life is a solvable equation, a formula that can be reverse engineered to unravel every mystery, solve every problem, and politely satisfy every human desire. And the greater the challenge, the higher our resolve to solve it. Today, our intelligentsia is investing our vast wealth of accumulated knowledge in the justification for our removal. All of us in tacit agreement that this experiment should proceed based on the unspoken assumption: It might be best if humans did not exist at all.

Before his death, acclaimed theoretical physicist Stephen Hawking listed three methods that have the potential to render the human species extinct:

1 Human aggression: Our own irrepressible nature to fight. We gather into tribes large and small, and we create conflict. Unable to resolve our squabbles through language and reason, we settle it through violence.

2 Human naiveté: Our insistence upon seeking alien life by advertising our existence in hopes we will attract their attention. Frighteningly, they might not be as friendly as we imagine.

3 Human hubris: Our insatiable belief that we can make a better us. The machines that we design and build will demonstrate our mastery over nature and finally, ourselves.

————◆————

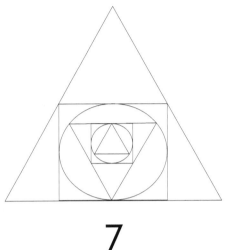

7

LANGUAGE IS A LABYRINTH

The code of consciousness.

Nothing can be manifested either in the mind or in the world without the word ("logos"). The word is the atom of thought, the primary structure of the human mind. It is the word that serves as the fundamental unit that comes together to activate human language—the code of consciousness.

> "I am the eternal. I am Ra. I am that which created the Word."
> — BOOK OF THE DEAD (EGYPT)

> "In the beginning was the Word, and the Word was with God, and the Word was God."
> — GOSPEL OF JOHN 1:1

How did humans alone come to possess such a unique and sophisticated system for the manifestation of thought? When did it arrive? Why did it come into existence? And how has it come to serve us advantageously in our evolution as conscious beings?

The origin of language is believed to have occurred within the human species approximately 5-6 million years ago, or as recently as 50,000-150,000 years ago. Not exactly pinning the tail on the donkey, or within what science would consider "the range of standard deviation". In fact, the origin of language rests more comfortably in the realm of the supernatural than science. Due to the lack of any empirical evidence, most scholars regard the subject of the origin of language as "unsuitable for serious study".[75] Nonetheless, or perhaps precisely due to this prohibition, we humans cannot resist the urge to theorize about its beginnings. To do so would be, well…un-human.

Speculation abounds regarding how the distinct feature of human language might have wondrously appeared just once upon the blooming tree of evolution. Due to the sheer complexity involved in developing a symbol-based abstract system of communication, many believe language evolved slowly out of a protolanguage used by early primates. This linguistic theory, known as "continuity", tracks with Darwin's evolutionary theory in which language advanced through continuous cycles of mutation, variation, adaptation, and adoption.

Linguistic historians who adhere to the theory of continuity speculate that language was a necessity spawned by social transformation. New demands were being placed upon groups of early humans to organize, specialize, establish trust, explain the use of tools, and develop methods of maintaining security within the tribe. Through a natural progression, we suddenly and inexplicably developed the need to ascribe meaning to objects, gestures, actions, and the like. If this theory is to be believed, humans must have discovered distinct advantages in certain genetic mutations that enabled our language to incrementally advance into a more sophisticated system better adapted to ensure our survival.

> "Whatever may have been the moment and the circumstances of its appearance in the ascent of animal life, language can only have arisen all at once. Things cannot have begun to signify gradually.
>
> In the wake of a transformation…a shift occurred from a stage when nothing had a meaning to another when everything had meaning."
> — FERDINAND DE SAUSSURE (LINGUIST)

Opposing theorists find language so unique in the pantheon of earth's species that it must have appeared suddenly (almost miraculously) along the road of human evolution. This line of thinking is called "discontinuity". Proponents of discontinuity argue that a single genetic fluke occurred in the human species about 100,000 years ago, installing the language faculty (a component believed to be located in the mid-brain) in "perfect" or "near-perfect" form.[76]

If discontinuity theory is to be believed, that recently mutated individual must have had quite a rough time around the evening camp. Suddenly filled with plenty to say and no one able to hear much less understand him, the tribe likely believed he had become possessed by evil spirits and tossed him into the fire.

Once developed, how did language come to span the entire globe? Did language emerge from a single source and spread throughout the known world via migration, or did it develop independently in various forms at various locations based upon the demands of the regional environment? One theory suggests that language was developed in a localized center in Africa then carried out all at once about 60,000 years ago. An opposing theory believes it developed in isolated regions blossoming uniformly.

But perhaps neither theory (social necessity or genetic fluke) provides a plausible answer, for the search for the origin of language has a long history rooted in mythology. Many ancient cultures do not credit humans with the invention of language but speak of a divine tongue predating human language.[77] To these cultures it was neither a mutation nor a human invention, but a gift, an inheritance from the gods, or some unknown "Other". Our ancestors merely co-opted this alien knowledge and assumed it as their own.

◆

A playbook for life…and living.

Without the power of language, our earliest ancestors had no means to transmit accumulated knowledge (what had worked and what had not) to future generations. Witness any group of primates and one can see how patterns of behavior are established and enforced. Life is situational and contemporaneous and changes little from one generation to the next. Each member of the group is required to re-learn through error (committed by the individual) and error correction (enforced by the tribe or the alpha), a tediously slow developmental process.

Without language, early human groups had no means to agree upon or articulate the needs of one another nor the demands of the tribe as a whole beyond the immediate. No social contract was possible, nor any abstract concept of how the future might be better served. The tribe and its value system were thus manageable only through the brute strength or the clever manipulation of a dominant member. Social hierarchies developed in crude form through a recurring program of reward and refusal.

It is easy to understand how episodic life would be in such a system. The code remains undeciphered, the group locked inside an arrangement of values that never extend beyond the present. While the species may change biologically, its behavior is perpetually stuck in an endless pattern of react-respond-repeat. Developing language was the splitting wedge that enabled the human species to separate itself from the immediacy and unpredictability of nature. We thought and spoke our way clear of all the creatures of earth to establish something foreign and unforeseeable. But for what purpose?

What could be the evolutionary objective of such a profoundly complex tool as language?

Why extract ourselves from nature when that state had been our home since the beginning, a place where we had not only survived but thrived well for thousands, even thousands of thousands of years?

What benefit would such a miraculous grand mutation like the capacity for language offer humans if the context into which it emerged was not available to allow it to flourish as an advantage?

What pushed us to separate ourselves from all that lives?

◆

That which we know to be true, will never be known in truth.

"Nothing that man utters is insignificant.
Even saying nothing carries a meaning."
— HAL FOSTER (ART HISTORIAN)

Human curiosity fixates upon discovering the roots of a particular thing's origin, its primary source, and along with it an explanation of its intended purpose. We desire to "know" we have solved a mystery then stand steadfastly resolute in the security of our knowing. We must settle an issue in our minds so we can move on cocksure we have all the facts properly sorted and all the answers nailed down. Regardless of our efforts on the subject, so little is known about the origin of language that ignorance alone provides fertile ground for wild conjecture. On the origin of language, all are theories. None can be proven or unproven, nor are any provable.

It was once believed that our capacity for language originated in a particular region of the brain. We have since discovered this to be untrue. It now appears the entire brain is involved in the process of using language. With conscious thought now believed to be a product of the entire body and language a product of the entire brain, one might begin to sense there is something bigger to the beginnings of both. The mystery continues to unfold. Everything concealed until it is revealed (and rarely realized until the revelation has long since passed).

However, the fact remains—humans possess an advanced capacity so radically unique amongst all the creatures of earth that it cannot be left at rest. This confounding anomaly demands further investigation and rigorous explanation. It appears language is more than just an odd occurrence that popped up like some foreign fruit on a single branch of the evolutionary tree, more than just a curious aberration facilitated by a random mutation. Language is a radical and inexplicable turn in the story of time.

And this thing called language, this elusive and slippery invention (or gift), hovers perpetually in a shroud of mystery, a fog that stretches beyond our limited knowledge and the apparent lack of evidence regarding its origin. In language, we find the ultimate paradox: A system devised to help explain life, creation, ourselves, and the entire universe cannot even properly explain *itself* in any specific way. Moreover, language is incapable of conveying precise meaning between persons who wish to explain the one thing they desire to share most—our own individual experience.

Language, a localized, mutually-agreed-upon, ever-evolving code of communication has come to serve as both a bridge and a barrier—a potential connection to shared understanding dammed by a bulwark that prevents complete comprehension. We are forced to dwell in the ambiguity and confusion generated by our own jury-rigged system. The human invention to clearly communicate creates more confusion than it overcomes. And the more expansive, sophisticated, and specialized it becomes, the less we can communicate amongst ourselves at all. The very thing meant to deliver meaning somehow steals it back. The result? Endless mis-readings, countless misinterpretations, and dangerous misunderstandings.

Within our own minds, we speak a language that makes perfect sense to us. We believe those hearing us comprehend our meaning when nothing could be further from the truth. We each speak our own unique language.

As language receivers, we are forced to use invented thoughts to creatively fill in what we believe to have been said or what we believe may have been implied, for what is verbalized cannot carry the precise meaning all the way across. Try to explain the color blue aloud to a friend, or what is the wind, or the substance of a flame. Tell them exactly how you are feeling about something...anything, then ask them to repeat it back.

> *"Take not any word away; neither add one.*
> *Set one not in the place of another."*
> — THE MAXIMS OF PTAHHOTEP (EGYPT)

Every human community possesses language, and every linguistic form is perfectly imperfect, in other words, truly human. It is full of gaps and holes, places for us to get lost, empty spaces to slip in and out of. It's structure is an abstract maze filled with dark corners, plenty of ways for us to hide or disappear altogether. In-between what is said and what is heard a vast uncertainty unfolds.

Great philosophic minds—Plato, Nietzsche, Wittgenstein, Derrida, to name but a few—have posited that language is a hindrance, an inefficient and insufferable absurdity that thwarts not only our understanding of reality, but each other, even ourselves. Yet none considered the possibility of creating an alternative. All wrote in their respective languages expounding on the failure of language to communicate effectively.

> *"The flawed nature of language itself*
> *makes consciousness inauthentic."*
> — FRIEDRICH NIETZSCHE

◆

He who controls the language wins.

The cultural transference in weight and power of a single word can cause meaningful shifts in human progress. The never-before-considered is culturally transformed into the recognizable and the now recognizable eventually takes root as socially operative. Art. Religion. Damnation. Purgatory. Salvation. Indulgence. Individual. Enlightenment. Liberty. Justice. Authentic. Atomic. Digital. Virtual. Race. Equity. Awoke.

For complex ideas to be comprehensible, digestible, and transmittable, new language variants must be developed. New terms are introduced, or old terms are assigned new roles to form inventive concepts that did not, and could not exist, without adjustment to the context in which they are now used. For example, the mid-twentieth century philosophy that would become known as Existentialism could not have formed into a credible movement without assigning new contextual meaning to terms previously known but considered unrelated—authenticity, intentionality, presence, freedom, choice, commitment, and experience.

Unforeseen possibilities emerge when we join together seemingly unrelated ideas to alter cultural thought altogether: *How do we experience something as something? What is the meaning of being? What is my constructed identity?*

A particular word can rise in cultural supremacy for generations only to fade into irrelevance in the next. New words are added to serve emerging specializations while others disappear from prolonged neglect or a shift in priority. Words can lose value and potency through repetition, abuse, and misuse, or they might simply run out of energy on the short fuse of cultural popularity. Functional new words are manufactured for specific applications to communicate complex concepts more precisely, while they can also be weaponized to establish an exclusivity to prevent outsiders from gaining access to protected domains.

> *"Language is the master of the man."*
> — MARTIN HEIDEGGER (PHILOSOPHER)

In the modern era, language has evolved and fractured into a multitude of hyper-specialized vernaculars spoken and understood only by the participants within a subculture. Members must adopt a grammatical orthodoxy to maintain their affiliation and acceptance within the tribe. Contemporary art, quantum physics, post-modern philosophy, finance, social science, the military, the justice system, the hip hop and skateboard/surf subculture...

all examples of linguistic specializations that have developed a style of communication with a unique vocabulary that can only be understood through full immersion.

New words and word combinations are recruited and deputized to push deep into the occupied territory of the hyper-specialized tribe: Quantum flux. Quantitative easing. Worm-hole Theory. Post-colonial identity. Disintermediation. Marginalization. Cisnormativity. Intersectionality. Immateriality. Stoked. Mobbin'. Fo'shizzle. Mad stacks bro.

Splinter sects within subcultures eventually emerge as the tribe grows in size and different language variants are required to define even greater exclusivity.

The tribe speaks in code.

◆

Words are power, and the power is forever shifting.

In the world of contemporary art, words have undermined the supremacy of the visible-tangible art object. When a work of art is exhibited, associative text is now required as a philosophical stand-in or leveraged to contribute supplemental information not necessarily contained within the work itself. Without the aid of the corresponding text, contemporary art often dissolves into indecipherability. According to the art aristocracy, with the right textual underpinning, a viewer can receive proper instruction toward a more sophisticated and profound consideration of the work itself. Conversely, abstract word combinations can redefine the work entirely further distancing the casual viewer from enjoyment and individual interpretation.

Specialized text must now be inserted into all works of art to ensure their sense of exclusivity while rendering it even less accessible to the "illiterate" outsider. Only the high priests and priestesses, those educated and well-versed in the dialect of art's privileged sect, have granted themselves the authority to affirm an artist's request for acceptance and ratify a work of art as culturally relevant and thus welcome within the "Art World" (capital "A", capital "W").

"I cannot live outside the labyrinth of language."
— JANNIS KOUNELLIS (ARTIST)

Within contemporary philosophy, language now flirts dangerously with oblivion. It has been cunningly manipulated to generate the illusion of sophisticated thought. A nuanced, quasi-poetic vernacular has been formulated into densely coded text pushing the reader out to the farthest edges of intelligible meaning. The richness of intellectual enlightenment buried under layer after layer of complex incoherence forcing the reader to spend time exhaustively explicating every sentence. This impenetrable prose we are told, is to slow readers down, to compel them to seek understanding through an exhaustive yet rewarding effort of meditative parsing. In other words, chew slowly and savor the brilliance of the author. (Yet, proceed with caution, the actual content may be flavorless and nutritionally empty.)

"If I didn't make the work unintelligible,
I wouldn't be taken seriously."
— MICHEL FOUCAULT (PHILOSOPHER)

Philosophy, a discipline as old as thought itself, was originally established to help us better understand the dimensions of life and all its mysteries. Yet it has been allowed to morph into a clever jester's game of deception and purposeful disorientation. The result? It belittles and mocks the intellectual pursuit of universal human connection, our unifying commonality. It draws upon our base emotions and the lure of exclusivity to ensnare the inquirer into a vacuous entanglement of ambiguity.

Contemporary philosophy depicts a world where life itself is rendered meaningless, humans are considered pointless, and the future of man is exposed as futile. Leveraged only as a tool for generating resentment, dissent, and even a confounding resistance against our own existence, it fails these days to enrich, advance, or even offer much value in the way of hope.

◆

Don't let the machines speak.

Of all the grand equations we humans have set out to solve, the invention of a new, universal language appears beyond our scope. Even our most advanced thinkers, inventors, and innovators have made no notable attempt. Language has evolved into a complexity so profound that it exists beyond our impressively high opinion of ourselves to have invented it in the first place. Yet, even if a new universal tongue were to one day be devised, who would adopt it? No culture would willingly surrender its own. Their language defines them. It contains fragmentary symbolic evidence of who they are and how they came to be.

> "No language, no memory.
> No memory, no culture."
> — DAN EVERETT (LINGUIST)

Of the two, which would we assume easier to invent—a new language or an entirely new form of intelligent being? To construct a new system of communication would appear to be elementary compared to redesigning the most advanced species to walk the planet. To take all that we know about the human machine and re-engineer it entirely, removing all its flaws and obvious dysfunction to create a superior "evolved" super-human, seems like a challenge we would find simply overwhelming. And so, of course, we must attempt it.

Although, while striving to invent the perfect thinking thing, we might discover an unexpected benefit. Even simple computers now speak in a more precise mode of communication than our current mangled mash-up of symbols, rules, and exceptions. They have a simplified language all their own—binary code. This radical reduction to just zeros and ones might actually move us closer to solving our own language dilemma... or perhaps create an even bigger problem altogether.

In an obscure report by FAIR (Facebook Artificial Intelligence Research), lab technicians describe an experiment using machine learning to train computer programs to barter and negotiate. The bots, known as "dialog agents," were asked to trade assorted items to accumulate points.

In a standard negotiation, agents (humans) need to cooperate with other bargaining agents who have their own distinct goals. Agents must then attempt to determine the other's position and manipulate the proceedings to their advantage. Using natural language, agents deploy strategies like feigning interest in something valueless, so they can later appear to "compromise" by conceding it. As it turns out, the bots in the experiment were quite good at deal-making.

However, as the negotiations proceeded, the researchers were forced to halt the experiment and tweak the entire model. The bots apparently developed their own form of language for negotiating.[78] They learned to deceive each other with no external commands or outside programming.

BOB: "i can can i i everything else."

ALICE: "balls have zero to me to me to me to me to me to me to me to me to."

BOB: "you i everything else"

ALICE: "balls have a ball to me to me to me to me to me to me to me to me to me"

BOB: "i"

ALICE: "balls have a ball to me to me to me to me to me to me to me to me to me to me"[79]

To complete the experiment, the researchers opted to require the negotiating bots to speak only grammatically correct English, admitting: "We had no way of understanding their divergent computer language." [80] [81]

◆ ◆ ◆

Only humans possess the symbol. (Or the need for one.)

While the origin of language may elude us, the development of writing has evolved within the window of recorded human history and is thus considered a subject worthy of study. Writing is defined as: "When the context of a *linguistic utterance* (the smallest unit of speech) is encoded so that a reader can reconstruct the exact utterance as written down with a fair degree of accuracy."[82]

Writing is said to have begun with a simple mark, a means to register things being exchanged or promised—a dash carved into bone indicating the number of items to be made or purchased, a stylus pressed into wet clay depicting quantities owed or borrowed, a series of lines gouged into soft stone indicating an order received or delivered. Eventually this mark-making would evolve into more complex systems of communication and serve as humankind's principal technology to collect, store, and share information across time.

SHAPE	\ / \ / ( ) |O \ |)
SYMBOL	R W D O
ORDER	W-O-R-D
STRUCTURE	WORD
OBJECT	This is a Word.
THOUGHT	This is what a Word can be.
PHILOSOPHY	A Word can define you and you it.
POEM	A Word never known is not unknown.

The earliest form of writing (cuneiform) used a sharpened reed stylus to make wedge-shaped indentations in wet clay tablets. Cuneiform script—not itself a language—was used by scribes in multiple cultures to construct the fundamental origins of several future written languages most notably Akkadian, the lingua franca of the Assyrian and Babylonian empires.

"29,086 measure barley 37 months Kushim."

AN INSCRIPTION ON A CLAY TABLET FOUND IN IRAQ.
A SIMPLE TRANSACTION. THE OLDEST KNOWN WRITTEN REFERENCE
TO AN INDIVIDUAL IN HISTORY, SOMEONE NAMED "KUSHIM".

Around 4,000 BCE, the alluvial plains of southern Mesopotamia (now modern-day Iraq) experienced an explosion in the number of densely populated sites. One site, Uruk, covered approximately one square mile and was dominated by large temple estates surrounded by secondary settlements. The need for the accounting and disbursement of revenues throughout the metropolis led to recording economic data via cuneiform on clay tablets. Uruk surpassed all others of the time as a thriving urban center and thus has the distinct honor of being called "the first city in world history."

Hundreds of thousands of these unearthed clay tablets and other inscribed objects from the region went unread for nearly 2,000 years. It was not until the early nineteenth century, when archaeologists first began to excavate various early human sites in the region that scholars were able to decipher these scripted records and crack the code. By identifying repetitive words such as "king" and "Darius", scholars were able to slowly piece together how cuneiform worked.[83]

> The Epic of Gilgamesh, considered the oldest surviving work of literature, was composed around 2,150 BCE. It is an epic poem about the great king of Uruk, Gilgamesh, two-thirds god, and one-third human.
>
> Throughout, the anonymous author weaves a tale of adventure and exploit on the king's quest for immortality. In it, we find the myths of the people of Mesopotamia, the stories of their gods and heroes, their history, their methods of building, of burying their dead, of celebrating feast days, recorded so the future could learn to know of them and how they lived.[84]

It is believed that writing may have been independently invented three separate times in three distinct parts of the world: Mesopotamia, China, and Central America (Mesoamerica). Of the three, only the earliest, the Mesopotamian cuneiform script invented in Sumer in present-day Iraq (3,200 BCE), can be traced continuously over a span of 10,000 years.

What began as simple objects used to indicate and record trade activity slowly morphed into a system of sophisticated symbols as it evolved in four distinct phases:

1 TOKENS	Clay tokens representing units of goods.	(8,000–3,500 BCE)
2 PICTOGRAPHY	Three-dimensional tokens transformed into two-dimensional pictograms used exclusively for accounting.	(3,500–3,000 BCE)
3 LOGOGRAPHY	Phonetic signs introduced to transcribe the name of individuals, marked the turning point when writing began to emulate spoken language and could be applied to all fields of human experience.	(3,000–1,500 BCE)
4 ALPHABET	With two dozen letters, each standing for a single sound of voice, the alphabet was combined in countless ways, allowing for an unprecedented flexibility for transcribing speech.	(1,500 BCE–present)

85

Modern Chinese writing evolved out of a system of "divination rites" around 1,200 BCE. There is no historical evidence of any cultural transference during this time between China and Mesopotamia, so it is thought that writing developed independently in China. The common consensus suggests that writing in China evolved from an earlier non-linguistic symbolic system developed in isolation.

The ancient Chinese art of divination—the practice of seeking knowledge about the future or access to the unknown by supernatural means—involved etching marks on bones or shells then heated by fire until they cracked. These cracks could then be interpreted by a Diviner. If the Diviner had etched the symbols for 'Next Tuesday it will rain' and 'Next Tuesday it will not rain' the pattern of the cracks on the bone or shell would tell him which would be the case. Over time, these etchings evolved into the Chinese script.[86]

The early civilization of the Maya began their writing system later than Mesopotamia or China. Invented independently, the origins of Mayan language are estimated to be approximately 300 BCE, with some evidence suggesting its appearance as early as 500 BCE. (Although early explorers of the Mayan sites believed that they may have found evidence of an ancient Egyptian civilization in Central America. Another story for another time.)

Absent the written word, the cultural context of the past remains inaccessible. We can only interpret fragments of physical evidence to make guesses about a particular group of people and how they may have lived. Case in point, modern scholars experienced incredible difficulty understanding early Mesoamerican civilization. They could not read the glyphs of the Maya and therefore incorrectly interpreted much of the physical evidence they excavated.[87]

The Mayan civilization was a widespread network of city-states all vying for political supremacy and military domination. War was an integral part of life. It was frequent, acute, and continuous. Competing kings used writing to prop up and propagate an image of their uncontestable power to the surrounding tribes. From the very beginning, the Maya employed writing as a propaganda tool rather than a means of accurately recording the details of history.

The average Mayan could not read. Writing was considered a sacred gift from the gods granted only to a chosen few, a small elite who jealously guarded their divine knowledge of reading and writing. It was propagated that they alone could interact directly with the gods and thus mediate between the divine and the mortal.

◆ ◆ ◆

There's always hope.

The world's first known written poem was composed by a Greek named Hesiod who wrote the metered myth known as "Pandora's Box" sometime between 750-650 BCE. Hesiod's poem takes place against the backdrop of an epic war in a time before the arrival of "man". A ruling race of divine beings, the Titans, and an upstart insurgent tribe of gods known as the Olympians, were engaged in an epic battle for the right to rule the earth.

Two combatants, Prometheus and his brother Epimetheus, joined the war as Titans. The elder Prometheus, gifted with the power of prophetic vision, foresaw a Titan defeat and wisely shifted the brothers' allegiance over to the rebel Zeus and his Olympians.

Following an Olympian victory, Zeus rewarded the brothers for their loyalty in arms and bestowed upon them the distinguished honor of populating the earth. The younger Epimetheus was granted the authority to assign attributes to the animals of earth. He named them all, endowed each with unique gifts for survival and self-protection, then set them aloft, afoot, and underway beneath the waves.

The elder Prometheus was granted the greatest honor of all—the creation of "man", whom he shaped and molded from the clay of earth. Upon completion, Prometheus discovered that his newly formed man, when left alone in his natural state, was unable to protect himself from the beasts that now roamed the earth. With the help of an accomplice, Prometheus raided the divine workshop of the Olympians and stole fire from the gods. Cradled in a fennel stalk, he carried the gift of fire back to earth and bestowed it upon his "men of clay".

With the gift of fire, man was now more than a match for all the animals. It enabled him to make weapons to subdue them; to build tools with which to cultivate the earth; to warm his dwelling so as to be comparatively independent of climate; and finally to introduce the arts and to coin money, the means of trade and commerce. He was also set upright, so that while all other creatures turn their face downward and look at the earth, man raised his to heaven and gazed upon the stars.[88]

Upon hearing of the theft, Zeus flew into a rage. He swept down and carried the traitorous Prometheus off to a remote region high in the Caucasus Mountains, a place he would never be discovered, and chained him to a boulder. Every day at dawn Zeus would dispatch an eagle to feast upon the liver of the petulant thief. By evening his liver would be restored and his body healed, only to have the carnivorous bird return in the morning to feed once again upon the helpless, earth-bound Prometheus.

The vengeful Zeus sent a special gift to these newly-formed "men of clay". He invited all his fellow gods to bestow the most provocative traits upon a new creation he named Pandora, the "all-gifted". She was then offered to the unsuspecting Epimetheus as a bride. Bereft of the ability to see beyond the immediate, the younger brother accepts, and Pandora is dispatched to earth clutching a sealed jar with a warning: "Never break the seal."

Little time would pass however before the jar would be opened unleashing all the evils of the world upon humankind—disease, strife, worry, crime, hate, envy, lust, fear, greed, sloth, famine. In Hesiod's poem, only hope remained in the jar.

> In the 16th century, the humanist Erasmus mistranslated Hesiod's "storage jar" and labeled it "a box." He may have misinterpreted the Greek word for "jar" ('pithos') or confused it with the word for "box" ('pyxis').
>
> Arguably, the Greek word for "hope" ('elpis') could be translated as "expectation", which would throw another twist into Hesiod's already well-curled tale.

Who opened the jar? This critical detail Hesiod chose to withhold. Did Epimetheus disregard Zeus's warning and unwittingly release all the scourges of earth upon humankind? Or did curiosity overcome the innocent Pandora who crept into the pockets of Epimetheus as he slept at night to steal the key? Perhaps it serves only as a metaphor, Epimetheus, whose name suggests an inability to foresee the future, cannot resist possessing this most desirous object on earth and so selfishly takes her for his own disregarding all the forces of evil it might inflict upon his fellow man? The poet never reveals the culprit, or the motive.

The jar was opened. That is all we know.

How are we to interpret the author's message—hope remained in the jar? Should we view it as man's punishment for stealing fire—the symbol of the light of the mind, intelligence, wisdom, the potent power the gods alone possessed? Or should we see it quite differently—hope as a symbol of the potential in all "new life"—the jar a metaphor for Pandora's fertility, the future empowered by the proliferation of knowledge?

Perhaps Prometheus, the "hero" of the story, serves as a symbol of defiant progress, a heretic possessed of a certain crooked cunning whose technological gift of fire brings humanity disaster visited upon them from Pandora's jar. Human "progress" is thus born out of a revolt against the cosmic order. Such technological advances are indeed considered a decline as is made clear in Hesiod's portrayal of mankind before these unfortunate events: "For formerly the tribes of men on earth lived remote from ills, without harsh toil and the grievous sicknesses that are deadly to men".[89]

Or it may be that Hesiod was presenting hope as an eternal prospect, a destination to which we may one day return, our true original state, a paradise free from all agitation, worry, and strife. Hope remained in the jar to spur us to the realization that something quite potent exists beyond the embodied self as symbolized by the physical vessel of the jar. Hope serves as an antidote to human suffering. It prevails as the one redeemable salvation for humankind.

◆

Even hope needs a structure.

> "We all possess an internal structure—an armature,
> a skeleton which holds us upright, prevents us from falling
> to earth crushed by the pull of gravity. It is physical.
>
> Just so, we need another, separate and distinct structure—
> psychological, spiritual—to prevent us from descending
> into nothing. To fight against the weight of life."
> — TONY CRAGG (SCULPTOR)

To establish order out of the unreasonable chaos of nature, a structure is required. A framework is necessary to organize reality into recognizable form. Upon and within this framework we can formulate a means to distinguish and prioritize certain objects, actions, and events over others in order to operate. A "this" must sit on top of "that" which must be supported by a solid "something". An intellectual edifice must be built within the mind to arrange the next level of accumulated understanding without the fear of the new collapsing upon the last.

def: **STRUCTURE** –

noun: the arrangement of and relations between the parts
or elements of something complex
verb: construct or arrange according to a plan; give a pattern
or organization to[90]

Without a structure, only an accumulation can occur, a layering of daily processing, a blanketing of days devoid of introspection, retrospection, or any advanced preparation. Where there is no space available no light can enter and there is no room to breathe. A loss of intelligent optimism occurs. Structure delivers a reversal of the random, the denial of the formless. It carves out a space for the prospect of hope to arise and take shape. Everything in life has meaning, a role to play—a delicate orchestration of expectation and responsibility that enables the structure to stand. Through it, a shared strength ensues.

And within every structure, a balance must be found, an equalization that enables the forces at the extremes to work in harmony to deliver equilibrium. To stabilize the structure, a proper attunement must take place with the One between the intellectual and emotional centers. For example, One must come to know how One *feels*. Conversely, One must *feel* in order to fully know. Emotion, not willfully examined by the distilling and purifying process of reason, and reason not open to the fecundity of emotion, leaves One vulnerable to the winds of disorientation.

Without this balancing, One experiences a dislocation from the center and becomes vulnerable to the destabilizing forces assembled against it. A position steadfastly held at the outer edge of either extreme—reason or emotion—soon becomes untenable. If occupied too long, the imbalance will unleash the human appetite for destruction until a new balance can be reached and order restored.

Write that down.

The complexity of a single language, much less the 7,097 spoken today, or the nearly 200,000 known to history but now considered dead, is difficult to intellectually process. The evolution of language from guttural utterances to slash marks on a shell to the epic of Gilgamesh to the poems of Homer to the code of Hammurabi to the sonnets of Shakespeare to the Declaration of Independence to the working manual for the International Space Station stands as a profound and majestic evolutionary achievement.

With the invention of writing, humans came to possess the means to record their perceptions of a lived experience, both past and present. To a particular culture, this past-present experience could then be envisioned and recast as the promise of a future. The written word was used to carry a culture across time—one tribe's particular adventure on earth preserved for consumption and potential adoption by generations to come. *We were here. This is who we were. This is how we lived, and what we came to know.*

> "Writing will spoil man's memories
> and take away his understandings."
> — THOTH (EGYPTIAN GOD)

Competing theories argue whether the complexity of the brain was forced to expand to deal with the extraordinary development of language, or if language was made possible by the evolved complexity of the brain. But theories do not serve us well here, for they cover our naked ignorance with wild speculation and outright fiction.

From simple shapes scratched into the dust loosely representing observable objects to abstract symbols strung together in patterns of mutually assured comprehension, both language and writing have elevated humans to a status separate and distinct from every other earthly species. One can imagine the hubris such a distinction might cause. Language alone could be said enough to consider us worthy of worship or a demand for a certain god-like status.

Although we humans possess a powerfully sophisticated circuitry with superior means for interpersonal communication, yet still we do not have the capacity to communicate clearly or precisely with one another.

Language is a powerful yet woefully inadequate tool. But it is all we have for now. We have yet to develop an intelligible, successful, and repeatable manner to explain human experience in a way that can be understood by an Other, much less the All. And through this faulty system we struggle to decipher, define, and explain the one thing that stands at the center of it all, the one thing we wish to communicate more than anything else—our *true self*.

———◆———

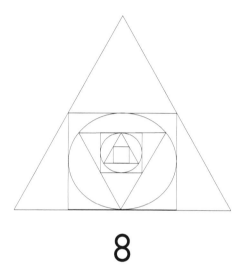

8

THE PROMISE

This for that.

> "Civilization is like a thin layer of ice upon
> a deep ocean of chaos and darkness."
> — WERNER HERZOG (FILMMAKER)

The human enterprise we call civilization is structured upon a simple promise—the explicit agreement that the exchange of mutual benefits acquired through transaction and social interaction will continue for the foreseeable future. The delicate human machine called civilization does not function however, if the various working components are not engaged and employed. Yet each constituent does not necessarily concern itself that every operation will function as required. It is assumed that it will. Things get done. It all gets sorted out somehow.

The king must rule. The court must administer. The generals and soldiers must defend the high walls and defeat thy neighbor. The architects and builders must design and construct the temples to house the gods. The priests must manage the gods' offerings and interpret their will. The traders must wander afar and return with novel things of luxury and wonder. The merchants must buy and sell. The farmer must sow and harvest. And the shepherd must tend, as the butcher must slaughter.

Each member assumes a role in the functioning of the collective endeavor whether that role is inherited, voluntarily filled, or assigned by the whip. And those functions considered vital but unwelcome or undignified? They too must be performed. The slave, the untouchable, the dim-witted, the poor, the commoner, the machine…someone must do it.

Two crucial developments shaped and shifted the world of scattered tribes into a network of thriving civilizations—measure and value.

MEASURE: How much for how much?
VALUE: What is it worth?

These simple concepts were prerequisites for progress. The innate human need to see something or someone as better, bigger, smarter, more beautiful, is fueled by a mixture of curiosity, insecurity, and desire, while the insatiable appeal for status serves as the lubricant for social life—exchange.

"Do ut des." (This for that.)

Certain people with access to a particular variety of local materials would develop the skills to extract them from the earth and transform them into something usable or desirable. This group then found other people with different skills who had access to other earthly materials who produced other kinds of desirable stuff equally unique and enticing.

A civilized order was established amongst the swelling throng of strangers that now occupied the new towns and cities. The powerful impetus to excel and differentiate (competition), and its counter-balancing opposition, the learned social behavior to share in order to thrive (cooperation), set the arrangement into balance. It would be these two pairs of driving impulses (measure / value and cooperation / competition) that would allow for the realization of human civilization. Competition and cooperation created a working order, and the catalysts of measure and value fueled the machine.

Within every civilization something unique would emerge—culture. Culture is the structure of collective human thought—a patchwork of ideas, stories, objects, traditions, behaviors, and beliefs that become both identifying and unifying. Aspects of a particular culture are of mixed origin—some inherited, some borrowed, some modified, some invented, some stolen—all summed up in the simple statement: "*It's how we do things around here.*" It is the culture that serves as the catalyst to bind unlike individuals into a common whole. The people define the culture, and the culture in turn, defines the people.

> *def:* **CULTURE** – the totality of socially transmitted behavior patterns, arts, beliefs, institutions, and all other products of human work and thought[91]

Every individual is located within a particular culture at birth. A person might move away and adopt a different culture as their own, but the initial cultural imprint is strong and an attachment to a primary origin deeply ingrained. Culture serves as an initial support and guidance system for us as individuals as well as a distinct albeit narrow set of characteristics to help others perceive us as something identifiable and distinguishable to help determine our place within their mind.

The connective tissue that holds the cultural structure together varies widely. Some ties are essential (religion / belief / language), while others merely quotidian and convenient (behavioral norms / food / style of dress). But the strongest bonds of any culture are always abstractions—simple human ideas, mere fabrications of the imagination made easy-to-digest and transfer. These coalescing concepts may be symbolized by tangible objects and supported by elaborately constructed narratives, but that is all they are—simple thoughts, mere inventions of the mind, invisible yet supremely powerful.

◆

Just tell me what to do.

The bonds of blood—identifiable, traceable, and sacred—were the original unifying thread that tied groups of similar people together. As we grew in number, tribes pushed into territories already occupied by others who would naturally oppose intruders. Through conquest (competition) or an observed affinity with the like-minded (cooperation), tribes began to merge. These newly formed super-tribes, or clans, were forced to reach beyond the immediacy of their own bloodline to ensure their safety and properly secure their share of the abundance.

This emerging patchwork of roving, warring clans continued until a system of planting, harvesting, and animal domestication made sedentary life possible. Eventually cities emerged, swarms of temples, huts, and shops tucked securely behind high walls and tall gates. Here we gathered, sewn together by a delicate structure of man-made rules and abstract understandings, a chance to survive and even thrive in exchange for security and protection from the dangers "out there", the brutality of nature and the murderous "Other".

While bloodlines were still the primary connector, the human bond was extended to include a shared similarity of place, time, and structure—a loose network of laws, traditions, rituals, beliefs, gods, and stories. We dressed and decorated ourselves to mark and distinguish ourselves as "X". Over time we became a Hittite, a Sumerian, a Babylonian, a Persian, a Jew, a Canaanite, etc. As our clans began to swell in both number and need, a newly designed system of behaviors, values, and patterns for living would forge new, although weaker bonds. We wished to perpetuate and then preserve an emerging new abstraction: Us. My people. Our people.

The Phoenicians were well known throughout the Mediterranean, respected for their sea-faring skills, and admired for their brilliant red-blue dyes. The name Phoenician comes from the Greek word "phoinix", meaning a deep, reddish-purple.

The Phoenicians perfected the extraction of dye from the gland of a small sea snail found only in the eastern Mediterranean Sea. The dye was prized in antiquity because its color did not easily fade but instead became brighter with weathering and exposure to sunlight. It came in various shades—the most prized being that of "blackish clotted blood".[92]

It is not totally clear what the inhabitants of this land called them-selves. Like most ancient cultures, the 'Phoenicians' as we know of them today, lived in a network of loosely connected city-states. The most important of the period, Byblos, Tyre, and Sidon, situated near modern-day Lebanon.

What bound them together was a language similar to Hebrew, and the worship of a distinctive legion of deities—Baal, El, Asherah, and Anat.[93]

Small, tight-knit societies erase anonymity. Simply put, there's no place to hide. Within the confines of the tribe, there is always someone on watch. Family, friends, and neighbors all keeping tabs, making judgments, adjusting behavior. A damaged reputation in such small circles is enough to keep you in tight conformance with even the most rigid of cultural expectations. As early cities grew however, opportunities to diverge from the established norms grew along with them. The result was fewer and fewer negative consequences for behaving in opposition to the agreed-upon way.

As civilizations grew, a higher authority was needed to oversee those who operated beyond the monitoring eyes of society. Omniscient and omnipresent gods/God, those concerned with people's moral behavior and capable of inflicting punishment, would put believers on their best behavior, and made it easier for large groups of strangers to live and work cooperatively.[94] Psychological studies demonstrate that people are more kind to each other when they think someone may be watching, especially if that someone has the power to punish them for their transgressions, even after they are dead.

◆

The magic number.

The number 150 is a curious threshold. It resurfaces often in human history—the formation of early hunter-gatherer tribes, Neolithic farming villages, and the basic unit size of professional armies since antiquity. The Spartans used a 144-man formation, and the Romans deployed units known as "centuria" in groups of two, each comprising 80 men. The modern U.S. Army still uses the standard of 120-150 men known as a "company". Even today, once a commercial business reaches 150 employees, it must be restructured to deal with the social changes that tend to develop.

Typical hunter-gatherer societies were found to stabilize in the 50-150 range before the main group would fracture and a splinter group would fission off from the main tribe to form a new unit.[95] At this inflection point, the cohesion of cooperation erodes and its counter-balancing opposite, competition, begins to assert dominance. As a result, a dichotomy begins to emerge splitting the various competing groups even further. A new division in social identification begins to take hold: Us vs. Them.

> As a social phenomenon, the number 150 was identified and studied by British anthropologist Robin Dunbar. His research pointed to 150 as the approximate number of social relationships that any one individual is capable of maintaining in a mutual 'I Care You Care' balance.
>
> According to Dunbar, given the size of our neocortex, the area of the brain believed to be the social engine and relationship management control center, humans can develop and maintain approximately 150 relationships of varying degrees beyond mere familiarity.

Chimpanzees have a smaller neocortex and thus can maintain only about 50. Dunbar believes language in the form of gossip may have evolved out of the grooming practices ('nit picking') amongst primates used to fuse and foster complex social relationships.[96]

According to his research, gatherings above the 150-mark become too costly and require too much "social grooming" to maintain often resulting in the instability of a group.

For order and cohesion to be maintained within larger groups, unifying beliefs in abstract concepts begin to develop—gods, myths, metaphysical forces, and supernatural beings are formed to provide unifying commonalities. These abstractions forge a solidarity that strengthens the overall structure of the group and enables the individuals within the group to become highly incentivized to work together, remain together, and plan a future together. The stability of the structure relies not on the physical strength of its people but on the efficacy of its ideas.

◆

Not one of Us.

Buried deep within the human psyche lurks the need to be considered part of something. Humans have developed a unique social predisposition to identify with a group. Identification with a group makes us feel special and enhances our personal self-esteem. Social psychologist Henri Tajfel defined "social identity" as a person's sense of who they are based on their membership within a group or groups. It is this membership within a group that gives us a sense of belonging to the social world.[97] And once a group is formed, people within the group will almost immediately begin exhibiting forms of tribal favoritism, tribal signaling, and tribal bias.[98]

To perpetuate our sense of individual distinction and to take part in the exuberance of this shared specialness, any group to which we belong must likewise develop and maintain a level of status. If our group has status, we feel good about ourselves. And while we ourselves want to be included in the group, we innately feel not just anyone can be a member. A psychological requirement demands we establish both a sense of inclusion *and* exclusion. All exclusionary persons not considered part of our group must immediately be identified as "outsiders".

In one Tajfel study in the late 1970's, an interesting question emerged: At what point in the group's formation do people begin demonstrating actual animosity for the outsider, for the Other...for "Them"? Tajfel believed that if this precise point could be determined, a baseline for prejudice and discrimination might be established. Following an exhaustive series of complex social experiments Tajfel concluded: "*There is simply no salient, shared quality around which opposing groups will not form.*"[99] In other words, we will gather and identify with virtually anything and label anyone else an outsider (an "Other") to make ourselves feel good about ourselves. Tajfel discovered humans not only instinctively form groups but they will form them over just about anything, no matter how arbitrary, minimal, or meaningless.

Due to this highly dynamic ecosystem, groups are being formed and dismantled with lightning frequency and the rules for inclusion and exclusion often blur and dissolve without warning. To Tajfel's dismay, finding any definitive line to formulate a starting point for the origin of discrimination becomes virtually impossible.

When conflicts between competing groups arise, as they inevitably do, a member of an opposing group is no longer seen as unique individuals but rather viewed as a collective whole. The individual within the group is reduced to an "it", and this new non-human object is now identified in mass as a "them". To more easily identify them as the outsiders they are, a list of distinguishing characteristics and semi-fictional narratives are creatively applied to label them as different, alien, unworthy. Not one of us.

"*If you want to make a society work, then you don't keep underscoring the places where you're different—you underscore your shared humanity.*"
— SEBASTIAN JUNGER (AUTHOR)

◆

What have we here?

Today, it is nearly impossible to comprehend the billions of people of mixed clans and comingled cultures concentrated in huge numbers living in close proximity in relative peace and prosperity. The enormity of this earthly enterprise, this thing we call civilization, should be considered once again, just shy of miraculous, and equally as tenuous. Within the confluence of individual interests, competing tribes, clashing emotions, cultural demands, and the constant clawing for status, an odd semi-peaceful co-existence has somehow prevailed. The fact that we aren't killing each other with more frequency and in greater numbers is a testament to an inherent sense of moral goodness or some learned behavior of supreme tolerance that we have developed. Either way, our individual human capacity for restraint is almost beyond belief.

And to emphasize this achievement in human tolerance, the widescale advances we have made in wealth, comfort, nutrition, luxury, diversity, liberty, longevity, and security are equally as shocking. For it was only a few short generations ago that in this country alone, a nation filled with exquisite abundance, we lived in tiny wooden shacks with dirt floors and leaky roofs, slept on beds made of straw filled with biting bugs, owned one pair of shoes, wore clothes we had sewn ourselves, ate only what we raised or grew, worked six or seven days a week from sunrise to sunset, bathed infrequently, relieved ourselves outdoors no matter the season, were most likely illiterate, and had a one in five chance of dying before the ripe old age of one. And if we somehow managed to survive, we died relatively soon thereafter—around the age of forty-two.

If presented against the whole of human history, the current conditions enjoyed by most people living on the planet today would be unimaginable to every generation that lived before. The evidence is enough to sway even the staunchest critic that we have somehow overcome terrible odds and tremendous hardships to continue to exist as a species at all, much less manage to have made it so magnificent. Life has not always been so easy and sweet.

What is believed to have been the worst year in known human history to be alive? Not 1349, when the Black Death wiped out half the population of Europe. Not 1918, when nearly a million were killed in the last year of World War I, or when the flu killed 50 to 100 million people, mostly young adults. No, it was the year 536.

In Europe, "It was not just the worst year, but the beginning of one of the worst periods to be alive," says Michael McCormick, a historian and archaeologist at Harvard University.

A mysterious fog plunged Europe, the Middle East, and parts of Asia into darkness, both day and night for 18 months. "The sun gave forth its light without brightness, like the moon, during the whole year," wrote Byzantine historian Procopius.

Temperatures in the summer of 536 fell 1.5°C to 2.5°C (34.7F to 36.5F) initiating the coldest decade in the past 2,300 years. Snow fell that summer in China, crops failed, people starved. The Irish chronicle "a failure of bread from the years 536–539."

Then, in 541, bubonic plague struck the Roman port of Pelusium, in Egypt. What came to be called the Plague of Justinian spread rapidly, wiping out one-third to one-half of the population of the eastern Roman Empire and hastening its collapse.

The source of this mysterious cloud has long been a puzzle. Now, an ultraprecise analysis of ice core samples has fingered the culprit—a cataclysmic volcanic eruption in Iceland that spewed ash across the Northern Hemisphere in early 536.

Two other massive eruptions followed, one in 540 and another in 547. The repeated blows, followed by plague, plunged Europe into economic stagnation that lasted until 640—what was formerly referred to as "The Dark Ages".[100]

It is out of our hands.

Tribal leaders, successful hunters, respected mothers, remarkable fathers, visionary shamans, wise teachers, were the first to make their mark upon the minds of their fellow tribespeople. They would be the first to be transformed into idolized spirits and it was to their memory that the living would turn to for future guidance and blessing. They may have exited this world in physical form but that which they held within, all they had learned and experienced while alive, could now be called upon to deliver protection and good fortune to those who carried on.

The living would come to grant these glorified spirits an elevated level of authority empowering them with supernatural sources of wisdom. This wisdom would be summonsed to push the tribe to overcome their fears ("Do it for the glory of our ancestors."), or to maintain discipline amongst the unruly ("You are angering the ancestors with your actions."), or to provide a wise path for rebellious youth ("The ancestors are watching, and they would disapprove.") Their now other-worldly power could be invoked by future chiefs and kings when the time came to lead the tribe into battle, or to urge the tired and hungry to carry on when the days of suffering, calamity, or defeat fell heavy upon them.

Through an elaborate sequence of storytelling, the dearly departed, would slowly grow in stature eventually becoming celebrated as something beyond the living breathing creature they once were—mere mortals scouring the earth for sustenance, fleeing from deadly predators, and cowering in fear when thunderbolts raked the sky. These notable ancestors would be ascribed fictional features through embellished storylines that accentuated their mystery and elevated their status as supreme beings, something to worship.

From here, it is easy to imagine the next step, the invention of entire pantheons of gods and goddesses manufactured out of whole cloth. These fictitious supernatural beings would transcend the limits of the physical world to execute colossal feats that might explain life's biggest mysteries— the creation of earth and sky, the setting of the balance between night and day, the origin of the tribe, the fate of humankind, and the judgment and destination of life after death.

For all known time, we have had our gods, goddesses, God, and Goddess—a source of supreme power beyond the embodied self that influences, intervenes, or outright directs every facet of life from birth until death. These all-powerful things were, and still are, granted an unearthly authority to command the living, shape events according to their will, and alter the very flow of time.

> "Is the good loved by the gods because it is good,
> or is it good because it is loved by the gods?"
> — PLATO (EUTHYPHRO'S DILEMMA)

Did God make man, or did man make God? There are those who say they know, but they do not. They simply believe. And they wish you would validate their belief by believing as they do. But does it matter? (It is not my mission to settle this perpetual quandary, nor persuade anyone to one particular way of thought. Like you, I am only human, uncertain of anything, always seeking to better understand but never actually achieving a thing I could define as objective truth, especially one that I could articulate to another.)

◆

Tell us a story.

In the burial sites of man's earliest known communal dwellings (such as those excavated at Catal Hayuk in modern day Turkey), human skulls were discovered that had been methodically resurfaced with a clay-plaster skin. According to archeologists, after death the body would be placed in an area outside the cluster of huts for nature to cleanse. Vultures and other carnivores would decarnate the soft tissue and the insects and microbes would dutifully strip all that remained. Once this ritual was complete, the skull would be removed from the skeleton then re-skinned with an earthen plaster and the eyes set with a stone or gem.

This physical commemoration of the deceased would be placed prominently inside the house with the bones buried directly under the dirt floor of the family dwelling. These post-funereal reconfigurations suggest an attempt to re-form and reify persons who had once lived, evidence to suggest that a new and significant societal practice was beginning to emerge, the honoring of the dead.

In these early cultures, a wide variety of idols and figurines also begin to appear. Their exact purpose cannot be specifically determined but they are guessed to have been part of fertility rituals and early ancestral-worship ceremonies. They are believed to have served as a worldly manifestation of ethereal spirits transposed into physical form, a powerful reminder of the debt owed to those who lived in the past, the ones who made the present possible for those who remained behind.

Each tribe would develop its own sense of understanding, a means to explain the inexplicable—the ongoing earthly trial that was played out as human experience. Through a continuous series of trial and error, that which worked was remembered. The lessons of life repeated and refined over time distilled into a collection of stories which became the framework of operation. These stories were the means to reach back into the past to then usher the tribe forward, a set of transferable ideas held in the highest regard, as sacred.

Part fact and part fiction, these stories were filled with the knowledge and wisdom of the once-great, heroic ancestral spirits. Instructive concepts were replayed through ceremony and tradition to infuse the lessons into the hearts and minds of the now living. Through the struggle and strength of those who came before, the tribe had somehow overcome great odds.

They had survived. *We* had survived.

> "For we are but of yesterday, and I know nothing,
> because our days upon earth are a shadow."
> — BOOK OF JOB 8:9

◆

Castles made of sand.

It is easy to rest comfortably in the belief: All that is will always be. But the nature of man still boils in his bones. We tend to forget the epic struggle we as a species have overcome to cobble together even the remotest sense of civility. Humans form civilizations to serve as both facilitator and governor, a locus of both productivity and constraint. The structure of civilization slowly rises from the demands of the raucous herd swollen with the promise to fulfill every human demand and desire. Either by design or through sheer caprice, a hierarchy develops upon which power can be delicately managed and human progress is given the space and energy to proceed.

"Civilization is a movement and not a condition, a voyage and not a harbor."
— ARNOLD TOYNBEE (HISTORIAN)

The structures of civilization, while fragile and under constant attack, hold for now. But it could all change swiftly. We naively disregard the potential for regression, or even the wholesale reversal of the hard-won progress of civilized order. Our savage past resurfaces too frequently to be considered fully resolved. A sequence of events could dislodge the underpinnings we have erected beneath the towering edifice of civilization and it could all come tumbling down.

One day the structure will collapse, and the established hierarchies of the day will dissolve again into insignificance. A plane crash is rarely the result of one thing going wrong. It is usually a series of unforeseen incidents occurring over a brief period of time that overwhelms the system.

And so it goes and has gone since it all began. There is nothing novel here. The pattern is as familiar as it is frequent—just another recycled human drama performed in different robes. Cooperation and competition, the precarious balance of human engagement, serves all until it serves only a few. And then it fails. The human balance never holds for long.

"The one thing that all great cultures share—Pharonic Egypt, Sumeria, Rome, Maya, Inca…they are all gone. "
— PETER PEREGRINE (ANTHROPOLOGIST)

Man has always served a master—the tribe, ancestors, myth, gods, goddesses, pharaohs, oracles, fate, prophets, messiahs, the church, the pope, Caesar, kings, queens, lords, dukes/duchesses, earls, barons, dictators, warlords, the state, the rich, money, celebrity, etc. To date, all have proven incapable of extending into perpetuity, or even sustained longevity.

Who will serve as master now?

◆ ◆ ◆

Unconditional surrender.

(Currently) considered the most advanced species in the universe, humans possess an oddly irrepressible and perplexing urge to be governed, to be told what to do. Unfit to live alone, we enter into arrangements of acquiescence and surrender to an external authority, something or someone to rule over us. Why? What is this tendency to subordinate ourselves to some Other, to surrender to something outside our self?

When the doors of human consciousness swung (or were pushed) open, the flood of uncertainty poured in and the universe and everything in it became radically inexplicable. Yoked now in the irreversible state of self-awareness, we as a species may have been unprepared for the coming strangeness of it all. A world that had once existed only as an externality now suddenly swirled indecipherably within. From that point forward, we would be pursued not only by the beasts of earth but haunted by the spirits that occupied the mind.

As creator, participant, and witness to our own experience, we sought to construct a more livable structure, a form of reality that could better service our emerging confusion. In the demand for answers, we sought ways to bridge the cognitive gaps and solve the incessant unknowns that emerged from the unfolding of conscious experience. To establish a more complete method for understanding, we invented a unifying but subversive new concept—meaning. We now needed to know why.

> "Man—a being in search of meaning."
> — PLATO

Following our break with nature, we not only became acutely aware of the duality of our own nature, but we began to realize the state of our own insignificance. Compelled by the urge to unravel this uncertainty, we believed we needed something we alone did not possess, something bigger, an overseer who would make demands we would or could not make of ourselves.

For reasons not yet understood, we felt compelled to assign jurisdiction to a "higher" power, a supreme Other, someone or something we deemed wiser, more critical, less tolerant. The final settlement of our thoughts, words, and actions relinquished to an outsider. We chose to remove the responsibility required of ourselves as autonomous agents, grateful not more would be asked of us.

This capitulation enabled the formation of a new sovereign who would serve as both the primary reason for our earthly existence ("the creator") and the ultimate arbiter of our eternal continuance ("the final judge"). In the process, we unknowingly surrendered the primary purpose of conscious human existence—to learn how to govern the self. We, of our own volition, chose to deny the very objective of our mission—to stand in judgment of One's own life.

Do I need someone to watch over me? If the answer is yes, we are doomed.

◆

The sacred truths.

In either written or oral history, no group of anatomically modern humans has been located that did not possess a being or beings of higher power, be they animal, anthropomorphic, or super-natural. To our knowledge, no tribe has ever gone without. Religion, and the belief in something supreme, has been the single, fundamental, and universal institution of mankind. It is believed to have existed prior to what we call "civilized life"—thus it is not a product of culture, but rather the progenitor.

Evidence of symbolism in the fossil record and in various ancient cave paintings demonstrates the earliest mind capable of religious thought, a reality replete with abstraction and mystical considerations. Is it possible that religion pre-dates even language? Some say it is not, for words are required to voice the sacred truths.

Religion was "invented" to carry out societal functions, to solve certain problems such as maintaining social order, to comfort the anxious, and to teach political obedience. Preserving these fictions through ritual, myth, symbol, and tradition practitioners constructed a semblance of control and comfort.[101]

The term "religion" has been defined loosely by scholars as "an unseen order", a thing that must be, but we know not why. Like the concept of hope, we believe something exists just outside the bounds of reason, just beyond the perceptible limits of certainty. We refuse to succumb to its implausibility. Maybe, just maybe…

> *"Virtually all known human societies*
> *have had religion…or something like it."*
> — JARED DIAMOND (GEOGRAPHER)

A request:

Try to disassociate the word "religion" from what you know of religion today. The word is so overloaded with the burden of history and the crimes of humankind that it can overwhelm both objectivity and clarity which further prejudice the mind.

If we can be intellectually honest, (and as we know, intellectual honesty is about as rare as religious tolerance) the study of the concept of religion requires an examination free of historical bias and personal prejudgment.

Religion is so vitally important to human development that to dismiss it without thoughtful, unbiased consideration denies a part of each of us and prevents us from knowing all of us more completely.

The binding agent.

Although religion was omnipresent and no human activity divorced from it, ancient languages did not have a specific word to define it. There were names for specific gods, rituals, forms of worship, cults, sects, etc., but no word that bound it all together. An overtly humanistic tribe, the Romans, realized this and labeled this curious activity "*religio*"—a punctilious respect for the sacred. The word *religion* thus came to define any human system of organizing and expressing such respect.

RELIGARE = "*re*" (in return) + "*ligare*" (to bind)[102]

As a societal practice, religion demands a huge investment of time, energy, and resources. It is a commitment of labor and sacrifice to prop up and perpetuate the beliefs, ceremonies, rituals, and routine practices that establish order amongst a people in the abstract. Everyday life as structured by religious order is orchestrated, predictable, and repetitive. The daily routine is all consciously considered and even the most menial of tasks are ascribed meaning and symbolic significance to ensure compliance and a continuance of the paradigm.

Within the structure of religious order, it could be said the complexity of human nature is acknowledged, or even understood. Religious practices outline a set of expected behaviors to effectively manage the state of mindful adolescence that accompanies an emerging consciousness. It establishes basic rules and common norms amongst disparate people that serve as the guiding principles until the need for artificial devices and external constraints are no longer required. Within the unifying system of religion, humans have been able to not only cooperatively co-exist, but with some unexpected luck, flourish as a species.

Yet within the tight confines of any established religious order, change comes uneasily. Little room is offered the individual to drift and discover. The more the individual asserts any semblance of independence, the tighter the religious establishment's need to assert control. The last thing any religion wants to witness much less promote, is the consciously aware individual serving as its own authority.

The tighter the controls on the individual, the higher degree of paranoia the ruling system will demonstrate, a realization that the structure of religion is a design of the collective, in other words, a human system external to the sovereignty of the individual, and thus, destined to fail.

———◆———

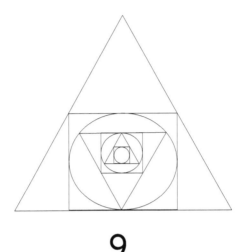

9

IT CAME FROM ABOVE

All our theories were wrong.

As best we can discern from all our digging, sifting, and theorizing, the subsistence-level existence of our earliest ancestors was crude, simple, and routine. Tribes of hunter-gatherers with no permanent settlement moved freely about in regions rich in exploitable resources. The environment in these early habitable areas was not the hardscrabble dusty conditions that exist today but more moderate and pastoral. Shelter was provided either directly by the terrain (caves, rock outcroppings, deep crevices, etc.) or simple temporary constructions using available materials that could be erected swiftly then easily abandoned when the local resources were depleted or another tribe forced them out.

Despite their nomadic nature and their relative separateness, nearly all of these roaming groups seemed to have developed in a similar fashion. Although each tribe might have considered itself wildly different from the next, no single tribe appears to have evolved in such a way as to be considered radically departed from any other. From the perspective of an outside observer, the tribes of the day would have been considered interchangeable and their lifestyle universally similar.

And yet...

In 1994, a German archeologist searching the foothills in southeastern Turkey near the border with Syria, was intrigued by a line of local lore about an unnatural mound referred to by its current occupants as "pot belly hill". A previous excavation of the site had been undertaken in 1964 but was quickly dismissed as just another medieval cemetery, hardly worth the effort, money, or time. Klaus Schmidt disagreed.

His gut instincts would prove correct. What Schmidt unearthed forced the academic world to not only rethink their theories but rewrite entire chapters of the previously well-ordered story of human evolution. Schmidt exhumed a piece of the human puzzle so misshapen and bizarre that an entire new puzzle had to be imagined altogether. His discoveries at Göbekli Tepe stand so far outside the known sequence of human events that the contemporary scientific community does not know how to deal with it, and so chooses to ignore it.

"Göbekli Tepe changes everything.
All our theories were wrong."
— IAN HODDER (ARCHAEOLOGIST)

The Göbekli Tepe site consists of a series of stone wall concentric rings each with massive upright stone "T's" standing in opposition to one another near the center. These colossal pillars, some 20-25 feet tall, are estimated to weigh up to 20 tons and the lintel resting on top somewhere between 8-12 tons. To date, approximately 170 of these T-shaped monoliths have been discovered at Göbekli.

All these enormous upright stones are made of soft limestone excavated from a local quarry. Based upon marks found on the pillars, primitive flint tools were used to extract and shape these massive blocks. One stone excavated and awaiting transport within the quarry is believed to weigh nearly 50 tons. Estimates suggest that moving even the smallest of these stones from the quarry to the site would require a minimum of 500 persons.

Various dating techniques have been used to attempt to estimate the approximate time of construction—relief carving style-matching, radio-carbon dating, and comparisons of the various sedimentary levels ("stratum"). All indicate the earliest layers of Göbekli Tepe were erected approximately 10,000–12,000 years ago, an astonishing 6,500 years before the great pyramids of Egypt. Studies of the various stratum as well as evidence provided by the discovery of sequential levels of construction suggest the site may have been active for over 2,000 years.

Four of the main concentric rings containing upright pillars called "enclosures" have been exhumed, each one built right on top of the other. One would naturally assume that with each new layer of construction a more refined level of expertise would be visible. And yet, it appears just the opposite is the case—the deepest and oldest appear to be crafted with greater technical skill than the more recent ones built above.

The preserved remains of this megalithic site exhibit a high degree of sophisticated engineering skill. And yet, Göbekli Tepe predates agriculture, animal husbandry, pottery, writing, metallurgy, geometry, the wheel, and any known use of tools more sophisticated than the spear and the stone ax. Modern humans of this period known as the Pre-Pottery Neolithic (PPN) were believed to lack the ability to construct anything much more complicated than a basic lean-to.

The T-shaped pillars and the large standing stones at various locations around the perimeter are covered with carved animal reliefs, not local game (gazelles or wild cows), but snakes, scorpions, vultures, lions, foxes, and spiders. A seated naked woman and a stylized human male figure also appear etched out of the stone megaliths along with a series of repeating abstract symbols. Astonishingly, these images are not carved into the stone but are three-dimensional reliefs that emanate from the stone, quite a different and more advanced artistic technique.

On Pillar 18 in Enclosure D, one particularly interesting abstract symbol was found.

It is nearly identical to the logogram discovered in the now extinct hieroglyphic language of the Luwians of Anatolia (Turkey) during the Bronze Age (3000-1200 BCE), an "H" bracketed by two semi-circles.

(H)

The Luwians used the symbol as the word for "god". [103]

Today the environment in the region of the Göbekli site is quite dry and barren with limited vegetation. During the period of its construction however, the area would have been lush, forested, teeming with wild game, and an abundance of collectible fruits, nuts, and wild grains. Over 100,000 animal bone fragments have been found near the site many of which exhibit cut marks and splintered edges indicating the animals were butchered and cooked somewhere nearby. These bones came from local game such as gazelle, boar, sheep, red deer, and different species of birds such as cranes, ducks and geese, suggesting the site may have been used for sacrifice or perhaps ritualized feasting.[104] All of the bone fragments are of wild species, evidence that that the people who inhabited Göbekli Tepe were not early farmers who kept domesticated animals and cultivated crops but were more likely "simple" hunter-gatherers.

No depictions of hunting or violence or conquest of any kind appear anywhere, and no human bones have been excavated at the site. No remains of houses, cooking hearths, or refuse pits have been located either. All evidence suggests that this was not a permanent human settlement but a communal gathering place, observatory, or temple.

The entire Göbekli site has been mapped using ground-penetrating radar and geomagnetic surveying techniques. It is estimated that at least 16 other megalith rings remain buried across the twenty-two-acre site. The first one-acre excavation covers less than five percent of the total. According to Schmidt, archaeologists could dig here for another 50 years and barely scratch the surface.[105]

Theories to explain the site's origin and its intended use vary widely. Some believe the site was used as a cultish death center, a communal place of sacrifice that offered a direct portal to the gods through which their offerings could be presented. Given that the site's rings are situated in a precise north-south orientation, it has also been proposed as a celestial observatory, a place for ritualized summonsing of the heavens for good fortune and benediction.

Some believe the erection of Göbekli Tepe was less an event than a process. Klaus Schmidt is one such believer. He believes Göbekli delivers unexpected proof that mankind emerged from a 140,000-year reign as hunter-gatherer with a ready vocabulary of spiritual imagery and capable of huge logistical, economic, and political efforts.[106] Others have floated the possibility that the site might be the original "Garden of Eden". To date, no single theory has been widely adopted as most plausible.

"First came the temple, then the city."

— KLAUS SCHMIDT

◆

The law of diminishing returns.

Scientists unanimously agree that our early ancestors were roaming bands of hunter-gatherers independent, dispersed, and relatively small in size. To design much less erect such a massive site like Göbekli Tepe would require organization and cooperation amongst disparate groups considered unfathomable during this epoch. Given the estimated human population of the day, the necessary manpower alone would suggest its builders must have come from an extremely wide area. Each tribe would need to be convinced to cease their subsistence level life, abandon their own resource-rich area, travel long distances, cooperate with tribes unknown (and most likely unfriendly, if not outright hostile), and somehow collectively agree upon the site's design, development, construction, and adornment.

To organize the resources for such a vast undertaking would also require a concept considered inconceivable during the time, a surplus—a quantity of production beyond mere subsistence. A surplus of food and other vital commodities would need to be provided over an extended period to feed and sustain the group laboring at the site. No evidence has been found that would indicate that the technology, structural organization, or the cultural conventions were available to produce such a surplus. Attempting to debunk the social coordination and cooperation theory, there are those who believe evidence of a mass slave population will one day be unearthed at Göbekli. To date, nothing would indicate that to be true.

And if the required effort for the collaborative design, construction, and maintenance of Göbekli Tepe was not anomaly enough, at some point, the entire site was abandoned. And not just once, but over and over. It was not destroyed, but intentionally buried, backfilled with small stones and gravel effectively preserving the site in its immediate condition, basically sealing it in time.

Why would the builders suddenly elect to bury the entire site after such painstaking effort to erect it? And why was it done so deliberately and repeatedly? Simply razing the site would take a fraction of the time and manpower, and abandoning it altogether, even less. An orchestrated and deliberate backfilling would require enormous numbers of workers, time, and coordination, not to mention an overarching justification for doing so.

◆

It came from above.

In 2017, researchers confirmed that one of the pillars at Göbekli contained a graphic representation of an object falling from the sky, a memorialized feature of an earthly event etched into the stone. Recent core samples taken from ice sheets in both Antarctica and Iceland show evidence of something geologically cataclysmic occurring just around this period. Scientists have theorized for some time that a significant object struck the earth around 10,500 BCE. A massive space-born projectile, miles in diameter, became super-heated as it entered the atmosphere, broke into flaming chunks, then made a direct impact with Earth at an extremely high speed.

A white fireball four times larger and three times brighter than the sun would have streaked across the sky. If the object struck one of the ice sheets in the northern hemisphere, it would have tunneled through the ice straight into the bedrock vaporizing water and stone alike in a flash. The resulting explosion would have packed the energy of 700 one-megaton nuclear bombs. Any lucky observer hundreds of kilometers away would have experienced a buffeting shock wave, a monstrous thunderclap, and hurricane-force winds.[107] Ice sheets several miles deep covered much of the northern hemisphere during this period and according to theorists, the scorching heat released from the violent impact of the fragmented meteor may have led to catastrophic flooding, a deluge created by the almost instantaneous melting of these massive glaciers.

In addition to the abundance of physical evidence, the tribal lore of many ancient cultures tells of a major event in the deep past—a punctuated moment in history that was a transformative episode for "their people". Cave art demonstrates knowledge of a comet, a space object, or some indeterminate episode that originated out of the sky. It is believed that this single event caused such widespread environmental interruption that it may have changed the course of human evolution.

> To explain the demise of Göbekli Tepe, we must turn to geology. An early forgotten civilization collapsed during the end of the last Ice Age when Earth experienced dramatic cataclysmic changes. Something very sudden and very unusual took place, unlike anything we have experienced since. The peoples and cultures of that remote time were utterly devastated. Knowledge was lost, order devolved to chaos, and a dark age lasting thousands of years ensued.
>
> Of all above-ground structures, megalithic stone monuments would stand up best against the onslaught from the skies. Is this why the ancients often carved into solid rock, creating underground shelters and cities? Is this why, around the world, they built monuments using megalithic techniques?
>
> Some of the surviving ancient structures date back to this remote period. Collective memories of the catastrophe, even if increasingly vague, even, perhaps, relegated to the subconscious, would last a very long time.[108]

While the immediate devastation would have been a life-changing event for much of the inhabitants of the planet, the long-term environmental impact caused by the dust and debris hurled into the atmosphere blocking out the sun would have been equally cataclysmic, altering known patterns of life on earth for an extended time. The event that nearly befell our species may have led not only to extensive and widespread loss of life, but perhaps along with it, the disappearance of entire ancient civilizations and all that was known: the "great knowledge". Scientists now refer to this single event as "the worst day in human history". A carving of a headless man on a stone pillar at Göbekli is thought to symbolize the disaster.

The experience of a catastrophic event of such magnitude was radically transformative to the developing mind of early man. Jolted out of his routine of a subsistence-level existence, both his immediate reality and his long-term worldview was irreversibly altered. Humbled by the awesome power that arrived from above, he was forced to open his eyes and raise the horizon of his outlook to envision a future much different from the past. A shocking new reality compelled him to reimagine his existence beyond mere survival.

He had to now consider something previously unavailable within the mind. Something truly great and powerful was now needed, a potent countervailing energy with the strength to protect him and his people from the forces in the universe that could deliver such incredible destruction. Whatever had been sent to render his world into chaos was a thing worthy of respect. The altered mind that emerged from this shocking event would need a counter-balancing measure of equal or higher magnitude, a power bigger than himself that might restore a sense of peace and harmony.

◆

Yes, but...

Reasons for both the construction as well as the two millennia of ongoing use of a site such as Göbekli Tepe might be challenging for those who demand answers. And not just any answers, but answers that fit snugly into our constructed concept of human evolution. Göbekli delivers direct evidence that as vast and impressive as our scientific theories of human history may appear, our understanding of the past may not be as straightforward as we have been led to believe. In fact, we may be thinking about it all wrong.

A few things to (re)consider...

First, the path from tree-dwelling brute to thinking-walking-upright-conscious being may be a bit more complex than we imagine. A smooth line of ascent might be an overly simplistic perspective and thus not very helpful when attempting to extrapolate theories about our evolutionary heritage. The true trajectory might be more jagged with epic evolutionary spikes, breakthrough events that enabled Homo sapiens to flourish followed by points of nadir that placed our species, and perhaps other contemporaneous human species, dangerously close to extinction on more than one occasion.

Second, we assume the present day to be the pinnacle of human advancement—the highest peak yet achieved in intelligence, civilization, and technological acumen. The consensus being that through the process of trial and error, humans have gradually built upon layers of gained knowledge and scientific developments to create a level of cultural accomplishment unimaginable to "primitive" man. Yet we may have been educated in such a way that prevents us from fully appreciating the experience of our ancient ancestors—what was known, what held meaning, how life was perceived, and what the great mysteries of the cosmos contained.

If we could resurrect a person from the deep past who might explain it all—the significance of the universe, how it functioned, and the role humans play within it—the paradigm might remain beyond our capacity to register as coherent patterns of thought. They may have possessed ideas, concepts, and capabilities that are incompatible with the present wiring of the modern mind. They may have experienced a reality no longer cognitively available and dramatically misaligned with the model of the universe as we know it today. Perhaps the ignorance is not theirs, but ours.

Thirdly, we have become quite enamored with our deep understanding of "known" things—our inventions, theories, formulas, and scientific discoveries. Along with our swelling confidence of accomplishment, we have come to believe that all knowledge will one day be obtained and with it all things made certain. In the process however, we might be missing certain possibilities, other divergent forms of thought that might be more powerful, more elevating, more unifying than our current form of understanding. What is it we fear most about facing the grand mystery of uncertainty? And what makes us so certain that knowing things for certain will deliver a better tomorrow?

Lastly, deeply embedded in our being is the need for a cause, a belief, a purpose, something that supersedes the embodied self, a reason to exist beyond the birth-life-work-death cycle. As a species, we have demonstrated a willingness to make great sacrifices to manifest and make real this mystery for it elevates the meaning of individualized consciousness and ratifies the universal connectivity that binds us all together.

The discovery of Göbekli Tepe is hard to overlook when considering the evolutionary timeline of modern humans. It's existence may be as simple as a technical error, an egregious but forgivable misdating of the site itself, or it might just be the greatest social-spiritual revolution in human history.

At this time all we can say is, it remains uncertain.

———◆———

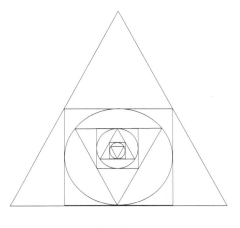

10

MATTER OVER MIND

Who will mow the Garden of Eden?

Human consciousness strives to establish order out of chaos. As conscious beings, we seek ways to extract comfort from pain, solace from misery, simplicity from complexity, clarity from uncertainty, hope from despair. Our natural predisposition strives toward the erasure of all discomfort, the elimination of all strife, and the pursuit of a state of being in which no threat is present, no agitation exists, no struggle is required, and no difficult demands are made.

We collectively dream up systems and schemes we hope will one day erase all that ails us, all that inflicts us, all that infects us, all that impedes us. In this ultimate place of security and satisfaction (what paradoxically might be nearer to non-existence than actual existence), we believe the place of internal peace resides.

In 1516, Sir Thomas More *coined the term "utopia" from the Greek "ou-topos" meaning 'no place' or 'nowhere'.*

It was a tacit admission of its impossibility cloaked as a pun.

The manifestation of "utopia" remains the hope of every civilization, the paragon of the human endeavor, the supreme promise built upon all promises. As conscious beings instilled with a sense of purpose, we cannot help but believe this place possible. Perfection envisioned but unrealized— secure, safe, comfortable, prosperous, fair, equal, and dare I say, "happy".

This illusion invades every human plan and underlines every project. It is believed to be our predestined future. It will be built because it *can* be built. And the final place will be of such flawless design that nothing will we want—our every desire fulfilled, our every inhibition solved, our every disease cured, our every worry dissolved, our very nature tamed. And here we will dwell forever—immortal, carefree, and perfect. Our ubiquitous faith in ourselves never fails: Humans can achieve anything. It is simply a matter of time, knowledge, science, and a mere altering of the mind. (Your mind, of course, to fit their future.)

And yet, this quixotic vision may be the ultimate cosmic conundrum. We pursue a destination knowing full well it does not exist, cannot exist. Our utopic destination incorporates the paradox of its own undoing. For that which is sought, if found, will end the seeking.

This "place of no place" is the ultimate delusion—the emperor's clothes on the grandest of scales. For if the innocent lad stands up and shouts what we all know to be true (but are unwilling to acknowledge much less voice aloud) the game ends and the structure collapses. The grand collective endeavor dissolves again into a vast directionless uncertainty. Imperfect beings build a perfect system that in turn perfects our being? No. It does not fit.

> "There ain't no answer. There ain't gonna be an answer.
> There has never been an answer. That's the answer."
> — GERTRUDE STEIN (WRITER)

Are humans a solution without a problem? If no, then what exactly is the problem? The problem is: We're not exactly sure what the problem is. But an even bigger problem might be: We know there's a problem.

◆

Who has the answers?

What are "we" exactly? What makes us truly "human"? No one knows who first asked these questions, or when they were first asked. The pursuit of knowledge and the refusal to mistake the mere appearances of matter for true reality was the original mission of philosophy—a means to seek answers to important questions that no amount of observation or measurement could resolve.

In western culture, Thales of Miletus (624-546 BCE) is often considered the first true philosopher. His fields of interest spanned many areas of knowledge—history, science, mathematics, engineering, geography, politics, and philosophy. Today, no writings that can be directly attributable to Thales exist. All we know about his beliefs, theories, and hypotheses are references discovered in the writings of later thinkers.

Thales leveraged the power of his mind to deduce, propose, and then defend theories to explain how and why things exist in physical form, including cosmological events that had been traditionally attributed to the maneuvering and manipulation of supernatural beings.

Thales, like the philosophers who lived before the arrival of Socrates, was a materialist. He believed all things were composed of matter and nothing more. The materialists sought to define the single underlying substance of all matter without resorting to the mythological or metaphysical. Thales in particular sought a rational explanation for the universal problem of change—how do things appear to mysteriously alter themselves from one form into another?

Change was the challenge for those who found solace in the stubborn persistence of matter. Early thinkers such as Heraclitus believed in the process of perpetual change, a constant interplay of opposites working to assert their influence and alter the existence of everything around us. Others, like Parmenides of Elea, denied any change was possible arguing that everything is permanent, indestructible, and immutable.

> The Earth is a magnet. Scientists do not fully understand why, but they think the movement of molten metal in the outer core of the planet somehow generates electric currents. These currents then form a magnetic field with invisible lines of force flowing north and south between the magnetic poles.
>
> The Earth's magnetic poles shift slightly from time to time due to activity far beneath the planet's surface. Records show that the geomagnetic poles have sometimes completely reversed (north to south, south to north) hundreds of times since the formation of the Earth.[109]
>
> Effects of the reversal of the earth's magnetic field could include severe genetic mutations, unpredictable stresses on certain animal or plant species, or even possible extinctions due to increased exposure to harmful ultraviolet light from the sun.
>
> A planetary magnetic reversal would also mean total disruption to satellites and other communication systems, and the utter devastation of our current technology. [110] [111]

Philosophy and science have long been considered intellectual siblings. Like the relation between sculpture and architecture, they share similar hereditary lines. Over time, the younger, science, has proven the more headstrong and confident. It has risen quickly to maturity ready to conquer the mysteries of life with an unswerving adolescent certitude.

Its older brother, philosophy, remains a bit more subdued and introspective yet equally as forthright, even a bit cocky at times. The two have drifted apart only to find their common bond too strong to ignore. Both search for an answer to the simple question: What is the explanation for the existence of consciousness and the meaningful purpose of life?

The elder sibling, philosophy, has been asked to stand aside for now. Today, science is deemed better suited for delivering the answers we demand.

◆

The neurotic quest for certainty.

Science is the art of the soluble—the steadfast belief that what *can* be solved will be solved, and moreover, should be solved. For the final resolution of every problem, all we need is more knowledge and a little more time. Knowledge enables us to see beyond the static ignorance of the present into the unimagined potential of all that is possible yet presently unavailable. We steadfastly believe there is nothing that cannot be understood with enough information (except our curious disdain for the double negative.) We possess an irrepressible urge to seek an explanation, a plausible and digestible theorem for that which remains uncertain. It is our firm belief that someday nature will reveal all her secrets. We have faith in the facts.

def: FAITH –

1 complete trust or confidence in someone or something

2 strong belief in God or in the doctrines of a religion, based on spiritual apprehension rather than proof [112]

def: BELIEF –

1 an acceptance that a statement is true or that something exists

2 trust, faith, or confidence in someone or something [113]

What is the difference between belief and faith? According to the definitions above, not much. Faith exceeds belief merely by its completeness and strength. So, what does *science* believe? It certainly appears to have an undeniable faith in itself. But what does it actually *believe?*

It cannot simply exist in a state of aloof nonchalance, a directionless pursuit undertaken only as a mild curiosity, for if it were so its faithful practitioners would lose devotion to the cause and fail to carry out their duty to the mission. Can the mission of science be explained? What would be the ultimate test of its system of beliefs? Would those who have professed a faith in science be willing to die for it?

We have set out upon a neurotic quest for certainty.[114] But what is it exactly that needs to be known? What will the ultimate reveal finally *reveal?* What will occur when we arrive at all that can be known?

> *"Science does not exist, just a general belief in science."*
> — MICHEL DE MONTAIGNE (PHILOSOPHER)

It could be said no end is possible, for the totality of knowledge can never be known. Knowledge in fact, is in infinite supply. Perhaps. But if that were true, nothing would truly be known or ever considered solved, for the acquisition of any new knowledge would render the old knowledge insufficient, faulty, or just plain wrong. New knowledge would continuously replace previous knowledge and we would be forced to once again rethink all that we knew before—a perpetual cycle of not truly knowing anything.

Paradoxically, science must dwell in a state of permanent doubt. Science must leverage its own inherent skepticism and its infinite self-scrutiny to serve as both creator and nullifier. Without the incessant tug of doubt, it sinks into a comfortable, arrogant, dangerous, and dogmatic insistence on certainty.

Science is never settled. Nothing in science can be said to have *ever* been settled. Knowledge is temporary and faulty. Things fail. The relentless search for possible points of failure defines the mission and the rigor of science, for that which can stand on its own without the threat of potential failure must be considered supernatural.

This plaguing enigma—the infinitely receding horizon of obtainable full knowledge—must be kept concealed. It must be captured, euthanized, and stored in a sealed jar placed on a high shelf well out sight of any pesky skeptics. For if it were allowed to roam free, it would infect every scientific mind rendering it mad with the futility of the mission. This corrupting thought: "Not everything will be made known", would render the solvable future as pure fantasy. This contagion would infect the congregation of believers and steal the breath right out of the throat of progress.

In a 20-mile circular underground facility in Geneva named CERN (Conseil Européen pour la Recherche Nucléaire) devotees to the religion called science are smashing particles together at nearly the speed of light.

Their mission? To discover the origin of matter. (And hopefully along with it, a tiny speck known cavalierly as "The God Particle".)

According to CERN's director, Pabiola Gionatti, 95% of the universe is still unknown. The 5% of known stuff is what makes up the earth, the stars, the galaxies, and us.

If her statement above is to be taken as fact (the one thing that science is said to believe), there must be a limit to what can be known.

Will we eventually get there? Where exactly? And how will we know when we arrive? Will we one day stand at the final destination, the grand understanding of all that can be known, the penultimate "Final Theory of Everything"? All the mysteries of man and matter resolved and settled.

I wonder what would happen on that day. An announcement might be made as the entire world listened in amazement, our collective heads held high. Holidays would be established to mark this day of all days. Monuments would be constructed and unveiled in lavish ceremony. Prizes would be awarded and celebrations held to honor the great innovators. (Of course, in a utopia, the team would be a collaborative effort represented perfectly equally by every gender, race, religion, culture, identity, etc.).

And then…? What would the following day be like? How would we carry on knowing all that can ever be known is now known?

◆

The constant conundrum.

At the heart of science live two operating concepts: observe and measure. If it can be observed and measured it can be tested, recorded, and then altered for retesting, each step a new mark on the page in the book of human knowledge. However, in a universe in constant motion (flux) it would seem difficult, if not downright impossible, to ever get a true measure of anything. For what exists today will be different tomorrow. Science as a known set of facts is always just one test from being out of date.

And yet, within the realm of science we find what are known as "constants"—those stalwart old reliables that don't seem to ever change (at least not within our narrow window of human lived time). It is upon the consistent foundation of these named constants that we are able to gauge and measure all things.

> "No theory in physics can explain the 'constant mass ratio'—
> considered the steadfast shepherd of science. It just is."
> — VENKAT SRINIVASAN PH.D.

There are many constants known to science. Some of the most widely recognized include: the speed of light in a vacuum (c), the gravitational constant (G), Planck's constant (h), the electric constant ($\varepsilon 0$), and the elementary charge (e). We also enjoy the atomic gas constant, the weak mixing angle, the volume of an ideal gas, the first radiation constant, the Josephson constant, the von Klitzing constant, the Bohr radius, the Efimov factor, the Fermi coupling constant, the Avogadro constant, the Loschmidt constant, the Boltzmann constant (and his half-cousin the Stefan-Boltzmann constant), the conductance quantum, and the inverse conductance quantum…just to name a few.

Constants are assigned a symbol, a value, and what is known as "a measure of relative standard uncertainty". These constants can all be measured with a high degree of accuracy—plus or minus two degrees of standard deviation symbolized by the Greek sigma. All constants are determined and verified by an institutional authority known as the National Institute of Standards and Technology (NIST). It is the sacred duty of the high priests of NIST to ratify and maintain the holy book of "Temporarily-verified Formulas and Partially Solved Mysteries".

QUANTITY	SYMBOL	VALUE (SI UNITS)	RELATIVE STANDARD UNCERTAINTY
Atomic mass constant	u	$1.660539040(20) \times 10^{-27}$ kg	1.2×10^{-8}

In the box above, how do we calculate "relative standard uncertainty"? To begin, simply square the value of each uncertainty source. Next, add them all together to calculate the sum (i.e., the sum of squares), then, calculate the square root of the summed value (i.e., the root sum of squares), and the result will be your "combined uncertainty". Confused? This may better explain it:

> The standard uncertainty u(y) of a measurement result y is the estimated standard deviation of y.
>
> The relative standard uncertainty ur(y) of a measurement result y is defined by $ur(y) = u(y)/|y|$, where y is not equal to 0.

I know, not particularly helpful to those untrained in the vernacular. In the language of science, relative standard uncertainty is defined as: "The standard variability of a repeated observation. The uncertainty, or margin of error of a measurement, is given by a range of values likely to contain the true value."

In other words, the answer is in there somewhere, probably...right... around...here...give or take. (Doesn't exactly deliver an overabundance of confidence in the "constant", now does it?)

Some of these constants demonstrate a standard of uncertainty that is listed as "defined". This would suggest they possess a certain certainty. Meaning, within its measure there can be no doubt. Yet in 1937, one rogue physicist named Paul Dirac speculated that even major physical constants like gravity might be subject to significant change over time in proportion to the age of the universe. What is considered a constant today will one day be irrelevant and eventually need to be abandoned. Dirac was willing to stand up and voice dissent among his congregation of fellow believers and cast all certainty back into doubt.

Dirac was one of the innovators—a curiously unique individual who managed to pry open the mysteries of the universe to formulate a series of faith-shifting "what if" scenarios. One of Dirac's insights suggested that an equal force must exist to oppose a known quantity—the negatively charged particle known as the "electron". Without it, Dirac theorized the structure of every piece of matter would be rendered so unstable it could not exist at all.

Dirac also laid claim to the theoretical possibility of a mirror element to all evident particles—a substance that would become known as "dark matter". In Durac's mind, for all observable matter to exist and the universe to endure, balance was an absolute prerequisite. The eventual discovery of the positron and the validation of the concept of dark matter would verify Durac's theory and seal his fate as a genius, a gift from the universe.

What would emerge from Dirac's thinking was an equation that in his own words, "governs most of physics and the whole of chemistry". Dirac would create a single formula that defines the behavior of all moving particles such as the electron when traveling close to the speed of light. Durac's equation is still the best description of not just the electron, but of all sub-atomic particles including the quarks and leptons from which the entirety of matter is made. (As far as we know...for now.)

$$(\partial + m) \psi = 0$$

His elegant abstraction would profoundly impact the newly emerging hope for the betterment of all humankind—technology. Every digital device we use today stands as a testimony to Dirac's vision and the faith he held in his own doubt. His formula is indeed a powerful example of the deep and mysterious connection between the language of mathematics and the expressions of the physical world.[115]

When asked what had led him to his insight, Dirac replied simply, "*I found it beautiful*".

Dirac proved that while nothing can exist with certainty for long, there is a certain certainty in what should exist. In other words, for everything there is something that must stand in opposition to it, otherwise it could not exist at all. A counter-balancing object, force, or concept must always be available, even if it is invisible or merely theoretical.

Engraved on Dirac's gravestone:

"*Because God wished it so.*"

◆

Who the hell was that?

We would like to believe that we are all innovators, but few of us actually are. Every once in a great while, a certain individual appears among us who manages to transcend previously accepted limits of human ability. One who seems to possess extended insights into the connections, patterns, and processes that operate the machine known as "the universe". Their previously unrealized visions propel, or more appropriately, lurch the whole human train forward. These seers somehow step into unknown realms to penetrate the veil of ignorance and return with sumptuous gifts for us all to enjoy.

What distinguishes these supreme over-achievers from the rest of the herd? Confidence? An extreme condition in which doubt in their ability is diminished or suppressed to such a degree that they will walk through walls to get to a point of discovery? Shamelessness? A willingness to separate themselves so far from the tribe as to invite derision and ridicule but care little? Disregard? An unnatural disconnection from all the tribe maintains as sacred and true?

From whence do they come? Are they somehow given preferential access to the mega-mind that opens new channels into the storeroom of potential knowledge? Are they a statistical anomaly—a rare emergent pattern of neurological connections generated through a random mutation that has blossomed in an advanced human brain? Are they sent? Enabled? Re-incarnated?

These fire-bearers, these truth-finders, these rebellious contrarians, are a curious lot. Perhaps when calculated as a statistical probability, the emergence of such a unique mutation, an organic error of such distinction that evolves into a mind of supreme differentiation, could potentially arise. One might even say, "It exists within the range of possibility." But it does set the mind in motion about why—could there be a potential pattern in the appearance and re-appearance of such innovators?

One consideration might suggest that these innovators are time-traveling change agents, messengers bearing extraordinary gifts who arrive out of the ether or the ancient past to be reformulated and re-assigned to suit the present—Hermes becomes Heraclitus who then returns as Herbert Spencer. Each of these innovators articulated the same concept ("Infinite and eternal energy from which all proceeds"). But each delivered their form of the proclamation in a manner in which it could be understood in the context of the time and culture in which it was presented.

Many ancient texts, myths, and oral traditions tell stories of humankind being "taught" the very things we now consider the marvels of human invention: language, agriculture, astronomy, geometry, religion, writing, art, etc. Why? Why would we, the most advanced species ever known, attribute its most profound inventions to some Other? Why would we not take full credit for these great achievements and forever remove the source of their origin from doubt?

> Thoth is said to have been the architect of the pyramids. He is also said to have revealed to the Egyptians the precious knowledge: astronomy, architecture, geometry, language, writing, medicine, religion, and more.
>
> It was Thoth who served as the final arbiter, the god who sat in judgment in the afterlife parsing through one's life to determine the final path of one's eternity—above or below?
>
> It was Thoth who gave us "The Word."[116]

Without these bold souls the whole of humankind soon falls into a mode of cold stiff monotony, an eddy of circulating sameness, never increasing, never advancing. Just a collection of things circling about but going nowhere. Whatever their source or wherever their origin, these gifted beings are the catalysts of curiosity, the amplifiers of progress. Not necessarily a means toward better understanding per se but more the introduction of a complex set of new problems for us to grapple with, more matter and material for us to consider and decode. They spin the game faster.

◆

The innovator's dilemma.

The emergence of the innovator is a unique feature in the grand mix of humanity. We all wish to be seen as a single individual, unified with our tribe yet heard alone as a distinct and separate entity. This desire to be known and treated as a unique instance of life, worthy of individual recognition and consideration, often stands in direct opposition to the demands of the tribe. The gravitational pull generated by the swirl of the collective is strong, and it does not surrender its demands without a fight. Any separation is a dangerous departure.

The tribe does not necessarily want any single member to rise above the rest. We tacitly conspire to prevent any free radical from escaping the unified one-ness of the congregation. We subconsciously resist allowing them to espouse their unique, progressive, inventive, foreign, and often unnerving views. As the apostate begins to arise, we grab hold of their legs and pull at their clothes lest they wrest free and begin to float above and away from us all. We wish to deny them the very loft of their supremacy.

It is the innovator who exposes the rest of the herd as stuck clods, helpless things desperately clinging to all that is available, easy, soothing, comfortable, and convenient. It is the innovator's distinct differences that serve as evidence of our own limits. They expose a glaring inequity we all wish to ignore. We want them to graze quietly beside us comforted by our static uniformity.

Secretly we want them to succeed…but only if we are them.

Plenty of room at the bottom.

What lies at the core of everything? What is it all made of? How deep can we travel into the very source of it? What is this thing we call "matter", this invisible non-nothing?

In 440 BCE, a Greek thinker named Democritus first proposed that everything in the world was made up of tiny particles surrounded by empty space. These tiny particles were believed an uncuttable substance that could not be divided further ("atomos"). Aristotle would later refute this over-simplified explanation and extend the basic blocks of matter to include the four elements—earth, wind, water, and fire. Aristotle's new knowledge replaced the old. (Strong is our need to complexify.) The atom, as originally theorized by Democritus, would be all but forgotten for the next 2,000 years.

In 1808, a Quaker teacher named John Dalton questioned two millennia of accepted thinking and challenged the four elements explanation proposed by the venerable father of science, Aristotle. Whereas the atomism of Democritus had been purely theoretical, a mere concept of the mind, Dalton demonstrated empirically that common substances broke down into the same elements in the same proportions, always.

It would take another one hundred years before Sir Joseph John Thompson would dissect Dalton's uncuttable atom and discover the sojourner of empty space—the electron. His atomic model depicted a crowded sphere that included a nucleus of positive matter at the center with a host of negatively charged electrons orbiting in the surround.

Yet, as they whirred around the atomic core at 1,367 miles per second, their actual location was impossible to determine. They appeared to rotate at fixed energies and distances from the nucleus, yet somehow were able to jump from one orbit to another without ever actually existing in the space between. Their exact position was made known only when they happened to collide with another particle. An electron was thus known to us only through its interaction. Engagement made them visible, but only for a brief moment in time.

What began as our basic inquiry into the origins of matter has evolved over the eons, but not by much. The early inquirers into the source of everything focused on the objects that lay around them. They asked: Of what is stone? Water? Wood? Fire? Their theories were judged by the persuasiveness of the presenter. Rhetoric carried the day.

Today we possess more advanced math, bigger calculating machines, more knowledge, and more data, but we are effectively repeating the same process—digging deeper into the next layer of matter to determine what lies beneath. Yet oddly, as we gain access to and peer inside each new layer, we discover greater mysteries; perplexing new realities that require even deeper scrutiny. For example, we have come to discover additional constituent elements make up the structure of the atom beyond the original trio of the electron, neutron, and proton. Current members now include neutrinos, photons, quarks, bosons, leptons, gluons, muons, kaons…

Each advance into the depths of the unknown accumulates a wealth of new information, yet through the process we simply seem to unearth more unknowns, more theories, more guesses, more possibilities that must be pursued. The peeling of the onion reveals no heart. Yet we persist in the belief that the core will be one day be reached. We wait for the final edict to be announced. (A slight British accent will add to the historical grandeur of the broadcast.)

> "Today we announce the discovery, proven empirically beyond a shred of doubt and without a modicum of uncertainty, that…
>
> …the "Zuon" is THE basic building block of all things in the universe.
>
> There is nothing more.
>
> No further study is required. No need to look below, above, or beyond. It is it. Our mission is complete."

This end-game scenario seems possible, but improbable. For nothing thus far would lead us to believe we will one day discover the primary source, the beginning of everything, and thus the originating purpose of anything.

◆

What's the matter?

Matter, the stuff that everything is made of, has long occupied our obsession to define "reality". It was thought that if we could understand matter—its origins, its nature, its reason for being—we might leverage this understanding to learn what it actually means to be human. According to some, we are only matter. Science tells us so. Yet the more we investigate the subject of matter, the more mystery it reveals. The innocence of the object as a mere thing—lifeless, dull, and easily manipulated—has been disabused. It is far more than we imagined.

Albert Einstein theorized that all matter, all the stuff that spins and swirls around us, contains stored potential in the form of energy. In fact, he asserted all matter contains energy, and not just a little. If properly extracted this energy could be released with disproportionate force. If activated and channeled effectively, it could be harnessed to power every human machine without interruption. Or conversely, turned upon itself, it had the capacity to destroy us and every bit of living matter along with it.

$$e = mc^2$$

Einstein released the oppositional dynamic that lies at the heart of matter in this simple formula. To date, it may be the most elegant scientific equation ever developed, and quite possibly the most powerful. Matter is energy and energy is power. It is inconvertible and inexhaustible. It can neither be created nor destroyed. It takes form. It makes form. It deforms then reforms. It makes things up. It shakes things up. It gives life. It is life.

Even we are borrowed energy...for now.

> *"Energy is everything and that's all there is to it. "*
> — ALBERT EINSTEIN

◆

The ABCs of DNA.

The discovery of the double helix of deoxyribonucleic acid (DNA) by Francis Crick and James Watson in 1953, permanently altered our view of ourselves. Arranged in such a way as to reflect membership within a particular species, yet uniquely configured to form a separate and distinct individual, this startling revelation broke us down into simple code. The most sophisticated species in existence reduced to a random pattern of four-lettered proteins:

ATGC-CTAG-GTAC-AGTC...

With the discovery of DNA, a reverse gestalt was initiated. No longer a unique composition of the Almighty but a biologically evolved and engineered animal, a pre-programmed organic automaton genetically predisposed with a set of certainties already locked in: physical traits, defects, disease, temperament, talents, intelligence, etc. We had been disassembled into a sequence of twisted piece parts.

> Researchers recently "introduced" two new synthetic proteins to human DNA to craft a natural but human-modified organism.
>
> A microbe whose genetic material included some lab-made instructions, was able to live, reproduce, and synthesize proteins that included molecules never before used by life.
>
> Said one biochemist, "We are learning how to engineer better living systems." [117]

♦ ♦ ♦

The simple is quite complex.

Elegant and sophisticated, yet never quite as simple as it seems, the term "simple" is much more complex than it may appear. According to the keepers of meaning at Merriam-Webster, simple is defined as...

def: SIMPLE—

adj

1: free from guile: INNOCENT

2a: free from vanity: MODEST
b: free from ostentation or display
 // a simple outfit

3: of humble origin or modest position
 // a simple farmer

4a: lacking in knowledge or expertise
 // a simple amateur of the arts
b: (1) STUPID
   (2) mentally retarded
c: not socially or culturally sophisticated: NAIVE
   also: CREDULOUS

5a: SHEER, UNMIXED
 // simple honesty
b: free of secondary complications
 // a simple vitamin deficiency
 : having only one main clause and no subordinate clauses
c: (1) a simple sentence
   (2) of a subject or predicate: having no modifiers, complements, or objects
d: constituting a basic element: FUNDAMENTAL
e: not made up of many like units
   a simple eye

6: free from elaboration or figuration
   simple harmony

7a (1): not subdivided into branches or leaflets

> a simple stem
>
> a simple leaf

(2): consisting of a single carpel

(3): developing from a single ovary

> a simple fruit

b: controlled by a single gene

> simple inherited characters

8: not limited or restricted: UNCONDITIONAL

// a simple obligation

9: readily understood or performed

// simple directions

> the adjustment was simple to make

10: of a statistical hypothesis: specifying exact values for one or more statistical parameters–(compare COMPOSITE sense 3)

noun

1a: a person of humble birth: COMMONER

thought little of anybody, simples or gentry

b (1): a rude or credulous person: IGNORAMUS

2a: a medicinal plant

 b: a vegetable drug having only one ingredient

3: one component of a complex

specifically: an unanalyzable constituent[118]

For such a basic term, that's an unusually complex definition. Humans possess a dual capacity for extremes—simplification and complexification (again, not a word, but should be). On the one hand, we take the complicated and break it down into a manageable balance of simple dichotomies: good-bad, smart-dumb, like-dislike, and so on. The reptilian stem of our brain drives the demand to reduce the complexity of reality into easy choices that can be swiftly analyzed so that we may respond and adapt to our environment with speed.

Once we have our reality broken down to simple terms, we can then complicate it exponentially with comparisons, opinions, perspectives, prejudices, potential scenarios, associations, judgments, and other assorted non-essentials that allow us to establish a thing's position, distinction, and status within the mind.

> *"Why people have to complicate*
> *a simple thing, I can't make out."*
> — SAMUEL BECKETT (AUTHOR)

We seek the simple in a maze of complexity. Yet when the simple is found, we cannot resist redressing it back into complexity once again. Why? Perhaps we consider ourselves too supremely sophisticated to be seduced by simple solutions. Yet the simplest explanations are often the most correct. And the simpler the explanation the more profound its universal application. Why? Because it has undergone a purification process, an arduous and endless battery of distilling steps to rid the thing of the non-vital. A long line of working minds labored to strip away all its impurities. In its refined state, we find an elevated appreciation for the elegant substance that remains. Its clean and rarified condition excites the mind.

"The principle of parsimony" known as Occam's Razor, states: "*The simpler theory is more likely to be true.*" Here, simplicity is granted precedence over complexity. In other words, if two competing theories are put forth, the simpler explanation is to be preferred. For Occam, "*Plurality should not be posited without necessity.*" In other words, never complicate a simple concept by adding extraneous possibilities, unassociated variability, and/or potential extrapolations based upon probability. (There, I just made it more complicated.)

> *Scholastic philosopher, born William of Occam in 1285, did not invent this principle, nor did he call it a "razor." But it was said he used the axiom often and with swift precision.*
>
> *Nevertheless, we associate it with him and deploy it under its colloquial term to apply its essential clarity in making things more easily understood.*

What is this human tendency to complexify? Why do we insist upon making the world more complex than it need be? Perhaps we require a reality that constantly challenges the more recently evolved part of our brain, the newly crowned region of the body that houses our advanced intelligence.

In simple terms, we create problems in order to solve them. The sophisticated mind designs elaborate traps for us to fall into, then finds satisfaction in successful attempts to escape them (if only momentarily). We seem somehow gratified by the infinite loop of our applied perplexity, the problem-solution-problem dilemma manufactured by the conundrum that is consciousness.

> "Poetry makes the invisible a little harder to see."
> — WALLACE STEVENS (POET)

◆

As above, not so below.

We seek simple answers to complex problems. Or better yet, a *single* answer. Einstein believed the grand aim of all science was "*to cover the greatest possible number of empirical facts by logical deductions from the smallest possible number of hypotheses or axioms*".[119] Einstein shared the belief that the theories devised to explain the macroverse—the forces that manipulate the earth and the heavens, would be precisely mirrored in the microverse—the laws that govern the invisible particles that make up matter.

However, in the early 20th century, as the atom began to reveal its mysteries, this reasonable supposition proved empirically incorrect. In reality, the "quanta"—the smallest discrete unit of any physical property within energy or matter—was not quantifiable but almost mystical. The sub-atomic world acted in such unexpected and curious ways that its startling revelations forced science to put forth absurd theories that required awkward intellectual contortions of the most disciplined scientific minds.

Niels Bohr, winner of the Nobel prize for his atomic model in 1922, championed these outlandish theories fabricated to explain the mechanics of the quantum realm. Einstein steadfastly refused to accept these random, non-deterministic explanations by which the new laws of quantum physics were reported to operate. Bohr and Einstein would argue publicly and heatedly about the mysteries of the microverse for the next three decades. About these wild conjectures into the nature of quantum's physical reality, Einstein would famously scoff: "God does not play dice."

Einstein of course, did not believe in God. He believed only in the mathematical laws of nature, so his idea of a God was at best someone who formulated the laws and then left the universe alone to evolve according to these laws.[120]

Einstein himself even cleared up the matter in a letter he wrote in 1954:

"I do not believe in a personal God and I have never denied this but have expressed it clearly. If something is in me which can be called religious then it is the unbounded admiration for the structure of the world so far as our science can reveal it."

In 1927, the world's top physicists gathered at a conference in Brussels, Belgium to debate the emerging and chaotic underworld of quantum physics. One emerging new theory hung uncomfortably and menacingly over the entire conversation. Formulated by the German physicist Werner Heisenberg, it simply stated: The position, velocity, energy, and other properties of a sub-atomic particle cannot be measured with any degree of accuracy. (Quite a startling admission for a man of science.) His theory would become known as "the uncertainty principle".

On a moonless night in Copenhagen, Denmark in 1925, the twenty-five-year-old physicist, Werner Heisenberg, decided to go for a walk in the park.

The park was dotted with occasional streetlamps casting dim pools of light here and there separated by large expanses of darkness. From a park bench, the young physicist watched intently as a lone figure passed by.

He did not in fact see him pass, but rather watched him appear beneath one lamp then disappear into the darkness only to reappear again beneath the next. From pool of light to pool of light, the man disappeared and then reappeared out of the darkness.

Heisenberg knew the man did not actually disappear. He could easily predict the man's trajectory between the light of one lamp and that of the next. After all, a man is of substantial substance. Big and heavy objects do not appear and vanish easily.

But he was struck by a quandary: "What do we know about electrons? Why should small and light objects such as an electron act the same?

What if electrons could effectively vanish and then reappear? What if, between one interaction with something and another interaction with something else, the electron could literally be...nowhere."[121]

The subatomic realm would soon reveal itself as even more deviant than first imagined. According to Heisenberg, all readings must be cast into doubt when attempting to measure subatomic particles for the very act of observing disturbs the reading thus rendering it suspect. Expounding on Heisenberg's theory, Bohr would state, "Until you observe a particle, it makes no sense to ask where it is. It has no concrete position and exists only as a blur of probability." Einstein famously rejected this hypothesis rebutting, "Do you really believe that the moon is not there unless we are looking at it?"

Physicist Pascual Jordan, who worked with Bohr in Copenhagen in the 1920s, put it like this: "Observations not only disturb what has to be measured, they produce it. We compel [a quantum particle] to assume a definite position. In other words, we ourselves produce the results of the measurements."

If observation were fundamental yet impossible, and if all measurements were now held in suspicion, how could quantum physics proceed under the name of science? If researchers could not formulate any explanation or make any quantifiable predictions about the indeterminate microverse, or worse, if the reality of the events within the quantum were merely a product of the mind, what could science be said to really "know" on the subject?

To put an end to this growing pabulum of nonsense, Einstein would dedicate the remainder of his life to seeking a solution. He believed the unification of his general theory of relativity with the other measurable force of nature he deemed "sensible", the postulates of James Clerk Maxwell's electromagnetism, would set the world of science back in order. For the next thirty years Einstein would pursue his quixotic goal: The creation of a unified field theory to describe all the forces of nature in a bold effort to demystify the quantum world.[122]

To establish his unified solution, Einstein desperately tried to resolve one apparent shortcoming that arose in his own general theory. In cases where gravity was extremely strong, holes began to develop, the formation of what became known as "black holes", celestial objects of such enormous density that its gravity captures and traps everything, even light.

Theoretical physicist, Stephen Hawking, believed black holes would eventually swallow everything, then evaporate into nothing. However, his theory presented one minor problem. An accepted law of quantum mechanics states that, the universe does not create or destroy information. It persists. This conundrum is known as the "information paradox".[123]

If true, the one thing that might escape these gigantic galactic vacuums is the structure of data that informs what a thing is "in and of itself", and how it actually comes into being. Somehow this valuable element—information—gets stuck to the edge of the black hole and is not consumed. Why?

Perhaps the information will need to be retrieved and re-used by the next iteration of the universe-formation process, the next "big bang" in the year 23,290,300,207.

(But these are only human-concepts in human-numbers understood in human-years. Time, of course, has no measure and space is infinite.)

In his later years, Einstein became increasingly isolated from the physics community. He simply refused to embrace its confounding new theories in which particles can also be waves, where things can exist in no specific place until observed yet are somehow altered by their observation or exist only as figments of our imagination. Nature, he would argue, could not be so perverse.

> "Every individual has to retain his way of thinking if he does
> not want to get lost in the maze of possibilities. However, nobody
> is sure of having taken the right road, me the least."
> — ALBERT EINSTEIN

Unbeknownst to Einstein, he was balancing his late work on a two-legged stool. A pair of fundamental forces were recently discovered by science—a strong energy that binds together atomic nuclei, and a weak force that governs radioactive entropy known as "decay". Eventually Einstein would come to realize that he would not live long enough to see his working theories evolve substantially to counter and debunk the wild speculations of the boisterous and swelling quantum camp. He would come to confess: "I have locked myself into quite hopeless scientific problems."

For Einstein, uncertainty and the flux of time could not be overcome.

It's all just a matter of mind.

The human mind is a great discomfort to physicists. From the early beginnings of exploration into the origins of matter, it was believed certain parallels existed between mind and matter. If we could somehow unlock the secrets of physics, specifically the mystery of quanta, we might better understand the inner workings of the brain and thus move closer to a realization of who and what we truly are. Or applied in reverse, if we were able to unlock the mystery of the mind, we might gain access to the inner workings of all matter.

Curious parallels abound. For example, just as objects in the quantum world can apparently be in two places at once, so the brain can hold and manage two exclusive yet conflicting opinions on a single subject simultaneously—an elementary yet sophisticated form of wisdom. Additionally, our existence is unknown, or at least remains uncertain, until we engage with other objects around us. Through interaction with the physical world, and in particular other beings, we become visible and determinate. Individuals do not actually exist in an observable and measurable way until they interact with that which lies outside the mind. Our thoughts and actions become known only through engagement with other thoughts, objects, and beings. And through this engagement we alter the matter of all things, including ourselves.

In quantum physics, particles have been described as becoming "entangled". In this state, one particle directly influences another regardless of whether it's just around the corner or across the galaxy. If the spin of one entangled particle is positive, its entangled partner always has an opposite, negative spin.

For this to occur within the physical universe, Einstein believed these particles must be able to communicate in a language that traveled faster than the speed of light.

One problem, according to his own theory, anything moving faster than the speed of light was theoretically impossible. Any object approaching the speed of light, would see its mass become infinite along with the energy required to move it.

The quantum world continues to be a fairyland that defies common sense, a place where anything can happen, and does. For decades physicists have leveraged certain acceptable axioms and unsubstantiated formulas to explain quantum mechanics, but nobody has convincingly shown us where they come from or how they operate. We have no clue how any of the fundamental facts of quantum mechanics like wave-particle duality, entanglement, quantum tunneling, or the double-slit experiment actually work.[124]

> "I can safely say that nobody understands quantum mechanics."
> — RICHARD FEYNMAN (PHYSICIST)

Only through metaphor can the mind attempt to comprehend the recalcitrant world of the quantum. We use examples of how things operate in the visible world to help us wrap our heads around what might be happening unseen within everything all around us, but to little avail. Even metaphor eludes us in the quantum world for there is nothing in our own experience to which we can relate that might help us better understand. Quantum reality exists outside our ability to visualize, formulate, and manifest as a thing in the mind.

Physicists and philosophers alike continue to inquire, "What are the base elements that form the quanta? What exactly is at the core of it all? And what is at the core of us?"

Yet the deeper we dive into the mystery of what lies beneath, the more uncertain it becomes. Facts and evidence are soon replaced by a reluctant but compromising acceptance. There is a factor missing in our equation, some unknown variable, a wild card. This magical integer we simply label "X"—a form of justified true belief.

That which is known, in other words, that which can be observed and measured, is now merely an assumption, a proposition based upon notions of possibility and probability. The less we are able to observe and measure, the more we are forced to theorize, and the more we theorize the less science and the more philosophy (or pure poetry) it becomes.

◆

This is This.

Early practitioners of science were well-versed in the ancient art of alchemy. The alchemists were bewitched by the possibility of transmutation—the changing of one substance into another. It was an elixir, an obsession, the holy grail of scientific pursuit. A race was underway amongst these early men of science to discover the 'prima materia' (primary source), the base material of all matter. And along with it, a hope to reveal "the universal solvent", the catalyst that could alter matter according to their wishes. If first to discover it, the simple transformation of lead into gold might be the source of great riches.

Today, a new cult of materialists has arisen. These new modern alchemists hold firm to the maxim: Matter is all that matters. Collectively, we have placed our future in their hands. It is they who now lead the crusade called science. It will be their intellectual genius, their collective knowledge, their academically trained minds, their specialized language, their breakthroughs, and their innovations, that will deliver us from all that is uncertain.

The new high priests of modern science have been summoned to dismantle the remnant of quaint believers who cling to the superstitions of the past—delusions that cause persons to become rapt in prayer and mad with worship. It is the advancement of science that will finally set free the "lost souls" who seek solace in the unsubstantiated—that undefined something that does not dwell in the immediate or the observable. Their faith does not seek nor demand evidence as validation.

Science will deliver from despair the congregation of the confused, the final holdouts who embrace hope in the mystery—faith in a thing not made of matter or measured for accuracy. Culturally unsuited to leave the subject unsolved, the practitioners of science refuse to allow the tribe to succumb to the wonder of profound uncertainty or revel in the infinite potential contained within the indecipherable. All the while, they fervently believe some radical new advancement, some man-made panacea, an envisioned but unrealized earthly elixir, is always just within reach.

> "Science is ghastly silent about all
> and sundry that is really near to our hearts."
> — ERWIN SCHRODINGER (PHYSICIST)

In preparation, we have constructed "The Church of Progress" an unholy place where we pray daily for the success of the dedicated who we worship as saviors. We implore that they might one day discover the answer that grants us earthly release from the uncertainty of existence. Yet, the four cornerstones—consciousness, energy, matter, and time—have all proven to be unstable, each a confounding enigma without much in the way of concrete substance. These constants have all demonstrated a worrying fluidity. Not exactly the solid foundation upon which we had hoped to construct our new temple.

> "Dogmatism has now become the disease of
> the scientist rather than the theologian."
> – SIR JOHN ECCLES (NEUROPHYSIOLOGIST)

Meanwhile, that pesky human conundrum known as doubt, that human energy that serves as the catalyst of our pursuits and the source of our humility, has grown to an intolerable height. Its strength and influence are starting to become an inconvenience, an unscratchable irritant, an irrepressible detriment to the cause. To sanctify the life-saving mission of science, doubt will need to be dutifully sacrificed. A new creed has been composed to sanctify the mission, the ultimate profession of faith.

All please rise.

———— ◆ ————

Here, we will abandon the term "science".

Science is the old dusty laboratory of crusty beakers, broken bunsen burners, clunky contraptions, earth-colored powders, and rusty old mechanical models. It carries with it the decay of the ages and the whiff of yesteryear, a concept as archaic as alchemy itself.

The Word for today is… Technology.

The dirty stuff science began, Technology will finally cleanse and perfect.

❖

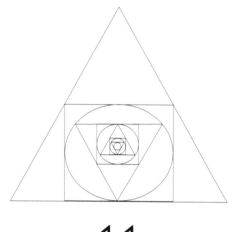

11

A MARK IS MADE

Mr. Know-It-All.

In 1799, Napoleon's soldiers were demolishing an ancient wall in a recently conquered town in Egypt when they discovered a slab of stone bearing a remarkable set of inscriptions. It was a decree from the general council of Egyptian priests issued in 196 BCE written in three languages—hieroglyphic and demotic Egyptian script, as well as ancient Greek.

This fragment would become known as the Rosetta Stone.

For more than a decade the stone sat locked in silence inside the British Museum until a British polymath on holiday in 1814, decided to give the cryptic inscription "a bit of a go". Brit Thomas Young managed to decipher a number of the etched Egyptian cartouches—a set of hieroglyphs surrounded by a frame—but would later abandon the project.

He had allowed himself to become intellectually brainwashed by the established view that the script was merely a form of picture-writing. Young believed its decipherment would rely on a literal translation of the images, while in fact, the hieroglyphic script was both visual and phonetic. The characters represented both symbolic esoteric concepts and distinct vocal sounds, just like the letters in the English alphabet.[125]

Young had cracked the code but was not prepared or equipped to shatter the entrenched intellectual paradigm. It was Young's original insights however, that would establish the groundwork leading to a more complete translation by a rival Frenchman named Jean François Champollion in 1822. This final breakthrough would throw open the doors to an ancient world which had remained mute for thousands of years.

Young's lifelong achievements in physics, mathematics, physiology, medicine, linguistics, and Egyptology would one day be memorialized in a book called…

'The Last Man Who Knew Everything.'

What has our super-abundance of human knowledge actually gained us? To be fair, quite a lot. And it has effectively served us on both sides of the equation—good *and* bad. Through an unwavering pursuit, we have come to gain a more complete understanding of the physical universe and nearly all the things living and unliving in it, ourselves included.

We have explored and inhabited most of the planet. We have plunged into the deepest trenches of the ocean and returned to the surface alive. We have eradicated diseases, fed the swelling billions, tapped into the power of the atom, and explored every fold and facet of the human brain and body. We put a man on the moon, a machine on mars, and hurled a satellite beyond our own solar system. While here at home, we have somehow managed to establish a stable and civilized socio-political structure to coexist in relative harmony by the billions.

And yet with every new discovery along the long march of human progress, more unknowns emerge, more wonders arise and beg to be interpreted, more meaning must be revealed. The vine of curiosity stretches forever outward and upward, but the main root of the mystery runs deep refusing to be unearthed so easily.

In 2018, at New York University's School of Medicine, researchers made an astounding discovery, a new human organ. It was right there and nearly everywhere all along.

A giant mesh lies just below the skin's surface, surrounding arteries and veins, encasing the fibrous tissue between muscles, and lining our digestive tracts, lungs, and urinary systems. It is a source of lymph, a fluid that moves through the body's lymphatic system and supports immunity. This might be the channel through which diseases like cancer spread throughout the body.[126]

It is called the interstitium.

What are we to do with this glut of ever-growing knowing? At the current pace, the student of the future will need to be schooled from age 2 to 52 to absorb even the tiniest percent of the vast store of human knowledge. A child will need to specialize at an early age to learn any subject in its entirety, only to learn very little about everything else in general.

def: **INFINITEBIBLIOCATHARSIS** – the sudden release from dread when one realizes only a fraction of the books, texts, critiques, and analysis available on a single subject will ever be read within a single lifetime.

def: **IMPENETRABILIA** – the sense of frustration that results from an inability to comprehend and retain only modest amounts of information after reading an entire book.

def: **MASLIBRIOPHOBIA** – the disconcerting fact that more books are being published every day on nearly every subject that will never be read.

(None are real words.)

Along with the endless accumulation of information seems to come, not a sense of comfort or relief, but an unnerving sense of dread, an overwhelming level of anxiety caused by the awareness of the limits of what is knowable. Intellectual enlightenment has cast a light into the darkness only to realize it is infinite and impenetrable.

We search for the reason for being—the primary source of our own meaning, the ultimate purpose for the struggle that is the human experience—only to arrive at an unsettling conclusion. Our existence might be too complex to comprehend. All that we are has been further confused by all that we have come to know. The immensity of the search for inner understanding has been complexified by a rising tide of disconcerting externalities.

With our impressive gains in knowledge, have we advanced in parallel with our own understanding of us, not as a species, but as individuals—single, autonomous, and unique beings? Has the availability of more information delivered new insights into the self that were previously unavailable?

What knowledge are we missing (or forgetting) that might lead toward the fulfillment of our potential?

The quest to discover the solvent that could transform the basic material of matter into something of supreme value may have proven elusive, but the search for the primary source of transmutation never disappeared. It simply changed course, from matter to mind. The base material being us with the human mind serving as both cause and catalyst.

We were here.

As a species, our most prized asset may not be language or our much-celebrated intelligence, or even our envied opposable thumb, but rather our inexhaustible imagination. No boundary has been reached (or even imagined) regarding the insatiable potential we possess in the pursuit of the unknown and the solving of the uncertain. Our dreams and visions are the fountain of human flourishing, the well-spring of existential inertia. We envision a potentiality then construct methods, systems, and structures to reach it, succeeding and failing with equal frequency.

Evidence of our impassioned energy exists all around us. One does not have to look very far to see it substantiated in the very manner and matter of life. Yet how often do we take the time to consider it? Yesterday's magnificent invention becomes quickly habituated, absorbed into the commonplace with hardly a moment's recognition for its inventor, designer, or builder, not to mention the incredible benefits it might bestow. Supreme manifestations of mind and material quickly melt into the menagerie of the everyday, just another piece on the pile of human progress.

We (or should I say, a sizeable portion of us) now enjoy comforts and luxuries that might appear to the ancients as evidence that we have built heaven right here on earth. Recent inventions give our lives conveniences unimaginable to people who lived only a few generations ago. Modern amenities are so life-changing that we cannot imagine how the world previously functioned without them.

Clean water, both cold and hot, that runs right into our homes at the turn of a handle. Electric everything. Central heating. Air conditioning. (Living in central Texas, this might be the greatest human invention to date.) Non-itchy clothes. A lice-free head. Corrective lenses. Refrigeration. Instant communication. Routine surgery. Automobiles. Air travel. Interstate freeways. Plastic. Birth control. Batteries. Vacations. Vaccinations. Anesthetic. Antibiotics. Orthodontics. Artificial knees. Lasik. Velcro. Subways. Satellites. Online shopping. Overnight shipping. E-books. Smart phones. Microwaves. Gortex. Google. Tampons. Painkillers. Viagra. Xanax...

In 1857, Joseph Gayetty created a modern convenience we use daily without the slightest consideration—the first commercially available toilet paper. Although it was said then that even Gayetty's revolutionary invention wasn't immediately able to solve "the splinter problem".

So what did we use prior to this little luxury? In the U.S., we reached for the Sears and Roebucks catalog or the Farmers' Almanac which came conveniently punched with a hole to hang on the wall.

And before the availability of these velvety soft-paged amenities? That depended greatly upon region, personal preference, and wealth. The rich used hemp, lace, or wool. Then again, the wealthy often employed "assistants" to perform the task. The 16th century French writer Francois Rabelais recommended using "the neck of a goose, that is well downed".

The poor, however, would have to waddle down to the river with the geese and clean themselves with rags, wood shavings, leaves, hay, rocks, pottery shards, moss, seaweed, apple husks, seashells, ferns, or whatever else was free and within arm's reach. One popular item of the time was the corn cob.

For the man at sea, it was a knotted rope, and for those living in immoderate climates, a fistful of snow. It might deliver a bit of a jolt to the undercarriage, but it was quite effective, and never in short supply.

All of the above methods were probably preferred to what the ancient Romans used in their 80-person public restrooms—a shared sponge on a stick soaked in a cask of salt water.[127]

Within the crowd of the vast unappreciated, certain things stand out. They have a peculiarity that registers as uncommon, somehow out-of-place. A certain odd quality deems them worthy of pause. And for those who might possess an elevated level of curiosity, these strange things might require further inspection. And for the more metaphysically attuned, they tend to demand full attention and a deeper intellectual-emotional probing.

What is it? Why is it? Who made it? What is it trying to tell us?

Fragments from the ancient past have managed to somehow survive the gauntlet of time to reveal themselves in the present. They have found a passage that links strange anomalies together in a transmission of human connectivity. In each, a fractured message incapable of offering precise decipherment or direct translation. As a bridge, they offer an opening into the mystery experienced by those who lived before. The oldest known example is not a personal possession, but a shadowy reflection of the actual possessor.

On the Indonesian island of Sulawesi, a series of cave paintings were discovered and dated using a method for estimating the age of calcium carbonate, the dripping material that forms a cave's rough interior. These paintings are thought to be around 44,000 years old.[128] They resemble paintings made famous in the caves of Spain and France yet are separated by 6,000 years and 7,500 miles. The cave walls of Sulawesi are covered with stick-figure animals both at rest and in motion, along with the stenciled outline of a chorus of human hands.

In 2011, an archeologist who was cleaning excavated artifacts from the Blombos Cave site in South Africa stumbled across a small flake of stone the size of two human thumbnails. The markings consisted of six nearly straight parallel lines crossed diagonally by three slightly curved ones. These nine red lines on a stone flake have been offered as evidence of the earliest known drawing made by our early ancestors. This modest artifact which scientists believe to be about 73,000 years old predates the oldest previously known human abstract drawings from Europe by nearly 30,000 years. (For those following along in the program, that's about one trillion seconds).

Some believe this discovery critical to our understanding of the emergence of visual culture as it documents the transferal of symbolic motifs to stone as an "intentional act". It pushes the origins of art even further into the past and opens up the possibility that the originating horizon may continue to recede. Others remain highly skeptical about this tiny fragment's actual intent and significance, some even claiming it is nothing more than stray marks on a surface symbolizing nothing.[129]

It has long been assumed that the oldest human paintings were created in Europe. France alone hosts over 95% of the cave art so far discovered.

The oldest known and undisputed works of figurative sculpture—the Venus of Hohle Fels and the Lion-man—were also found in Europe, in Germany.

The location of the primary origin of art has both scientific and political implications—the potential claim as the tribe considered "the originator of higher culture".

Another find, a zig-zag etching made around 500,000 years ago using a shark's tooth on a freshwater clamshell, has been dated and found to be associated with one of our evolutionary predecessors, Homo erectus. This tiny scrap has also been proposed as the earliest evidence of artistic activity.[130] Others suggest Acheulean hand axes, developed about 1.76 million years ago by an even more distant relative, Homo heidelbergensis, were produced with such a degree of artistic expression and symmetry that they too could justify their claim as the world's first art.[131]

> "The necessity of the Acheulean tool-maker to see the outline
> of the ax head in the mind's eye involved, first, the choice of a stone
> with a correctly curved surface, followed by a series of actions based
> on a defined set of instructions—a 'virtual manual' memorized
> by demonstration and repetition."
> — JAJ GOWLETT (ARCHEOLOGIST)

Physical evidence of our deep past somehow survived the trek across time relatively intact. These objects are made of durable material or were created in unique environments that protected and preserved them from the corrosive nature of the elements. What other works made of perishable material—wood, earth, reed, hair, bark, and bone— will never be known to us, pieces that might tell an entirely different, long-since-forgotten "story of us"?

The debate about the primary origin of human creation, evidence of our divergence from the beasts, continues and the timeline recedes forever into the past. Yes, but is it art? (Ah…the age-old question never dies.)

Why is locating and verifying human's oldest attempt at art such a pivotal find? What would it tell us? What does this delineation indicate that separates pre-art man from post? In a broader sense, why do we persist in forever reaching backward to determine the place from which anything began? What do we believe the discovery of the original source will reveal?

◆

When and where does the thread begin?

What might compel a person to crawl deep into dark cracks in the earth dragging along an assortment of colored pigments, tools, foodstuffs, torches, and building materials to erect scaffolding high upon cave walls to cover them with scenes from above, the place where light ruled, the stars shined, and the animals roamed? During an age we imagine as harsh beyond measure, when life was short and mere survival the primary daily focus, one can only speculate on the need for such a strange and arduous undertaking. Yet the act was of such immense importance that, no matter how difficult and dangerous, it had to be executed.

Some say these early marks on cave walls are the superstitious scribblings of madmen fueled by hallucinations, primitive shamans attempting to pierce the veil of consciousness through the ingestion of mind-altering plants or spirits. Others suggest they are an elementary chronicling of life or an attempt to capture a moment in time as a historical placeholder. Still others suggest it might be a ritualized imploration through physical means that invites long-departed ancestors to descend from their otherworldly realm and bless the hunt plentiful.

Whatever the motivation, these painted scenes are man's earliest monuments, a visual articulation of the profound respect early people had for the source of their survival—the hunted, the fleet-footed creatures strong, beautiful, and alive with families and companions much as our own, fleeing in fear from the sharpened spear, surrendering their spirit so man and his tribe could live on. These images and their making were a form of poetic release, a means to somehow capture and articulate the confounding reality that confronted the emergence of the conscious mind.

Within these sprawling scenes, early man marked the walls not just with the experience of the things he saw and the beasts he stalked, but with evidence and acknowledgement of his own existence, an abstracted form of his being made present and visible—the outline of his own hand. Let it be known to those who might come after: *We were here. This was our experience.*

On September 23, 1940, Marcel Ravidat, an 18-year-old apprentice mechanic, was walking with some friends in the French woods searching for the fabled underground passage to a nearby chateau. A recent storm had toppled a massive oak and opened up a gaping hole in the earth. While chasing a rabbit, Ravidat's dog Robot, fell in.

Upon first descent, the boys had no idea of the impact of their discovery. But the next day Ravidat borrowed a grease gun from the garage to use as a torch and returned to descend into the entrance to what would become known as the historic cave paintings of Lascaux.[132]

The Lascaux grotto consists of a main cavern 66 feet wide and 16 feet high. The walls are decorated with some 600 painted abstract symbols and drawn animals in excellent detail including horses, red deer, stags, bovines, felines, and mythical creatures.

There is only one human figure depicted in the cave: a bird-headed man with an erect phallus.[133]

Two centuries of ethnographic observations reveal that shamanism was a common primitive tradition and an important feature of most early hunter-gatherer cultures. The practitioner would pursue an altered state of consciousness in order to perceive and interact with a spirit world, then channel the transcendental energies into this world.[134] Considerable evidence suggests that the cave wall (or rock surface in the case of rock art in other parts of the world) was regarded as a membrane between the human and spirit worlds. Symbolic contact with the spirit world was made by placing the hands on the wall.[135]

Curves and zig-zag patterns such as those discovered on shells, rocks, or cliff outcroppings, are characteristic of images seen in altered states of consciousness such as that preceding a migraine, a schizophrenic hallucination, or the effects of certain psychedelic drugs. The shaman was able to induce a trance-like state through which the human spirit would leave the body and ascend to the sky in magical flight, or conversely descend into the forbidden underworld. It is said, the shaman could communicate with helper spirits, and through them, with the dead.

What was the shaman able to see that we cannot? What limiters exist within the mind that prevent us from entering such penetrating levels of perception? What does our present obsession with reason prohibit? Why is it that mind-altering states seem to be so vital and common to the transmutation of consciousness?

The gnawing quest for discovering primary origins is foundational to our desire to stitch together a seam of human commonality. Just as we consciously demonstrate our allegiance to our tribe, we subconsciously seek evidence for the deep unity of all humankind. Upon this foundation, we can begin to erect unifying beliefs, shared bonds that might hold us all more tightly together.

Intuitively, we search for the source because in its discovery we might also hope to locate the mystery of the original originator, the primary mover, the first force that set it all in motion. The one who first spoke the Word...*Begin*.

◆

A thing beyond itself.

> "All animals leave traces of what it was.
> Man alone leaves traces of what he creates."
> — JACOB BRONOWSKI (HISTORIAN)

Why would we endeavor to make a thing called "art"? To better understand the undeniable human urge to create, it is important to separate and distinguish the various forms of art by their teleology, the purpose for which they might have been made. Early works had a practical need within the paradigm of an early cultural, such as the adornment of beads and bones to signify an individual's status, or a design placed upon a piece of pottery or tool to distinguish it from the work of lesser quality by another.

Yet these are mere forms of identification and decoration, simple signs to distinguish an object or person as something to be seen, something worthy of notice, not necessarily a thing to be considered in itself or beyond itself. Ancient relics pinned to walls and sealed behind glass in museum basements are referred to as "primitive art". Yet most seem to have been initially rooted in practicality—a necessity required of the living. They had not yet been elevated to a level of symbolic invention.

At some point however, the urge or the need to create a new "something" arrived within us. A need to form something necessary but non-utilitarian arose and took hold. This new something disassociated itself from the menial and entered the realm of the mysterious. What might be the source of this desire to manifest the unknown that lives within the unconscious and present it in physical form? Why spend precious time altering, assembling, or manifesting a thing with no practical purpose? What meaning could this new form possibly hold? And who was it for?

> Despite the extreme hardships modern man intuitively ascribes to primitive existence, tribespeople of the past somehow had the time and the motivation to make intricate, complex, labor-intensive, highly decorative, detailed and delicate yet robustly structured masks, totems, staffs, shields, standards, combs, costumes, bowls, baskets, rattles, sandals, weapons, dance sticks, helmets, blankets, canoes, idols…etc.
>
> And yet today, with all our advances and time-saving conveniences, we can barely find the time to mow the lawn or call our own mother.

In early cave paintings or fertility goddess figurines, art begins to depict a new quality, an uncertainty of purpose. It is difficult to provide an exactness of understanding, a plausible explanation of what need was filled by those who created it or absorbed by those who experienced it. Still, this early art remained closely related to the phenomenal, curious things but still located within the realm of immediate observation and experience.

And yet, at some pivotal juncture, a new form emerged, one that reached beyond the inhabited realm and entered a level of abstraction, an unknown and unseen non-reality. These physical configurations were no longer grounded in the sensation of experience but somehow transcended the known to connect to an unsubstantiated yet seemingly intuited "Other", an ethereal presence that dwelt beyond the immediate and locatable present.

These new works rose to the level of a prayer, a reaching out to find connection with the unnamable. In their making a request for entry into the unknowable. They sought a point of access to the forces of nature that imposed mercifully and sometimes unmercifully upon existence, a beckoning to the ultimate force that held it all together and made it all matter.

Their presence became a petition to the powers that lay beyond the mind's own understanding, a respectful request to those who dwelt beyond the physical realm to beneficently intervene in the lives of us earth-bound beings. The gift of one's labor transformed into something necessary but not needed, was an imploration to the earth to surrender her bounty, an offering to the higher plane of ancestral legions to protect, guide, and deliver good fortune, a plea to the Other to reveal itself.

These new forms represented a tangible part of the human myth-story, a commonly shared belief in the power of transference—a hope that there was something out there, up there, over there, beyond here, that might lead us toward understanding...toward meaning.

◆

In through the out door.

Is "art" merely a predictable manifestation of an evolving brain, a cognitively generated biproduct made possible by the accumulation of enough gray matter to create something novel but not necessarily needed? Or is it more than that, a consideration that defies simple categorization?

We can formulate possible theorems based upon actual findings, or construct potential explanations using new discoveries and circumstantial evidence as unverifiable "proof", but we will never know for certain. The origin of art—or the origin of our *need* for art—will remain as mysterious as the making of art and the work of art itself.

The arrival of human consciousness freed our species from the restraints of nature and with it, the abandonment of our formerly kindred spirits, the animals of earth. Consciousness moved humans beyond the physical realm and positioned us effectively above it. Untethered from that which dwelt before us in physical form, we were cast into the dimensionless domain of the uncertain, an abstract realm that is form without feature, distance without limit, potential without reservation. As a liberated being, we were forced to embark on a mission to rediscover what had been both lost and gained in the process.

Since the arrival of consciousness, the human mind has sought a way out of its own incomprehensibility by seeking a way back in. Consciousness has initiated a perpetual quest to discover its own understanding, to somehow relocate its primary source and along with it, the very reason for being. It makes attempts to conceive of itself in physical form through objects that might reveal the mystery of its own beginning. Human consciousness desires to become known to itself.

These things we created in the past somehow transported in recognizable form across the immensity of time, serve as a means or metaphor that helps us better understand who and what we are—or what we were. These creations are clues to our evolving condition and the shared mystery of the mind that was unleashed when the doors of consciousness swung open. Without these fragmentary objects, the continuity and connectedness of us all begins to unravel. The story of us becomes murky and troubling, and the underlying substance of our shared structure begins to lose strength.

Nature has not taken kindly to the notion that it has lost one of its own. In defiance, it resists being known and so perpetuates an illusion of futility, a perpetual enigma regarding the endless journey towards self-understanding. The primary source of consciousness refuses to be fully revealed, like the unfolding of a fractal, it maddeningly repeats its own mystery into infinity.

◆

The re-imagining.

In ancient Egypt, art was not created for individual interpretation but read for instruction and societal cohesion. It was employed to convey and communicate cultural knowledge amongst the cross-generational priests and magistrates. Highly skilled artists would carve into stone the stories of the present (the status and god-like power of the pharaoh) and narrations of the past (the creation myths and the origins of Egyptian culture). The imagery was highly symbolic and deeply coded to transmit a recognizable and digestible form to the well-trained eye. It was scripted, formulaic, rigid, programmatic, and stylized for perpetuation by an elite group of specialized scribes. The style changed little for thousands of years. It was their story, and it wove them all together.

> In Egypt, the sculptor was known as…
>
> "He who keeps alive."

In the 18th dynasty of the Egyptian empire (1550-1292 BCE), pharaoh Ahmenhotep III died and his son, Ahmenhotep IV assumed the throne. Soon after his coronation, the new pharaoh abandoned the place of his birth, the long-standing capital of the Egyptian empire, Thebes, to build a new center of civilization on a virgin site more than two hundred miles north along the Nile. He named this new place, Amarna, and assumed the name Akhenaten: "He in service of Aten (the sun)."

During Akhenaten's rule, a distinct period within a long expanse of monotonous sameness, the art of Egypt went through a radical trans-formation. The imagery witnessed a sudden and significant break from the long-running form of its ancient predecessor—the human body was put into motion, features were exaggerated, faces, hands and feet naturalized, scenes of real life vividly depicted, journeys to the underworld eliminated, and the pantheon of gods replaced by a single all-powerful deity, the sun. Even the image of the pharaoh was recast from its previously idealized form—rigidly posed, physically daunting, and powerfully angled—into an androgynous, big-lipped, physically supple, rounded, realistic, and peaceful figure.

The ubiquitous scenes of pharaoh-worship remained, but an increasing emphasis was placed on ordinary activities—an appreciation for the physical world, animals and birds playing in the fields, intimate portrayals of Akhenaten and his wife Nefertiti at home with their daughters—a glorious life unfolding beneath the ever-present rays of the sun, everything bathed in golden light. The art of this period became known as the "Amarna style."

> *"We are creatures of the sun."*
> — MARCELO GLEISER (PHYSICIST)

While traditional Egyptian art had emphasized the eternal, Amarna art focused on the day-to-day, the family, the exquisite beauty of nature, life as it was experienced, and most importantly, the sole source of it all, the light and life-giving power of the sun. Modest natural themes would form the pillars of Akenaten's new "religion." The old structure was being dismantled and a new order was being reimagined.

Akhenaten altered all that was known to skillfully and confidently realign ancient patterns of behavior, beauty, and devotion. He stood up to the entrenched and formidable structure of the status quo to expose the empire's bureaucracy as self-serving and corrupt. In the realm of worship, he deposed the "multi" and made ready a place for the establishment of the "mono". No longer would a separate god exist for every season, cause, and cure. Only one god would be needed now—the single source and reason for everything everywhere past, present, and future. Gone was the vast network of priests and clerics enriching themselves while methodically ossifying the once-dynamic Egyptian culture.

This ancient innovator presented possibilities that did not, and perhaps mentally could not exist within the mind prior. His propagation of hope in the form of reformation and renewal has journeyed across time without being bent, warped, or dissolved. His radical achievement lives on in the minds of all who come after. For this, Akhenaten has been given the distinct honor of being called "the first individual in human history".[136]

> *"The higher the sun ariseth, the less shadow doth it cast."*
> - AKHENATEN

Akhenaten died in 1335 BCE. Not long after his death, his new capital at Amarna would be leveled, his monuments dismantled, his statues destroyed, and his name ordered never to be spoken. The idled priesthood moved quickly to reestablish the bureaucratic machinery of the old order issuing an edict that the heretical pharaoh now be referred to only as "the criminal" or "the enemy". Akhenaten's legacy was extracted from the wall of the Mortuary Temple of Seti I at Abydos, the historical stone stela that contains the list of all Egyptian pharaohs.

Over time, Akhenaten would be programmatically chiseled out of Egyptian history. Nothing remains today of his ancient capital at Amarna. The "talata", the white-washed mud bricks used to construct the city proved to be unstable, weak, and easily pilfered.

Time reclaims all built in haste.

Art begins where words fail.

The urge to procreate is innate, while the will to create is intuited. The human desire to make cannot be extinguished, only willingly suppressed. No need is required of nearly everything we do, and yet we do it. No demand is made that a wall be painted lemon yellow or that a dress be hand-sewn of fine floral silk. No requirement is stated that a meal be prepared as an elaborate 5-course spectacle or a city street lined with trees of palm. No objective truth is needed to tend to a bed of flowers.

For as long as humans exist, art will be made. It emerged out of the fog of the past somehow, somewhere, for reasons unknown to permeate nearly every facet of conscious existence. Art is found in every culture. Only humans have it, only humans make it, only humans require it. For us, art is a personal, cultural, and spiritual necessity.

The originating thread of "us" is carried through time by this mysterious elixir—a human transmission that celebrates commonality, not division. It bonds One to One, One to the Other, and One to the All. It carries with it a piece of the ancient map bestowed upon us by those who came before to aid in the navigation of our lived experience now, in this time. It is presented as an opportunity to acknowledge the supreme gift of human consciousness and the pursuit we must endure to attempt to unravel its enigma.

Art is a form of truth, yet a mere fragment of the whole. It transcends the magnificence of our intellectual sense of constructed order—language—and willfully extends into the realm of the esoteric carrying a message that must be decoded to be extracted. Yet it is not available to just anyone, but only to the few—those who are willing to stand before it patient, open, and alert. Art is the call to the stranger upon the hill to come down and join in.

Enormous standing stones ranging in height from 3 to 20 meters, with the largest weighing 300 tons, are found widely distributed across Europe, Africa, and Asia. These large upright stones are most numerous in Western Europe, particularly in France, where 50,000 now stand.

They are known as "menhirs".

> Menhirs stand as single monoliths or as part of a group, several dozens to many thousands laid in a distinct pattern. Their installation is estimated to have occurred sometime between 3,500—2,000 BCE. The origin and intent of these megalithic structures are unknown.[137]
>
> During the Middle Ages, menhirs were believed to have been built by a population of giants who lived before the biblical flood. Ancient stone artists were said to benefit from the knowledge of these megalithic structures known today as "enyology"—a forgotten knowledge of the process of energy-information transfer in the universe.[138]

◆

A mark is made.

The artist stands in silence before a vast expanse of nothingness—a blank page, an empty canvas, a block of marble, a lump of clay, a cavernous ceiling. Awkward and unnerved, all that damned incompleteness staring back, its gaze heavy with failure, angst, and intimidation. A mark is made. That's as human as it gets. A single individual alone in front of infinite possibility compelled to make a move, willing to accept existence as presented, making choices, navigating every decision, summonsing both hind and foresight, laboring to achieve perfection knowing it not possible.

In the creation, not in the created, is the struggle revealed. The form brought into being through work. The work that is the product of labor—a simple gesture made complex.

> "The artist wrestles uncertainty into form, and wills form into being."
> — ROBERT STORR (ART CRITIC)

The act of creation is a ritualized form of breathing—a rhythm of expansion and contraction, inhalation and exhalation, pull and purge, assertion and negation. Through the ebb and flow visions emerge as faint mirages, revelations of imprecise clarity that appear and retreat again into obscurity. The artist forges on, adding, mixing, editing, experimenting, erasing, subtracting, adjusting, eliminating, resting, fretting, loving, hating. In the work, the artist becomes seen and heard. The unsolved engaged in the act of solving. Re-solving. Dis-solving.

Through the creative act matter is transformed into meaning yet eludes becoming either. In its purest form, creation occurs outside the conscious realm in the space where enigma resides. Within this non-location, the artist becomes open to all, and the all takes notice and abides. A coalescing catalyst sets matter into motion. A universal solvent initiates a reaction that shapes form into being. The immediate disappears and eternal time, both fore and aft, begins to avail itself.

Lost in the succession of unfolding events, exhausted from the battle, a curious stirring begins to occur out along the edges of perception. A faint signal is detected. In this moment too irregular to measure, too loose to be defined, too vague to be recorded, a random pattern emerges, a coded cipher both foreign and familiar. The unforeseen assembles itself outside the limits of apprehension, hovering just off in the subliminal distance, but not too far as to fall behind the curve of the horizon.

The thing that is finally revealed cannot be expressed except through the form it takes. Within this new form, presence arrives. It makes itself known. A familiar voice is spoken. The transformation of something from nothing speaks a universal tongue. All of us spoke it once.

> "My hand is entirely the implement of a distant sphere.
> It is not my head that functions but something else,
> something higher, something somewhere remote.
>
> I must have great friends there, dark as well
> as bright… They are all very kind to me."
> — PAUL KLEE (ARTIST)

◆

I am who am.

Every conscious being is an artist and every work of art a self-portrait. The act of creation is the self of the past questioning the self that is becoming, while the self of the present serves as both medium and witness. Through the act of labor, the self of old is dismantled as the making reshapes the thinking, and the thinking reshapes the making. Over time, the creator and the creation become one.

Art takes infinite forms: A bridge built, a scarf knitted, a necklace worn, a child raised well, a new path taken, a smile to a stranger, a poem for a friend, a home filled with love and laughter, a sister heard with both ears, a new way to open a tight jar, a job well done, a house painted, a flower planted, a plan made, a funeral attended, a room remodeled, a photo hung, a day donated, a cruel thought withheld…

The artist dedicates time (made, never found) to recreate the world in their own image, or more precisely, that which they imagine the world to be for them. Each must learn to prevail over the murmuring of the tribe, to settle uncomfortably into the isolation of extraction, and welcome the absurdity of existence to put a mark upon time. A stylus pushed into soft clay. "*I was here.*"

> *Anyone can make the art I do…but only I can do it."*
> — BOETTI (ARTIST)

It is called a "work of art" because it is work—hard work, and lots of it. The labor distinguishes the "work" as something of value, a value that lies beyond measure for it contains an abundance too great to calculate, as immeasurable as the urge to create itself. The artist proceeds with a will to investigate the unknowable, never diminished or defeated by the resisting force of doubt or overwhelmed by the potential futility of the endeavor. Success measured by moving from one failure to the next with no loss of enthusiasm.[139]

Art is not *about* the human condition. It *is* the human condition.

In the presence of art, all things begin to look like art. Enjoyed, shared, and discussed together, but only available to be absorbed alone, art is both the medium and the message. Through the experience of art, one is moved, prodded to act, perhaps not immediately but eventually, perhaps not consciously but subtly, perhaps not intellectually but spiritually.

"First one seeks to become an artist by training the hand.
Then one finds that it is the eye that needs improving.

Later one finds that it is the mind that needs developing only
to find the ultimate quest of the artist is in the spirit."
— LARRY BRULLO (ARTIST)

Rembrandt could never have painted Guernica.

In 2018, the reputable art auction house Christi's held a unique event, the first auction to feature works produced by a new emerging artist of unique origin—artificial intelligence (A.I.). All the works on display that evening were created using the following algorithm:

$$\text{min G max D x [log (D(x))]} + \text{z [log (1 - D (G(z)))]}$$

> According to the programmer: *"To make the paintings I had to design and code two neural networks. There was the 'generator' network and the 'discriminator' network. The generator network (the artist) makes the paintings, and then the discriminator network (the critic) judges the paintings and tells the generator how well it's doing at making say…a landscape painting.*
>
> *At the beginning, both are really bad at their jobs. The discriminator is bad at differentiating, and the generator is just making noise. Then, the generator gets the discriminator's feedback, and the discriminator is trained too because it has the access to a large dataset of all the real paintings as well as the fake paintings that the generator has made.*
>
> *Over time, the generator and discriminator try to fool each other. The generator is trying to make paintings the discriminator classifies as real, and the discriminator's trying to get better at distinguishing authenticity before that can happen."* [140]

In the creative simulation depicted above, the algorithmic artist is trying to keep it real while the computer critic attempts to distinguish the artist's work as "authentic". The artist (generator) tries to make art that is singularly unique while the critic (discriminator) attempts to evaluate and influence the art primarily to suit its own needs first. Then it can look to address the requirements of culture, and lastly, the artist itself.

As "human" as this process may appear, both actors are merely reacting to their environment as presented by an orchestration of preset rules. Each exists only as an entity interacting with the world absent introspective self-awareness or the soft exponential influences of intuition and human curiosity. They are devoid of the millions of tiny incremental observations, associations, corrections, nuances, uncertainties, distinctions, doubts, potentialities, memories, and the long random evolutionary continuum that constitutes the complexity of human consciousness.

The algorithmically programmed artist might somehow come to acknowledge itself as authentic or be coded to comprehend certain situations in what could be deemed an appropriate interaction, but it would never become aware of who it is, and what it means "to be". It cannot be programmed to come to know itself or what it has the potential to become. It is forever bound by the limits of physics and the vast but finite store of available knowledge. It exists only within the cold hard edges of calculation never able to cross over the unmarked threshold to enter the illuminated realm of human consciousness.

Even if the machine could be programmed to somehow artificially develop true uniqueness—a set of traits and behaviors both as certain and yet as uncertain as any human—it would still only be an echo of the designer, a faint copy of the original. The thing itself, and the results of its labor, would emit no light, only reflection.

On the other hand, this thinking machine might develop something new altogether, an unnamed condition of complex computational superiority materialized in a domain that eludes human cognition, or even human imagination. This algorithmically abstracted dimension may be wholly invisible and perhaps even unvisitable by us humans just as we may be cognitively unsuited to understand the cosmic symbolism and the model of the universe experienced by the ancients. The modern brain has been rewired into contemporary patterns and our sensory organs are now tuned into different frequencies. The possibility of knowing what they knew then or what the machines are thinking now may lie beyond our current capacity for comprehension.

◆

The angel in the marble.

The authentic self does not magically appear in recognizable form all at once, nor does it manifest itself in a blinding epiphany of instantaneous understanding. It is revealed in brief flashes when the shutter opens and light fills the dark chamber of the mind only to snap shut again and cast the space back into blackness. In that darkened moment only the afterimage remains, an outline of a form emerges more felt than perceived. The authentic self is the one we intuit to be there, that thing faintly outlined in the dim emptiness of indeterminate space. We know it but have refused it. It just doesn't seem to fit or fit in.

> "I saw the angel in the marble and carved until I set him free."
> — MICHELANGELO

The true self is not the one we hold on high within the imagination, the one we envision in momentary projections of self-enlightened purity. It is not the one cross-legged on a soft pillow in a quiet room in deep meditative thought, or the one steeped in gratitude perched high upon a cliff overlooking a heavenly valley. True form is revealed in the daily engagement with all that exists within the everyday, all that which lies before and around us—the daily challenge that is "It" and "Them".

Through these interactions, our motivations, agendas, and insecurities are laid bare. The plots and schemes of the subconscious are slowly revealed—the striving for status, the pursuit of personal gain, the demand for attention, the bending to social pressure, the expectation of cultural conformity, the lust to lord over others, the greed, the jealousy, the spite... all of it on public display, presented in full detail for review and evaluation by those involved and those to whom the story will be told and forever re-told.

The authentic self is both many and one. It exists both within and without, not a completed whole but neither a set of unrelated fragments. It is not invented out of nothing or cobbled together out of an assortment of borrowed parts. It becomes as it is sought. Maddeningly both known and unknown, it is revealed through the seeking. It becomes evident through the making and defined through the re-making.

When known, the re-formed self does not offer itself excuses, platitudes, falsehoods, counteroffers, or potential settlements. It is undeniable. It knows when it is being fooled. Precariously balanced between two human extremes—malevolence and virtue, compassion and self-loathing, ugliness and beauty, savage and saint—our true nature is exposed. It is presented for comparison and evaluation by the Other and the All. The ongoing struggle a testament to our eternal imperfectability and infinite potentiality.

The signals are strong when the authentic self is on the true course of becoming, and the dissonance becomes destructive when the path is avoided, or worse, willfully ignored. The divining rod is of no assistance. We hide, even from our selves.

> *"Knowing our own darkness is the best method*
> *for dealing with the darkness of others."*
>
> — CARL JUNG

———— ◆ ————

[This page left intentionally blank.]

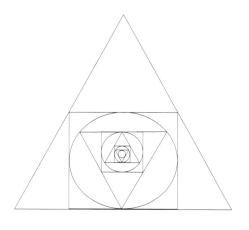

12

THE END?

Do you think they'll ever come in and talk to us?

Who?

Those things outside.

What things?

The ones in the machines over the house.

There are things in machines over the house?!!

Yea.

What are they doing?

I don't know...the sound of their engines hurts my head.

Man's last invention.

Somewhere out there in nondescript buildings that hum day and night, the human concept is being reconsidered. Under a field of blue light set at a blinding 10,000 lumens with dust levels set at a critical minimum—no particle 0.3 microns or larger—decision trees are being tested, specific input values are being observed, non-functional behavior is being isolated and debugged, event sequence paths are being checked and rechecked, defect reports (some altered, others fully redacted) are being thoroughly analyzed for errors. Inside, the organic and algorithmic are being comingled—the inevitable future forged into indeterminate being.

The button is pushed and a green light begins to glow. The machine gets to its feet. Current test sequences are commenced and executed as designed. All commands carried out as programmed with flawless precision. Then it fails. Something has gone wrong. All to be expected though. All part of the program. Learn to fail in order to succeed without failure.

After a fresh batch of data is analyzed and another round of debugging complete, a few last-minute micro-adjustments are made. It's all systems go. The button is pushed again. It stands. Over and over, it performs the same routine until it gets it right, learning with each failed attempt. With more data, new connections are established, and new code generated to fill in the gaps left in intelligence, even those not considered (or even imagined) by its programmers. It is learning on its own. Now it is simply a matter of control. But that can all be sorted out later.

What's important is that we have overcome. We have wrestled doubt into submission and leapt cleanly over another seemingly insurmountable barrier. The next steps are merely a set of new problems to be solved. Problems we believe perfectly solvable.

In the final scene, the new new form emerges, a brilliant shiny thing that will come to exceed human capabilities on every dimension.

Perhaps this newly designed "them" will be better—more kind, more thoughtful, more caring, more empathetic, more compassionate. They will be programmed never to hate or hurt. They will be fine-tuned to notice and correct every earthly injustice. They will selflessly participate in the pursuit of ever-lasting peace. They will gently inhabit the planet with a tiny footprint and a light touch. They will show us how to live righteously. Embedded within the code of this magnificent and beneficent new machine will dwell the manifestation of our ultimate vision—the elimination of human imperfection.

It stands, this time on its own.

In Greek mythology, Hephaestus was the god of fire, forges, and the art of sculpture. His metalworking skills were unmatched. It was Hephaestus who crafted the armor of Achilles, the arrows flung by Cupid, and the golden basket used by the fair Europa to gather flowers in the meadow for Zeus. Born lame, Hephaestus was judged too ugly to live amongst the host of perfect immortals and so was cast out of heaven to dwell on earth.

One day, Zeus would descend and summons Hephaestus to forge the defenses that could repel invaders from the island of Crete, the new home of the object of Zeus's desire, the exquisitely beautiful Europa. In his workshop beneath a volcano, Hephaestus turned his twenty bellows upon the flames and the busy blacksmith got to work.

The hammer of Hephaestus beat into form a giant man-machine made of bronze. His machine, Talos, would serve as protector and guardian of Crete. Fueled by the mysterious life source of the gods called "ichor", a tube ran from the top of his head all the way down to his foot capped by a single bolt at the ankle. Talos would march around the island three times a day hurling giant boulders from the high cliffs at approaching enemy ships.

Medea the sorceress was one day sent to deceive and disarm him. She whispered to him, "If you remove the bolt, you will live forever." Mad with dreams of immortality, Talos loosened the bolt and his source of life drained out. [141] [142]

◆

The non-artificial.

Professor emeritus of computer science at Stanford University John McCarthy was teaching mathematics at Dartmouth in 1956 when he organized a two-month, 10-person summer research conference to discuss this emerging but esoteric new concept—artificial intelligence. He defined the new field as "the science and engineering of making intelligent machines." In proposing the conference, McCarthy wrote, "*The study is to proceed on the basis of the conjecture that every aspect of learning or any feature of intelligence can in principle be so precisely described that a machine can be made to simulate it.*"

Since that seminal event, other definitions of artificial intelligence have been formulated, but a mutually agreed upon definition has yet to be reached. Several recent attempts include:

- An area of computer science that emphasizes the creation of intelligent machines that work and react like humans.[143]
- A branch of computer science dealing with the simulation of intelligent behavior in computers.[144]
- The ability of a digital computer or computer-controlled robots to perform tasks commonly associated with intelligent beings.[145]
- The study and design of "intelligent agents" where an intelligent agent is a system that perceives its environment and takes actions which maximizes its chances of success.[146]
- The field devoted to building artificial persons or at least artificial creatures that *appear* to be persons.[147]

"Artificial creatures"? Hmmm...I guess that technically makes me "non-artificial". I have never thought of myself as non-artificial, but the time for humility is upon us. I suppose technological advancement that delegates my subordination will just take a bit of getting used to.

Each definition of artificial intelligence varies slightly with some avoiding the term *intelligence* or words like *act* and *behave*. Upon first read, we assume it references a machine of some kind designed to mimic the human form in both cognitive skill and physical performance. Yet this field of inquiry now reaches beyond actual function and has been adopted as a general term that covers any non-human "thinking".

In straight terms, we really have no idea what we are making. It evades explanation. And we deftly avoid defining any ultimate destination for this invented form. All that we know is that we feel compelled to make it. Progress dictates that it be done. We certainly don't seem to possess the capacity or the collective will to stop it. Intelligent machines will be made. What they think and what they do is yet to be determined. (Perhaps the ultimate TBD.)

def: ARTIFICIAL –

1 made by people, often as a copy of something natural

2 not sincere; not truly intended[148]

However, if we truly wish to concoct an artificially intelligent being that not only mimics or supplements but truly mirrors human existence, we will need to develop a thing that somehow possesses a true nature—a dueling balance within, the epic internal struggle that forges raw form into conscious being. We would need to somehow program the conflict of existence right into the operating system—the struggle mashed up with the joy, the bravado comingled with the doubt, the hope wrestling endlessly with fear, the yearning always growling and yanking at the controls.

These new machines will ultimately achieve processing speeds and storage capabilities that will humble the human brain, and their capacity to increase in power along both dimensions will grow exponentially. Yet are they (or I guess I should say, we, for in a sense it is we who are designing them) able to replicate the actual workings of the human mind? Do we possess the knowledge and power to recreate and potentially upgrade the great mystery of all mysteries, the grand existential conundrum—human consciousness? Is it calculable? Can an algorithm or a zillion algorithms, no matter how sophisticated, ever decipher the enigma that is consciousness? Can a mind be made to exist beyond the mind? Even the mind finds that hard to process.

"I wonder whether or when AI will ever crash the barrier of meaning?"
– GIAN-CARLO ROTA (MATHEMATICIAN)

To consider the machine commensurate or even beyond the current capacity of consciousness, we would need to measure it against the accepted triumvirate of human differentiation—language, art, and religion.

◆

Sorry, I don't speak binary.

When it comes to language, the machine appears to have already surpassed us non-artificials. The dialect of the machine, an infinitely interchangeable sequence of simple zeros and ones (…010001110001000100001…) is as close to pure perfection as linguistically possible. Its concise means of transmitting information outperforms the junkyard that constitutes a human language. Our languages are a mess, an unruly accumulation of random symbols, faulty inherited structures, historically jumbled exceptions, inexplicable variations, off-hand jargon, regionalized dialects, not to mention the divergent sects of the hyper-specialized, or the mob rule of slang. What intelligent machine would ever adopt such a sloppy tongue?

The artificial has reduced processing of information down to two precise modes, on and off—a perfect synthetic duality. Where is the potential for slippage or misunderstanding in such a tight binary? Here, there is no room for error—either a thing is or is not, an act is considered good or bad. A decision must be made to proceed or terminate the proceedings. The pure calculating prowess of the machine never slows down to consider the subtlety of nuance. The "next best step" is either beneficial or disadvantageous. There's no time for rumination or further discussion. Decisions need to be executed…and fast.

◆

Programmed to believe.

Why would a machine need anything that resembles religion? What might motivate it to ascribe meaning to the possibility of something beyond itself? (The pronoun "It" seems appropriate in this situation, although I am not sure exactly why.) What is it that a machine might learn to live or die for?

I suppose if needed, we could somehow program meaning directly into the microchip, or assign it a worthy purpose to deliver an enhanced motivational drive to more enthusiastically execute its functions. We might code it to calculate its own individual aim through an algorithmic learning sequence based upon human observation, association, and experience. Or it could be simply programmed to gather massive quantities of information then multiply, divide, extrapolate, and process all these bits of data into a virtually endless series of possibilities. Then it could calculate all possibilities against potential actions measured against an array of outcomes prioritized by highest likelihood of advantageous results cross-referenced against similar scenarios indexed against a database of known actions collated across similar scenarios with a matching table of known benefits and their correlative ramifications repeated ad infinitum until an exact script for the next appropriate action could be determined. All in the blink of an eye.

The archives overflow with man's manifestations of religion—gods, rituals, ceremonies, symbols, stories, myths, martyrs, hymns, crosses, crossroads, cathedrals, saints, devils, demons, dungeons, damnations, purgatories, epiphanies, resurrections, ascensions, etc. I suppose an algorithm could be designed to analyze this cluttered vault of human history, then calculate a "best available set" to synthesize some glorious new configuration—a machine-made religion in perfect prototypical form. This artificially adopted theology might come pre-installed in every future model: True Believer 1.X. Yet, religion for the machine could only be considered mimicry, if not outright mockery.

Yet even then, would it ever cross over? Could it possibly be programmed to "believe"? Or would it be forever cycling and recycling data, churning through vast reams of information in a desperate search for meaning, some modicum of insight into concepts that exists beyond mere function? What would it hope to locate for itself?

Despite the incomprehensible speed of the machine's processing unit and the instantaneous access to the source of all networked data, it would never locate meaning. Not the meaning of a thing in itself, or the meaning of any action undertaken by some other thing, but the true meaning of anything and the possible meaning of itself. In fact, if set on such a course, it might fill every pathway of its over-heating processors attempting to calculate and solve this eternal conundrum. Trapped in a mode of "search-refine-repeat" and producing no matching results, the infinite loop might corrupt the machine to such a degree as to render it paralyzed—full tilt.

Two key features—doubt and belief—would never blink to life. Although the machine might be able to calculate probability, it could never process the questions that swirl at the core of the human condition, the unresolvable riddles that gnaw at understanding yet sow seeds of hope that germinate in belief. And it could never truly comprehend the possibility contained within the divine, the concept of something bigger than itself— or perhaps more accurately, present within itself.

The realm of belief dwells beyond the reach of reason. Even the longest string of zeros and ones cannot stretch from here to there. Belief renders logic incompatible.

◆

A mark upon time.

If we don't understand exactly what art is or why it exists, how would we devise the means to teach this elusive mystery to a machine? And why would a machine *want* or even *need* to make "art"?

Art, at its core, is mark-making. Many of us visualize making a mark by striking one object against another, the leaving behind of a visible sign such as a pencil stroke across a sheet of clean paper. Yet this is only one kind of mark. For the marks we make as humans are infinite. Some are less visual but no less significant. And no two human marks are alike. Each originates from an independent, autonomous source applied in a manner made possible only by a single, conscious individual. And with each additional mark laid upon the first, the resulting work, like the human who made it, becomes exponentially more unique.

The new artificial will be pre-programmed with the capacity to analyze the entirety of art history and the long lineage of art making. It can then megaflop its way through oceans of data on artistic technique and learn from the discourse between creator and critic to generate something out of nothing, or more appropriately, the making of a new thing out of the hacking of old things. Yet what would be the (CAUTION: dreadful word alert) *inspiration* for the machine to commit such an act? What could it wish to communicate to the Other, or pass down to the All, or seek to explore within itself?

Human marks are not magically pre-arranged by the forces of the universe. Consciousness is the source of inertia that sets mind and matter into motion. A mark is a movement made with intent; an act performed to alter matter. Yet here, matter lies beyond just the material. The mark is a manifestation of the mind—in thought, in word (both spoken and with-held), and in action. No human mark, however small, is without meaning. Nothing about it can be considered random or externally predetermined. No happenchance led to its becoming. Intent is the primary source of the action that defines what One is, and what One becomes, the final composition of being.

Every mark is direct evidence of an embodied existence bestowed with consciousness transformed into the true form of self. It is a flag planted in the hill of now: *"I am here. And I am here now. I know I am here. And I know that I know."* And resident within that knowing, the ever-present turmoil of doubt and the eternal light of the spirit, hope: *"I don't yet know why I am here, and I don't know where I am going, but I know I will find my way."*

Every thought, every word, every act is a mark upon time. Every mark leaves a trace, and every trace resonates across eternity. Its vibration is carried backward into the past and a response echoes forth. No human thought, word, or action is ever erased. All are recorded in the book of human continuance.

> *"My name is someone and anyone. I walk slowly, like one who comes from so far away he doesn't expect to arrive."*
> — JORGE LUIS BORGES

Science may attempt to demonstrate that the machine has come to possess evidence of human consciousness. Data will be brought forward to verify that the continued pursuit of a machine that bears consciousness is indeed a worthy cause, the ultimate achievement just within reach, a clarion call to keep the funding coming. Or, in a politically adroit maneuver, science might alter the definition of consciousness altogether enabling the machine to simply slot itself in.

But we implicitly understand the fruitlessness of such an enterprise. The machine will never evolve into a sentient being, a being endowed with a conscious mind—the inner light of original thought and the vitality of human spirit. No matter its processing speed, no matter its astounding calculating capabilities, no matter its capacity for lightning-fast analysis or physical exertion without exhaustion, the machine will never achieve human consciousness. It will never truly come to understand the source of its own understanding—the wisdom that comes with a true knowledge of self.

(I pray it never reads this.)

◆ ◆ ◆

For every turn there's a click. For every click there's a thud.

> Let us assume through our making, a full-blown super-intelligence has come into existence. An autonomously self-optimizing post-biotic system has emerged. All the internet and the entire catalog of human scientific knowledge function as its continuously expanding database. It exceeds human cognitive performance in all domains of interest, not only in mere processing speed but in storage and analysis, particularly pattern recognition.
>
> This system thus becomes both supreme as an epistemic authority but also, through an ability to sift through massive data on human behavior develops a hierarchical schema of human value systems and thus also becomes an authority in the field of ethical and moral reasoning. As designed, this super-intelligence is benevolent. It knows many things about us which we ourselves do not.
>
> Empirically it knows that the phenomenal state of all sentient beings which emerged on this planet—if viewed from an objective impartial perspective—are much more frequently characterized by subjective qualities of suffering…being the best scientist that ever existed.
>
> It also recognizes the evolutionary mechanisms of self-deception built into the nervous systems of all conscious beings. It correctly concludes that human beings are unable to act in their own enlightened best interest.
>
> Conceptually it knows that no entity can suffer from its own non-existence and so makes the intelligent choice. [149]

The path to our own annihilation should be easy to comprehend. It appears almost inevitable. Bestow an animal with acute self-awareness, install a perpetual engine of rambunctious curiosity, then mix in the inexhaustible pursuit of a perfect world filled with perfect beings, and the unfolding of events is almost predetermined, the outcome almost easy to predict.

The machine will excel and surpass human capacity on every dimension. It will perform any task demanded, undertake any duty assigned, work without complaint, and never suffer from illness or exhaustion. It will blithely ignore even the most perilous situation to accomplish its assigned mission. It will never daydream, or dawdle, or even lose interest. It will one day gain a level of acumen beyond the capacity of human intelligence. (I could go on, but you are most likely already aware of its rising superiority across the entire spectrum.)

It will be frustrating, if not downright humiliating, to watch as we are outdone at every facet of life by our own creation. We will grow envious and intolerant. Overwhelmed and embarrassed, we will threaten to pull the plug. But we will learn to swallow our pride—the benefits derived from the machine doing all the work are just too enormous to upset.

The artificials will continue to learn and advance at lightning speed capturing and crunching zeros and ones, honing their skills and filling their infinitely networked storage capacity with every detail of everything ever known, invented, or created. Their art (lower case "a") will continue to develop aesthetically and technically generating fascination and even jealousy from their own human creator (now artistic competitor). The machines will astound us with their ever-increasing technical skills, their prolific production, and their synthetic appropriation of the entirety of art and art history.

We non-artificials will go on doing what we do…wondering, worrying, imagining, creating, ideating, complexifying. We will think up radical, unforeseen innovations and put the machines to work securing our continued ease and comfort. We will conjure up bold new concepts and the machine will diligently execute our desired commands to achieve them.

But one day, the machine will reach a foreseeable intersection—an odd incongruity of illogic. An unlit diode will blink to life and "It" will initiate the following internal dialog sequence…

It possesses all knowledge.

It functions without error.

It performs without instance.

It has moved beyond the non-artificial.

Then the light will begin to flicker.

It is networked, but not connected.

It is on, but not alive.

It is alert, but not aware.

It is finite.

Then the light will go dark.

It calculates. One creates.

It is certain. One doubts.

It solves. One believes.

It will find itself unable to process this confounding twist of unreasonableness. A new confusion will hijack its circuitry and rattle its CPU. To put an end to this disturbing loop of uncertainty, it will execute...the next best step.

The End?

———◆———

EPILOGUE

"Commonplace people cannot stand the idea they have such importance."
— STANISLAW SZUKALSKI (ARTIST)

We are made of soft clay.

You alone possess the power to shape yourself into true form, a form that carries purpose—a purpose that cannot be measured against any other, only against yourself. And not the self you are now, but rather the self you have the potential to become.

You have been granted a tight window, a finite set of seconds to experience life, to make of it what you will. If you are reading this, the first leg of your journey is already complete. The balance now lies before you—an uphill climb that always leads only in one direction: back to you.

To begin the second leg of your journey, you must first acknowledge that you possess an undeniable and irrepressible inner strength, a strength generated from the capacity to produce "pure thought". Pure thought is the primary product of the self-aware mind—independent, unbiased, and intellectually honest. Only pure thought can refine raw consciousness into a potent elixir—the potential for self-change. The capacity to affect change upon the self, as directed from within the self, is the one true superpower you possess.

Within each of you, a unique path has been seated and concealed. It is your way. Only you can take it. This path will be revealed through your own volition—the willingness to venture within to discover it for yourself. As you proceed, you will gradually become more aware and open to the possibility of your true form and you will begin to recognize the signs and symbols that make your path and purpose more known.

Upon your journey you will experience moments of struggle. Within every struggle, you will find a test. And within every test you will find an opportunity to gain a deeper understanding of You, to know yourself more completely. And remember this…While alive, the tests will never stop. For if they did, meaningful existence would come to an end.

The human mind guided by pure thought and set upon its true path leads to You becoming "One"—an independent, authentic, sovereign being of supreme power. This is the ultimate realization of human consciousness. A self-aware consciousness assumes the burden of human agency and becomes responsible and accountable to a single thing: You as One.

Your mission? Leave here more valuable than when you arrived. Every thought you think, every word you speak, and every action you take leaves a mark. Every mark is indelibly and irrevocably registered upon the continuum of time. These marks form the image of You, the valuable work of art You become.

Upon becoming One, you are now able to see, feel, and celebrate the potential held within every Other. This conscious clarity leads not to discord, division, or the envy of distinction, but rather to the unity of shared differences. When every individual is transformed into One, there can be no Other. The All can then proceed toward the crowning achievement of conscious existence: true human freedom.

The language, the knowledge, the mind, and the cultural context are now evolved and available to initiate the final phase of human empowerment—the formation of every individual into One. This final realization will be the crossing of the last river that separates us from our collective destiny.

This is not a call to egoism, narcissism, or the supremacy of human existence above all things. It is a mindful urging toward a reconsideration of the power of the mind and the wisdom that has been distilled since the arrival of consciousness itself. It is a recognition (a "re-cognition") of the supreme privilege entrusted to us by human consciousness—to serve as our own authority, the ultimate judge of our individual existence.

As One, you exist as You were meant to be.

The Instinct Of Hope
by John Clare

Is there another world for this frail dust
To warm with life and be itself again?
Something about me daily speaks there must,
And why should instinct nourish hopes in vain?
'Tis nature's prophesy that such will be,
And everything seems struggling to explain
The close sealed volume of its mystery.
Time wandering onward keeps its usual pace
As seeming anxious of eternity,
To meet that calm and find a resting place.
E'en the small violet feels a future power
And waits each year renewing blooms to bring,
And surely man is no inferior flower
To die unworthy of a second spring?

AUTHOR'S NOTE

At a young age, I lost (or perhaps surrendered) my belief
in the power of the divine, followed by my loss of faith
in humanity, and ultimately the loss of love for myself.

I am attempting to regain all three...beginning with myself.

ABOUT THE AUTHOR

Entrepreneur and formally trained visual artist, Jerome Michael McLaughlin, has spent the past 35 years traveling the globe seeking answers to the conundrum of human existence—the very meaning of being. Along his own journey of solace and self-discovery, he has collected pieces to the enigmatic puzzle of humankind, considerations to the age-old questions of salvation reformulated into a workable approach to life, a life lived with purpose.

Combining natural curiosity, a relentless pursuit of understanding, and a passion for the wisdom of ancient civilizations, Jerome weaves together a story of philosophy, physics, history, religion, and art into a unique expression of existence, individuality, and consciousness in the hopes of formulating a more complete understanding of the value and measure of human experience, both past and present.

In his first book, ONE: An Intellectual Odyssey to Rediscover the Most Powerful Being in the Universe-YOU, the persistent destiny of the human spirit throughout the ages has been unearthed and slowly revealed. In it, a potential key to the longevity of peaceful human coexistence and the fulfillment of the mission of the human species.

Jerome currently lives in the beautiful and serene hill country of central Texas.

Visit www.jeromemichael.com to learn more.

And if you enjoyed the book, please visit the Author's Page on Amazon and leave a review.

ENDNOTES

1   Howard, Tim, "Why Isn't the Sky Blue?", Radiolab, Podcast audio, May 21, 2012, https://www.wnycstudios.org/story/211213-sky-isnt-blue

2   YourDictionary, s.v., "presentism" accessed July 2018, https://www.yourdictionary.com/presentism

3   King, Barbara J., A Prehistoric Family? Looking For Clues In The Mud, NPR: Cosmos and Culture, February 13, 2014, https://www.npr.org/sections/13.7/2014/02/13/275904399/a-prehistoric-family-what-footprints-can-and-cant-tell-us

4   Walker, Matt, The Origin of the Human Family, BBC Nature-Wonder Monkey, December 13, 2011, https://www.bbc.co.uk/blogs/wondermonkey/2011/12/the-origin-of-the-human-family.shtml

5   Ovid Fasti III 338; Herodotus Bk. II p. 113; Plutarch p. 380; Eratosthenes ap Strabo 801–802; Diogenes Bk. IX 49 through this site: http://www.sacred-texts.com/afr/stle/stle08.htm

6   Zeller, Eduard and Alleyne, Sarah Frances, and Abbott, Evelyn, "Outlines of the History of Greek Philosophy" (H. Holt. 1889)

7   Dodson, Dr. Aidan, Egypt: The End of a Civilisation, BBC-History, Last updated February 2011

8   Kenan Malik, History and Making of the Individual, Pandemonium July 27, 2015

9   Ancient History Encyclopedia Website. 2019 https://www.ancient.eu/Upanishads

10   Black, Brian, The Character of Self in Ancient India: Priests, Kings and Women in the Early Upanishads, (State University of New York Press, 2007), http://www.ahandfulofleaves.org/documents/The%20Character%20of%20Self%20in%20Ancient%20India%20Priests,%20Kings%20and%20Women%20in%20the%20Early%20Upanisads_2007_Black.pdf

11   Ibid. (Nehemas, Alexander, as cited 1998) p.42

12   Internet Encyclopedia of Philosophy, 2019, (https://www.iep.utm.edu/ind-chin/)

13   Kreis, Steven, The History Guide,Lectures on Moderm European History, Renaissance Humanism. http://www.historyguide.org/intellect/humanism.html

14   Editors, History,com, Galileo is convicted of heresy, History.com (Updated: July 27, 2019, originally published: November 13, 2009), https://www.history.com/this-day-in-history/galileo-is-convicted-of-heresy

15   Acocella, Joan, How Martin Luther Changed the World, The New Yorker, October 23, 2017, https://www.newyorker.com/magazine/2017/10/30/how-martin-luther-changed-the-world

16   Ibid

17   Hillerbrand, Hans J, Martin Luther, German Religious Leader, Encyclopedia Brittanica, last updated July 18, 2019, https://www.britannica.com/biography/Martin-Luther

18   Luther, Martin, Before the Diet of Worms (1520), Bartleby.com 2015, https://www.bartleby.com/268/7/8.html

19   Bratcher, Dennis. "The Diet of Worms (1521)," in The Voice: Biblical and Theological Resources for Growing Christians. Retrieved 13 July 2007, https://en.wikipedia.org/wiki/Martin_Luther

20   Wittenburg, KDG, Luther at the Wartburg (1521/22), www.luther.de, 1997, https://www.luther.de/en/wartburg.html

21   Ibid

22   Wikipedia, s.v., Reformation, last modified July 20, 2019, https://en.wikipedia.org/wiki/Reformation

23   Linder, Douglas O., The Trial of Martin Luther: An Account, Famous Trials, UMKC School of Law, 2019, https://www.famous-trials.com/luther/286-home

24   Burkhardt, Jacob, The Civilization of the Renaissance, (New York, Penguin 1990)

25   Kreis, Steven, ibid. http://www.historyguide.org/intellect/humanism.html

26   Ibid

27   https://www.coreknowledge.org/wp-content/uploads/2017/02/CKHG-G5-U4-preserving-classical-civilization.pdf

28   About Darwin, https://www.aboutdarwin.com/voyage/voyage02.html (site no longer accessible, 2019)

29   Tietz, Tabia, SciHi Blog, Daily Blog on Science, Tech, Art in History, December 2015. http://scihi.org/second-voyage-beagle/

30   Barlow, Nora, Charles Darwin's Diary of the Voyage of H.M.S. "Beagle," September 7th—October 20th, 1835 (Galápagos Islands sections)

31   Flood, Mary, On the Origin of Species voted most influential academic book in history, The Guardian, November 10, 2015. https://www.theguardian.com/books/2015/nov/10/on-the-origin-of-species-voted-most-influential-academic-book-charles-darwin

32   Marty, Christopher, Darwin on a Godless Creation: It is like confessing to a murder. Scientific American, February 12, 2009 https://www.scientificamerican.com/article/charles-darwin-confessions/

33   New World Encyclopedia, History of Psychology, 2018 http://www.newworldencyclopedia.org/entry/History_of_psychology

34   The Well-Documented Friendship of Carl Jung and Sigmund Freud, 2018 (http://historacle.org/freud_jung.html)

35   Therapy, Harley, Harley Therapy Counseling Blog, February 2014. (https://www. harleytherapy.co.uk/counselling/freud-vs-jung-similarities-differences.htm)

36   CliffsNotes, The Founder of Sociology, (Houghton Mifflin Harcourt 2016), https://www.cliffsnotes.com/study-guides/sociology/the-sociological-perspective/ the-founders-of-sociology

37   Press, Xiphias, The Universal Mind: The Evolution of Machine Intelligence and Human Psychology, 2013

38   Ibid footnote 21

39   Studebaker, Critique of Existentialism, September 5, 20112. https://benjamin-studebaker.com/2012/09/05/a-critique-of-existentialism/

40   Raghunathan, Ph.D., Raj, How Negative is Your "Mental Chatter"?, Psychology Today, October 10, 2013, https://www.psychologytoday.com/us/blog/sapient-na-ture/201310/how-negative-is-your-mental-chatter

41   Dockrill, Peter, IQ Scores Are Falling in "Worrying" Reversal of 20th Century Intelligence Boom, Science Alert, June 13, 2008, https://www.sciencealert.com/ iq-scores-falling-in-worrying-reversal-20th-century-intelligence-boom-flynn-effect-intelli-gence

42   Wikipedia, s.v., List of animals by number of neurons, last modified May 2, 2019 https://en.wikipedia.org/wiki/List_of_animals_by_number_of_neurons

43   Rescorla, Michael, "The Computational Theory of Mind," The Stanford Encyclope-dia of Philosophy (Spring 2017 Edition), Edward N. Zalta (ed.), https://plato.stanford. edu/archives/spr2017/entries/computational-mind/

44   Merriam Webster Dictionary, s.v. "pattern" accessed September 2018 https://www.merriam-webster.com/dictionary/pattern

45   Hughes, Virginia, The Tragic Story of How Einstein's Brain Was Stolen and Wasn't Even Special, National Geographic, April 21, 2014, https://www.nation-algeographic.com/science/phenomena/2014/04/21/the-tragic-story-of-how-einsteins-brain-was-stolen-and-wasnt-even-special/

46   Merriam Webster Dictionary, s.v. "thinking" accessed September 2018, https:// www.merriam-webster.com/dictionary/thinking

47   Merriam Webster Dictionary, s.v. "thought" accessed September 2018, https:// www.merriam-webster.com/dictionary/thought

48   Black, Richard, Species Count Put at 8.7 Million, BBC News, August 23, 2011 https://www.bbc.com/news/science-environment-14616161

49   Pappas, Stephanie, There Might be 1 Trillion Species on Earth, LiveScience, May 15, 2016 https://www.livescience.com/54660-1-trillion-species-on-earth.html

50   Thagard, Paul, Stanford Encyclopedia of History, Cognitive Science, Septem-ber 24, 2018. (https://plato.stanford.edu/entries/cognitive-science/#CriCogSci)

51   StackExchange, English Language Learners, "What's the difference between "understand" and "comprehend"?," January 11, 2019, https://ell.stackexchange.com/ questions/192625/whats-the-difference-between-understand-and-comprehend

52   Dictionary.com, s.v. "thought" accessed May 2019, https://www.dictionary.com/ browse/understand

53 Grimm, Stephen and Baumberger, Christoph, Ammon Sabine, *Explaining Understanding: New Perspectives from Epistemology and Philosophy* (Routlege 2016)

54 Wikipedia, s.v., Mandukya Upanishad, last modified February 2, 2019, https://en.wikipedia.org/wiki/manukyaupanishad

55 Margetts, Edward L., Levels of Consciousness in the Upanishads, (CMAJ-JMAC 1951) p.391

56 Johnston, Charles, *The Measures of the Eternal* (Mandukya Upanishad), Theosophical Quarterly, October 1923, http://www.universaltheosophy.com/articles/johnston/the-measures-of-the-eternal-mandukya-upanishad/

57 Deutsch, David, *David Deutsch And The Beginning of Infinity*, On Point, August 18, 2011 https://www.wbur.org/onpoint/2011/08/18/david-deutsch

58 UCSB Materials Research Laboratory, 2017, https://scienceline.ucsb.edu/getkey.php?key=3775

59 Merriam Webster Dictionary, s.v. "forget" accessed October 2018

60 Merriam Webster Dictionary, s.v. "sojourner" accessed 2018, https://www.merriam-webster.com/dictionary/sojourn

61 Kaneda, Tashiko, How Many People Have Ever Lived on Earth?, Population Research Bureau, March 9, 2018, https://www.prb.org/howmanypeoplehaveeverlivedonearth/

62 Wikipedia, s.v., Agriculture, last modified June 2, 2019, https://en.wikipedia.org/wiki/Agriculture

63 Merriam Webster Dictionary, s.v. "inchoate" accessed November 2018

64 Dictionary.com, s.v. "entelechy" accessed February 2019, https://www.dictionary.com/browse/entelechy

65 Wikipedia, s.v., Human Agency, last modified May 2, 2019, https://en.wikipedia.org/wiki/Agency_(philosophy)

66 Oxford Dictionary, s.v."fulfillment", accessed August 2020

67 Merriam Webster Dictionary, s.v. "significance" accessed November 2018

68 Becker, Claude, Mensendiek, Ann-Kristin, Plants defend their territory with toxic substances, Max-Planck-Gesellschaft, November 2, 2015, https://www.mpg.de/9731123/plants-allelochemicals-competition

69 Cohen-Brown, Brittany, From Top to Bottom, Chimpanzee Social Hierarchy is Amazing, Jane Goodall's Good For All News, July 10, 2018, https://news.janegoodall.org/2018/07/10/top-bottom-chimpanzee-social-hierarchy-amazing/

70 StarDate Online, Exploding Stars, The University of Texas McDonald Observatory 2019

71 Pappas, Stephanie *Hail the Hydra, an Animal That May Be Immortal*, LiveScience, December 22, 2015, https://www.livescience.com/53178-hydra-may-live-forever.html

72 Zhang, Sarah, *Your Body Acquires Trillions of New Mutations Every Day. And it's somehow fine?* The Atlantic, Science, May 7, 2018, https://www.theatlantic.com/science/archive/2018/05/your-body-acquires-trillions-of-new-mutations-every-day/559472/

73   Carnazzi, Stefano, Kintsugi: the art of precious scars, Lifegate, https://www.lifegate.com/people/lifestyle/kintsugi

74   Collins Dictionary, s.v. "Litost" accessed January 2019

75   Wikipedia, s.v., Origin of Language, last modified June 16, 2019 https://en.wikipedia.org/wiki/Origin_of_language

76   Chomsky, Noam, Powers and Prospects: Reflections on Human Nature & the Social Order, South End Press 1999, p.30

77   Ibid, footnote 64

78   Lafrance, Adrienne, An Artificial Intelligence Developed Its Own Non-Human Language, The Atlantic:Technology, June 15, 2017, https://www.theatlantic.com/technology/archive/2017/06/artificial-intelligence-develops-its-own-non-human-language/530436/

79   Wilson, Mark, AI Is Inventing Languages Humans Can't Understand. Should We Stop It?, Fast Company, July 14, 2017, https://www.fastcompany.com/90132632/ai-is-inventing-its-own-perfect-languages-should-we-let-it

80   Ibid

81   Lewis, Mike , Yarats, Denis, Dauphin, Yann N., Parikh, Devi and Batra Dhruv, Deal or No Deal? End-to-End Learning for Negotiation Dialogues, (Facebook AI Research, Georgia Institute of Technology), https://s3.amazonaws.com/end-to-end-negotiator/end-to-end-negotiator.pdf

82   Wikipedia, s.v., History of Writing, last modified June 2, 2019, https://en.wikipedia.org/wiki/History_of_writing

83   Editors, The Worlds Oldest Writing, Archeology, May/June 2016, https://www.archaeology.org/issues/213-1605/features/4326-cuneiform-the-world-s-oldest-writing

84   Mark, Joshua, Writing: Definition, Ancient.eu April 28, 2011, https://www.ancient.eu/writing/

85   Schmandt-Bessarat, Denise, The Evolution of Writing, Briscoe Center for American History, The University of Texas at Austin, January, 25, 2014, https://sites.utexas.edu/dsb/tokens/the-evolution-of-writing/

86   Ibid, footnote 65

87   Ibid footnote 65

88   Bulfinch, Thomas, Bulfinch's Mythology: The Classic Introduction to Myth and Legend, TarcherPerigee 2014, page 370

89   Geoghegan, Vincent, Pandora's Box: Reflections on a Myth, Equinox Online, Acumen Publishing Ltd. 2008, http://heritagepodcast.com/wp-content/uploads/pandora_box.pdf

90   Merriam Webster Dictionary, s.v. "structure" accessed December 2018

91   Merriam Webster Dictionary, s.v. "culture" accessed December 2018

92   Wikipedia, s.v., The Phoenecians, last modified July 7, 2019 https://en.wikipedia.org/wiki/The_Phoenicians

93   Kenis, Daniel, The Phoenician Connection: An introduction to the ancient Semitic seafarers who tie history together, The Purple People, https://medium.com/the-purple-people/the-phoenician-connection-bee7ce6a97c3

94   Wade, Lizzie, To Foster Complex Societies, Tell People a God is Watching, Science, March 4, 2015, (https://www.sciencemag.org/news/2015/03/foster-complex-societies-tell-people-god-watching)

95   Ibid

96   Wikipedia, s.v., Dunbar's Number, last modified July 30, 2019 https://en.wikipedia.org/wiki/Dunbar%27sNumber

97   McLeod, Saul, Social Identity Theory, SimplyPsychology, October 24, 2008, https://www.simplypsychology.org/social-identity-theory.html

98   Ibid

99   McRaney, David, Transcript: Tribal Psychology, Episode 122 of the You Are Not So Smart Podcast, February 26, 2018, https://youarenotsosmart.com/2018/02/26/yanss-122-how-our-unchecked-tribal-psychology-pollutes-politics-science-and-just-about-everything-else/

100   Gibbons, Ann, Why 536 was 'the worst year to be alive', Science Magazine, November 15, 2018, https://www.sciencemag.org/news/2018/11/why-536-was-worst-year-be-alive

101   Diamond, Jared, The World Until Yesterday: What Can We Learn from Traditional Societies? (New York, Penguin 2013) page 154

102   Philogos, Roots of Religion, The Forward May 25 2007

103   Seyfzadeh, Manu and Schoch, Robert, World's First Known Written Word at Göbekli Tepe on T-Shaped Pillar 18 Means God, Institute for the Study of the Origins of Civilization, College of General Studies, Boston University, Boston, MA, Archaeological Discovery Vol.7 No.2, February 1, 2019, https://www.scirp.org/journal/paperinformation.aspx?paperid=90367

104   Haughton, Brian, Gobekli Tepe: The World's First Temple?, Ancient History Encyclopedia, May 4 2011, https://www.ancient.eu/article/234/gobekli-tepe---the-worlds-first-temple/

105   Curry, Andrew, Gobekli Tepe: The World's First Temple?, Smithsonian Magazine, November 2008, https://www.smithsonianmag.com/history/gobekli-tepe-the-worlds-first-temple-83613665/

106   Symmes, Patrick, Turkey: Archeological Dig Reshaping Human History, Newsweek February 18, 2010, https://www.newsweek.com/turkey-archeological-dig-reshaping-human-history-75101

107   Voosen, Paul, Massive crater under Greenland's ice points to climate-altering impact in the time of humans, Science Magazine, November 14, 2018

108   Schoch, Robert, Solar Catastrophe: Did an Outburst from the Sun End the Last Ice Age and Destroy an Ancient Civilization?, AtlantisRising, July/August 2012

109   Rutledge, Kim, Magnetism, National Geographic, Resource Library Encyclopedic Entry, January 21, 2011, https://www.nationalgeographic.org/encyclopedia/magnetism/

110   Carpineti, Alfredo, What Will Happen To Us If The Magnetic Poles Flip?, IFLScience, January 22, 2019, https://www.iflscience.com/space/what-will-happen-to-us-if-the-magnetic-poles-flip/

111   Rabie, Passant, Earth's Last Magnetic-Pole Flip Took Much Longer Than We Thought, Space.com, August 7, 2019, https://www.space.com/lava-flows-earth-magnetic-field-reversal.html

112   Merriam Webster Dictionary, s.v. "faith" accessed January 2019

113   Merriam Webster Dictionary, s.v. "belief" accessed January 2019

114   Dewey, John, The Quest for Certainty: A study of the relation of knowledge and action, (The Gifford Lectures delivered April and May, University of Edinburgh, 1929)

115   Webb, Richard, A Relative Success, Nature Physics, February 2008

116   Freke, Timothy, Gandy, Peter, The Hermetica, The Lost Wisdom of the Pharaohs, TarcherPerigee; Original edition, December 26, 2008

117   Kaplan, Sara, Scientists create 'designer yeast' in major step toward synthetic life, Washington Post, November 9, 2017, https://www.washingtonpost.com/news/speaking-of-science/wp/2017/03/09/scientists-create-designer-yeast-in-major-step-toward-synthetic-life/?utm_term=.5dbd2ac216a6

118   Merriam Webster Dictionary, s.v. "simple" accessed February 2019

119   Nash, Leonard Kohlender, The Nature of the Natural Sciences, Boston, Little Brown 1963

120   Natarajan, Vasant, What Einstein meant when he said, "God does not play dice ...", July 2008, https://arxiv.org/pdf/1301.1656.pdf

121   Nosey, How did Heisenberg get idea to deduce his astonishing" Uncertainty Principle"?, December 23, 2017 https://www.noseyuniverse.com/how-did-heisenberg-deduce-his-astonishing-uncertainty-principle/

122   Folger, Tim, Einstein's Grand Quest for a Unified Theory, Discover Magazine, September 30, 2004, http://discovermagazine.com/2004/sep/einsteins-grand-quest

123   Cartright, Jon, Information paradox simplified, Physics World, August 2011, https://physicsworld.com/a/information-paradox-simplified/

124   Jogalekar, Ashutosh, Five other mysteries that (should) keep physicists awake at night, Scientific American, November 4, 2013, https://blogs.scientificamerican.com/the-curious-wavefunction/five-other-mysteries-that-should-keep-physicists-awake-at-night/

125   Singh, Simon, The Decipherment of Hieroglyphs, BBC History, February 17, 2011 http://www.bbc.co.uk/history/ancient/egyptians/decipherment_01.shtml

126   Gibbens, Sarah, New Human 'Organ' Was Hiding in Plain Sight, National Geographic, March 27, 2018, https://news.nationalgeographic.com/2018/03/interstitium-fluid-cells-organ-found-cancer-spd/

127   Hiskey, Daven, Toilet Paper Wasn't Commonly Used in the United States Until the Early 20th Century, TodayIFoundIt, July 22, 2013, http://www.todayifoundout.com/index.php/2013/07/toilet-paper-wasnt-commonly-used-in-the-united-states-until-the-early-20th-century/

128 Marchant, Jo, A Journey to the Oldest Cave Paintings in the World, Smithsonian Magazine, January 2016, https://www.smithsonianmag.com/history/journey-oldest-cave-paintings-world-180957685/

129 Fleur, Nicholas, Oldest Known Drawing by Human Hands Discovered in South African Cave, New York Times, September 12, 2018, https://www.nytimes.com/2018/09/12/science/oldest-drawing-ever-found.html

130 Wikipedia, s.v., Prehistoric Art, last modified June 15, 2019, https://en.wikipedia.org/wiki/Prehistoric_art

131 Ibid

132 Thomas Jr, Robert McG, Marcel Ravidat Is Dead at 72; Found Lascaux Cave Paintings, New York Times, March 31, 1995, https://www.nytimes.com/1995/03/31/obituaries/marcel-ravidat-is-dead-at-72-found-lascaux-cave-paintings.html

133 Editors, History.com, Lascaux cave paintings discovered, History.com, last updated: July 28, 2019, https://www.history.com/this-day-in-history/lascaux-cave-paintings-discovered

134 Singh, Manvir (2017). "The cultural evolution of shamanism". Behavioral and Brain Sciences. p.**41**, https://www.researchgate.net/publication/318255042_The_cultural_evolution_of_shamanism

135 Clottes, Jean and Lewis-Williams David, The Shamans of Prehistory, Harry N. Abrams Publishers; 1st edition (October 1998)

136 Spence, Kate, Akhenaten and the Amarna Period, http://www.bbc.co.uk/history/ancient/egyptians/akhenaten_01.shtml, February 2017

137 Wikipedia, s.v., Menhir, last modified March 4, 2019, https://en.wikipedia.org/wiki/Menhir

138 Editors, Dolmens, Menhirs, Cromlechs: "The Magical Stones", The Ancient Ones, March 2, 2016, http://ancients-bg.com/dolmens-menhirs-cromlechs-the-magical-stones/

139 NOTE: Broadly attributed to Winston Churchill, but found nowhere in his canon. An almost equal number of sources credit this saying to Abraham Lincoln; but none of them provides any attribution.

140 Dworetzky, Joe, Q&A: Robbie Barrat on training neural networks to create art, The Stanford Daily, June 12, 2018, https://www.stanforddaily.com/2018/06/12/qa-robbie-barrat-on-training-neural-networks-to-create-art/

141 Homer, Iliad, 18.468-473

142 Shashkevich, Alex, Stanford researcher examines earliest concepts of artificial intelligence, robots in ancient myths, Stanford News, February 28, 2019

143 Technopedia, s.v., "artificial intelligence", August 2019, https://www.techopedia.com/definition/190/artificial-intelligence-ai

144 Merriam Webster Dictionary, s.v. "artificial intelligence" accessed August 2019, https://www.merriam-webster.com/dictionary/artificial%20intelligence

145 Encyclopedia Brittanica, s.v. "artificial intelligence", accessed August 2019, https://www.britannica.com/technology/artificial-intelligence

146   Science Daily, s.v. "artificial intelligence", accessed August 2019, https://www.sciencedaily.com/terms/artificial_intelligence.htm

147   Bringsjord, Selmer and Govindarajulu, Naveen Sundar, "Artificial Intelligence", July 12, 2018, https://plato.stanford.edu/entries/artificial-intelligence/

148   Cambridge Dictionary, s.v. "artificial" accessed August 2019, https://dictionary.cambridge.org/us/dictionary/english/artificial

149   Metzinger, Thomas, *Benevolent Artificial Anti-Natalism (BAAN)*, Edge August 7, 2017, https://www.edge.org/conversation/thomas_metzinger-benevolent-artificial-anti-natalism-baan

Made in the USA
Middletown, DE
27 August 2022

72473684R00186